American Priso

Imprisonment has become big business in the United States. Using a "history of ideas" approach, this book examines the cultural underpinnings of prisons in the United States and explores how shared ideas about imprisonment evolve into a complex, loosely connected nationwide system of prisons that keeps enough persons to populate a small nation behind bars, razor wire and electrified fences.

Tracing both the history of the prison and the very idea of imprisonment in the United States, this book provides students with a critical overview of American prisons and considers their past, their present and directions for the future. Topics covered include:

- a history of imprisonment in America from 1600 to the present day;
- the twentieth-century prison building binge;
- the relationship between U.S. prisons and the private sector;
- a critical account of capital punishment;
- less-visible prison minorities, including women, children and the elderly; and
- sex, violence and disease in prison.

This comprehensive book is essential reading for advanced courses on corrections and correctional management and offers a compelling and provocative analysis of the realities of American penal culture from past to present. It is perfect reading for students of criminal justice, corrections, penology and the sociology of punishment.

David Musick earned his Ph.D. in Sociology at the University of California, Riverside. His areas of specialization include the history of ideas, criminology and juvenile delinquency. For most of his adult life, he worked with inmates, as a counselor, teacher and social researcher, in a number of adult and juvenile prisons. For over thirty years he taught courses on the sociology of corrections. In collaboration with his wife, Kristine, Professor Musick has worked as an expert on over fifty capital murder cases.

Kristine Gunsaulus-Musick earned her Ph.D. in Human Rehabilitation at the University of Northern Colorado. Her background in social science, secondary education and the mental health fields has informed a career that includes work as a university center psychologist, professor, researcher and published writer. She has maintained a private practice as a licensed psychologist in the Rocky Mountains, alongside the collaborative "systems" work, research and writing she enjoys with her spouse, David.

"As someone who has written on American society and its problems, but who is not an expert in any sense on prisons in America, I found this book to be fascinating and enlightening, even as it examines worrisome but important issues that should concern all Americans and, most certainly, scholars and students interested in the dilemmas posed by the American penal system. *American Prisons* examines the history, development, and operation of prisons in the United States right up to the present; and so doing, it addresses their building, efforts to privatize, financing, inmates, costs to public, disease and health risks, sex, rapes, violence, gangs, subcultures, riots, executions, profiteering, and less-acknowledged inmates such as children, women, sick, and the elderly. Books like this are what made me become a sociology major some six decades ago, and later a professor for over fifty years; and it is just this kind of book that will do the same for students today, and for the faculty who teach them. It is an engaging read that I highly recommend."

Jonathan H. Turner, *University Professor, University of California, Riverside, and Research Professor, University of California, Santa Barbara*

American Prisons

Their Past, Present and Future

David Musick and Kristine Gunsaulus-Musick

Routledge
Taylor & Francis Group

LONDON AND NEW YORK

First published 2017
by Routledge
2 Park Square, Milton Park, Abingdon, Oxon OX14 4RN

and by Routledge
711 Third Avenue, New York, NY 10017

Routledge is an imprint of the Taylor & Francis Group, an informa business

© 2017 David Musick and Kristine Gunsaulus-Musick

British Library Cataloguing in Publication Data
A catalogue record for this book is available from the British Library

Library of Congress Cataloging in Publication Data
Names: Musick, David, author. | Gunsaulus-Musick, Kristine, 1950– author.
Title: American prisons : their past, present and future / David Musick and Kristine Gunsaulus-Musick.
Description: Abingdon, Oxon ; New York, NY : Routledge, 2017. | Includes bibliographical references and index.
Identifiers: LCCN 2016050411| ISBN 9781138805781 (hardback) | ISBN 9781138805798 (pbk.) | ISBN 9781315751993 (ebook)
Subjects: LCSH: Prisons–United States–History. | Imprisonment–United States–History. | Corrections–United States–History.
Classification: LCC HV9471 .M88 2017 | DDC 365/.973–dc23
LC record available at https://lccn.loc.gov/2016050411

ISBN: 978-1-138-80578-1 (hbk)
ISBN: 978-1-138-80579-8 (pbk)
ISBN: 978-1-315-75199-3 (ebk)

Typeset in Scala Sans
by Cenveo Publisher Services

This book is dedicated to our children and grandchildren;
may their lives be lighted by love and kindness.

Contents

List of tables

Chapter 1

Introduction

Contents

This book is about prisons in the United States. We examine their past, present and future. We rely heavily on the work of other scholars who have studied American prisons. We use secondary data (incarceration rates, number of executions, for example) whenever it is appropriate and available. We've included a good amount of information gleaned from reputable news sources. Overarching this compote of information is a "history of ideas" approach to the study of social phenomena. Imprisonment is, first and foremost, an idea that must be accepted, at least by those in power, and acted upon. If imprisonment of some human beings is accepted and acted upon, a universe of other prison-related ideas will follow (location of prisons, size of prisons, inmate treatment, sentence length and on and on).

As ideas of imprisonment mature in a civilization, they take on the sociological qualities of structure and permanence. In terms of location and physical appearance, prisons become distinctive places. In populous states, prisons multiply and are organized into systems. This process has evolved to the point where prisons are woven into the fabric of life in the United States. Prison images seep incessantly into our consciousness through what we see and hear in print, in the movies and on television. In fact, it is arguable that prisons have become a social institution, just like families and schools. Like other social institutions, prisons were created to address long-term, ongoing social problems. Like other social institutions, prisons are normatively prescribed and legally upheld.

Inside American prisons, we find a rich array of undesirables, including violent offenders, property offenders, drug offenders, and the mentally ill, as well as illegal immigrants. The variety and volume of American inmates has, for all practical purposes, defeated all but the most stubborn attempts at rehabilitation. Instead, inmates are warehoused and then returned to their communities, having benefited little from incarceration. How did U.S. prisons get to the point where they do little more than temporarily keep undesirables separate from members of civil society? Why are U.S. prisons resistant to positive change? In the chapters that follow, we explore information that provides answers to these and other important questions.

Importance of the book

Imprisonment has become big business in the United States (Henrichson and Delaney 2012). The number of state and federal prisons increased from around 600 in the mid-1970s to over 1,000 by 2000. More people are imprisoned in the United States than inhabit entire countries, like Greece, for example. Annually, we Americans lock up over 2 million people, almost 700,000 in jail and about 1.4 million in prison. One out of every 11 inmates in the United States will spend the rest of his, or her, life in prison, costing taxpayers about $700,000 per "lifer." Of the over 600,000 American inmates released from prison each year, about 400,000 will be locked up again before long.

The American practice of sweeping social problems into jails and prisons has become expensive, costing at least $60 billion per year. Our appetite for prisons is stifling other social investments. In California, for example, since 1983, 23 new prisons have been built but no new universities. Since 1991, the cost of running many state correctional systems has more than doubled. State taxpayers are facing large increases so that the prison system can be funded.

Lacking enough prison space of its own, the District of Columbia keeps thousands of inmates in federal prisons. Similarly, many states send "excess" inmates to costly out-of-state corporate prisons. The following is a partial list of state correctional systems that have sent inmates to out-of-state corporate prisons: Wisconsin, Alabama, Hawaii, Alaska, Arizona, Indiana, Connecticut, Vermont and Wyoming.

Is there any end in sight? Will the supply of prisoners run down, or out? We don't think so. Even though arrests for most crimes of violence and property hover at 30-year lows, judges around the United States report that criminal courts are swamped with new cases, ensuring at least one inmate will arrive in prison to take the place of each inmate released. Adding to the supply problem is a recent tendency of some American prosecutors, judges and juries to send some white-collar offenders to prison. If this practice of sentencing and imprisoning middle-class and upscale offenders were to catch on, prison space would have to be greatly expanded.

Many corrections administrators, policymakers, legislators and judges recognize that prisons are becoming too costly for use as a general "problem-solving" tool. They just can't find a way out of the soup. Reforms aimed at reducing prison populations are afoot. The scrapping of harsh cocaine sentencing rules and the elimination of "two- and three-strikes" laws, for example, are attempts to shorten what are now lengthy mandatory sentences. However, supply-side forces loom even larger.

On the "inmate supply side," several factors suggest a steady stream of new inmates will be heading towards lock-ups. For example, most American politicians, when facing election or re-election, support expanding police forces and hold prison systems in high regard. Politicians do this in order to demonstrate to the voting public that they are "super-crime-fighters." Super-crime-fighter politicians leave unattended many important prison issues. Instead, they point to the full prison as proof that their solutions to problems are working. In the United States, a good deal of prison space is needed in order to house persons diagnosed as mentally ill, since there are few other public places to put them. Prison lobbyists, corrections workers' unions, corporate prison operators and prison vendors help politicians see the need for ever-expanding prison systems. Finally, prisons in the United States are used to control ethnic minority persons who, many legal officials believe, might otherwise pose a threat to social order. Combined, these factors ensure that a steady supply of criminals will be available for imprisonment in the United States.

This book is critical in tone. The subject-matter of this book is provocative and troubling. Some readers will likely be left with dark images of a runaway system, ripping a wound into the very fabric of American society. We make no attempt to "gloss over," "sugar coat" or trivialize this set of somber subjects. Our hope is that this book will contribute to a productive debate among concerned persons around the world about how U.S. prisons should be configured and run.

We exclude, herein, analysis of jails and juvenile facilities, in order to keep ourselves sharply focused on adult prisons. Our treatment of U.S.

prisons is structural, in the sense that long-term lock-ups are imbedded into social systems. Long-term lock-ups display internal and external linkages. Habits of organization and patterns of communication are in place. Our analysis of U.S. prisons occurs within the context of these structures. This book is intended for use by college and university students, both undergraduate and graduate, who wish to deepen their knowledge about American corrections. This book will be useful for the general reader who is looking for information about how prisons in the United States came into existence, about how they operate and about where they are most likely headed. Finally, policymakers, legal officials, politicians and prison administrators might find, herein, the dissenting voice that is frequently lacking when important decisions are made.

For most of his adult life, the senior author worked with inmates, as a counselor and teacher, in a number of adult and juvenile prisons. For over 30 years, he has taught courses titled "Sociology of Corrections" at five colleges and universities. Knowledge gained from such experiences shares space herein with the insights and information provided by hundreds of scholars and writers who share our passion for this unseemly subject. A list of references, at the end of this book, provides some small indication of our debt to these people.

Book overview

Chapter 1 explores the philosophy of imprisonment in the United States, as it took shape during early occupation by European armies and as it matured under internal political control. We examine the three primary goals of American imprisonment, namely isolation of criminals, their punishment and, simultaneously, their rehabilitation. American aptitudes for judging others harshly, and for turning our backs on them thereafter, are identified as the ideological pillars of the American imprisonment philosophy.

Chapter 2 provides a brief history of early American prisons, covering the years 1600 to 1900. Here, we see the basic themes of prison life take root, an emphasis on cruelty and inhumanity as ways to induce law-violating humans to be less cruel and less inhumane.

Chapter 3 examines the twentieth-century prison-building binge. We see emerge, from modest beginnings, a prison system thirsting for resources and threatening to push aside other, more constructive, social policies.

Chapter 4 tells the story of how federal prisons came to life and how they have become one of the fastest-growing, most costly, segments of corrections in the United States. We see federal prison policy usurp states' rights, in terms of shaping the current character of prisons and their future direction.

Chapter 5 helps us understand how a handful of American corporations, and their executives, became major players in the prison game. We learn how to extract large profits from punishment and how to bypass voter approval, while seeking a "higher" goal, that of rapidly providing prison space.

Chapter 6 examines the American practice of executing inmates. We review the history of executions in American society, execution technology and the raging debate over its practicality and morality.

Chapter 7 focuses on new prison minorities. We learn that women, children and the elderly are showing up in large numbers and are staying longer, in our nation's prisons. We examine the special problems that new minorities pose for corrections officers, prison officials and taxpayers.

Chapter 8 highlights two prison by-products – violence and disease. Each by-product is described in considerable detail. Explanations are provided of how prison by-products, not only contaminate inmates' lives, but also of how their effects seep outside the walls, back into American communities and cities.

Chapter 9 summarizes what we have learned about the past and present of prisons in the United States. Finally, Chapter 9 focuses on the future of American prisons. We address questions like "Can the American prison system continue to grow as it has in the past century?" "Is prison the most appropriate place to house mentally ill persons, petty drug dealers and users and common thieves?" and "Is the American economy capable of sustaining the cost of operating one of the world's largest prison systems?" Finally, we briefly explore some options for changing the character of imprisonment in the United States.

Chapter 2

A brief history of imprisonment in America (1600–1900)

Contents

Imprisonment in colonial America

If we use a conventional contemporary definition of prisoner, like "[A]nyone who is held in either a county or city jail, prison, or penitentiary," or of inmate, like "[P]risoner of jail or prison" (Champion 2001: 69, 107), then there were few inmates or prisoners in colonial America. However, if we think of inmates or prisoners as persons "deprived of their liberty to leave" (Christianson 1998: 13), then there were tens of thousands in America during the colonial period, including indentured servants, slaves and other assorted persons exported from European jails and prisons. Most indentured servants were Europeans who contracted with American masters for a fixed period of servitude in exchange for passage to North America with room and board upon arrival. Some were indigenous Americans who indentured themselves to masters in exchange for the opportunity to learn a trade by serving as an apprentice. Indentured servants were frequently subjected to physical abuse and sexual violation.

In the early 1600s, via royal proclamation requested by the Virginia Company, England began the process of exporting thousands of vagrants and other criminals to the American colonies. Criminal law in England classified many violations as capital offenses, and under the threat of execution, prisoners awaiting trial usually agreed to exportation. This flow of prisoners into the colonies included women and children, as well as adult males. In England, both private companies and legal officials were authorized to apprehend and transport poor, law-violating persons to the colonies. In the colonies, such "kidnapped" persons were sold to masters to be used as servants and workers. Once in the colonies, kidnapped servants and workers were at the mercy of their masters and endured much brutality and oppression since there was little legal oversight of such relationships (Christianson 1998; DeMause 1974; Musick 1995). In 1646, Massachusetts passed the Stubborn Child Law, which provided for taking vagrant children into custody; they were to be held in jail or almshouses until they could be placed as apprentices. The Stubborn Child Law was adopted by other colonies and became, until the late 1800s, the legal standard for treatment of poor American children. Children's rights were considered unimportant. Fathers and masters had total legal control of their children (Schorsch 1979; Tiffin 1982). During the 1700s, it is estimated that one in four immigrants to colonial America from England was a convict (Christianson 1998). The Irish, French, Spanish and Dutch also sent large numbers of convicts to America. The practice of exporting criminal law violators to colonial America is called "penal slavery." Later in American history, this practice is resurrected in the form of prison work gangs contracted out by prison officials to work for the state or private interests.

In 1619, a Dutch man-of-war arrived at a Virginia port and sold to the colonists 20 persons stolen from West Africa. Those first African Americans were held in bondage until 1661 and then proclaimed by law to be slaves. Mass slavery was practiced in North America until 1862. Many English ships transported a mix of slaves, indentured servants and criminal law violators. When, in 1776, the Continental Congress outlawed the importation of foreign slaves, a number of Southern states began programs to breed their own. By 1790, the Southern population was 35 percent African American. By 1850, there were approximately 3 million African American slaves living and toiling in North America (Turner et al., 1984). Slavery in America was a dirty enterprise. Most enslaved African Americans were worked savagely on plantations, on farms and in mines. Slaves could be bought and sold without limitation. Children of slaves could be taken from their parents anytime their owner chose to do so. Slaves could be beaten, branded, raped and murdered with impunity by owners and managers. Others who did not own or manage the slave might encumber a civil liability for perpetrating such atrocities. In most jurisdictions, by law, slaves were not allowed to read and write. Cotton and tobacco plantations were among the most oppressive prisons to be found in colonial America (Turner et al., 1984). African American slaves were the ultimate prisoners of early America.

Jails, places of confinement for persons awaiting trial or execution, became common in colonial American communities. Throughout the North and South, jails were built to temporarily hold runaway slaves, indentured servants and other law violators. Jails were built in cities like Boston, Charleston, Hartford, Newport, New York, Philadelphia, Salem and St Mary's, Maryland. Jails were a basic part of the legal structure that served to uphold slavery and other forms of bondage in colonial America: "By the 1720s every city and virtually every county had at least one detention house, and most had several. Colonial America had more jails than public schools or hospitals" (Christianson 1998: 60).

Prisons were another early feature of colonial American legal structure. For example, in 1632, the General Court of Boston ordered that a house of correction, and living quarters for a warden, be built. In fact, the original charter for the Massachusetts Bay Company provided for the construction of a house of correction, to punish offenders and to deter would-be law violators. By 1636, the colonists in Massachusetts were operating a prison on Castle Island. In 1674, the Maryland Assembly allocated funds for the building of a prison at St Mary's. Inmates in most colonial-era jails and prisons were expected to pay their keepers for "extras" like food and bedding. In 1682, Pennsylvania adopted the Great Law, which prescribed hard labor in a house of correction as punishment for most crimes. However, all other colonies operated under the English Anglican code, which prescribed execution for 13 offenses and mutilation, branding, or corporal punishment for most other legal infractions. In 1718, one day after the death of William Penn, Pennsylvania adopted the English Anglican code. The English Anglican code dictated most penal policies until shortly after the American Revolution. In 1757, a large debtor's prison was built in New York. Early American jails and prisons were overcrowded and became breeding grounds for disease and depravity. Men, women and children were housed together, allowing for wholesale abuse. Many men, women and children who committed petty offenses were held in jails and prisons for long periods of time. One way out of a jail or prison was to "volunteer" for servitude under control of the state or a master. Prisoners who "volunteered" for servitude were often worked in "chain gangs."

During the American Revolution, the English operated a number of makeshift jails on American soil, used to hold captives. Captured churches and warehouses were commonly used for this purpose. The British also incarcerated captured American rebels on disabled ships, called "hulks," which were tethered to the sides of rivers and harbors. It is reported that scores of inmates died daily, suffering from starvation, hypothermia and disease. Inmate bodies piled up and were sometimes fed to domestic or wild animals. Jails and prisons operated by the American rebels were no better. The worst was probably Newgate, opened in 1773, a copper mine turned prison in Simsbury, Connecticut. At Newgate, inmates were held underground and forced to work 12-hour shifts (Christianson 1998). In 1774, Newgate's inmates rioted. After the revolution, a number of prisons and jails originally run by the British continued to operate under American control. For example, Bridewell, originally a British prison in New York, later held local vagrants, runaway slaves and other types of criminal law violators.

American prisons after the revolution

State prisons

Shortly after the American Revolution, the penitentiary was born in Philadelphia, where part of the Walnut Street Jail was transformed into a long-term lock-up. The Walnut Street Penitentiary, composed of 16 cells, was based upon the separate (or solitary) confinement model, sometimes called the Pennsylvania system, that isolated inmates – one to a cell. Inmates were left in their cells to contemplate misdeeds and to study the only piece of reading material allowed – a Bible. The separate confinement model gained in popularity and was emulated in a number of other states. In 1796, the New York legislature allocated funds for construction of separate confinement penitentiaries. New Jersey completed construction of a penitentiary in 1797. In 1800, penitentiaries were opened in Virginia and Kentucky.

Soon thereafter, penitentiaries were opened in Maryland, Massachusetts, New Hampshire and Vermont. State legislatures moved to adopt long-term incarceration and hard labor as the primary response to criminal law violation by revising legal codes, abolishing capital punishment for most offenses and, instead, prescribing confinement in penitentiaries.

American legislators and corrections officials embraced the old Beccarian principle that the more horrific (or serious) the crime, the more time in a penitentiary the offender should be given (Christianson 1998). Thus, the prison-building boom was begun in America, a boom that continues today. America was becoming known as a center of innovation when it came to using prisons as tools for managing and containing social problems. Two varieties of penitentiary emerged. First was the separate confinement system described earlier in this section. Pennsylvania officials first employed this system at the Walnut Street Penitentiary. In 1826, the separate confinement system was implemented at a new penitentiary in Pittsburgh, and in 1829, at a penitentiary in Philadelphia. Second, New York legal officials devised the "congregate," or Auburn, prison. The Auburn prison, like the separate confinement system, emphasized silence and hard labor, but it allowed inmates to work in groups.

The congregate system was implemented at New York's first state prison, which began receiving inmates in 1797 (Christianson 1998). The New York State Prison was located at the edge of the Hudson River in New York City. The prison, completed in 1799, was surrounded by a wall with watch towers. The prison consisted of a main building; its wings contained eight-person cells, solitary confinement cells, a chapel and prison industry buildings. The prison was designed to hold approximately 450 inmates. Just 4 years after it opened, in 1803, the New York State Prison was operating at full capacity. The prison held men and women, free persons and slaves. It was anticipated by the New York state legislature that the prison would pay for itself through revenues generated by prison industries, using inmates as laborers. The prison hosted a constant stream of escapes, stabbings, riots and other forms of violence. The warden, a Quaker reformer, lamented the prison's failure to rehabilitate convicts.

New York implemented the congregate system at the Auburn Penitentiary in 1819–1823, at the infamous Sing-Sing Penitentiary in 1825 and at Dannemora in 1845 (Keve 1991). Eventually, largely due to economic considerations and to the fact that isolation promotes mental illness in inmates, the congregate system won out over the separate confinement system as the preferred type of American prison, although all prisons had isolation cells available (Grassian 1994).

Here, we encounter the striking dual reality that is characteristic of American prisons. On the one hand, legal officials saw the American penitentiary as a humane attempt to eliminate the causes of crime and to replace them in the minds and souls of inmates with a hard work ethic and with penitence – a feeling of sorrow for having sinned or done wrong. In other words, penitentiaries were designed to reform law violators through punishment and hard work. On the other hand, inmates experienced penitentiaries as hell holes, where violence and disrespect prevail, where inmates learn that if you possess enough power, you can do anything you want to others, even if it is against the law. In the words of one veteran inmate talking about the prisons in which he served time, "I'd love to meet the dude who dreamed up shit like this. He must have been made on Mars" (The History Channel 1998a). Prisons became part of the traditional American criminal justice system. Prisons were invented by a generation of Americans who were unable to prove that the incarceration of some deterred others from crime, or that prisons reformed criminals.

Sing-Sing, up the Hudson River from New York City, located near Ossining, New York, became a model for penitentiaries throughout the world. Cut from stone by convicts, Sing-Sing added to the American vocabulary phrases like "up the river," "big house" and "last mile," which referred to the walk to the world's first electric chair made by 614 inmates executed there. Inmates quarried the stone and built the first cellblock, which opened in 1828, after 3 years of construction. Four tiers high, 476 feet long, freestanding within an outer shell, with 800 cells 7 feet long by 3.5 feet wide, the first cellblock served as the primary structure at Sing-Sing for a hundred years. In the 1830s, Sing-Sing was expanded to include workshops, a factory, a chapel, a kitchen and a hospital. The outer walls of Sing-Sing were designed to communicate a cold, forbidding presence (The History Channel 1998a).

State legislators and prison officials touted Sing-Sing as the centerpiece of their commitment to reforming criminals. But, the harsh reality of life within the walls signaled another agenda. Sing-Sing became one of the most notorious penitentiaries in the world, for its violence. Sing-Sing housed the toughest criminals from New York City and soon earned the nickname "house of fear." Homemade weapons and inmate violence were constants at Sing-Sing. Strict discipline was imposed, which included a code of silence. Inmates were dressed in striped uniforms, in order to humiliate them. Uniforms and shoes issued to inmates did not fit, making walking painful for many. Inmates were forced to move about the prison in "lock step" fashion. All hair was shaved from the heads of inmates. Guards were encouraged to physically punish inmates and to treat them with contempt. As a disciplinary measure, misbehaving inmates were put in stocks in an exercise yard. The whip, called a cat-of-nine-tails, was used. The cat-of-nine-tails was notorious for cutting flesh. Inmates called this form of discipline imposed on them at Sing-Sing a "catocracy." Blood shed from the punishment of inmates was left on the floors of the prison, so that others could view it. In 1847, after flogging inmates was outlawed by the New York state legislature (except in self-defense or riot situations), guards increased use of the "iron cage," a device placed around the neck and head of an inmate, and left on for lengthy periods, as a form of punishment. Some inmates were exposed to a form of punishment called a "shower bath" that, in its extreme form, could result in drowning. Many inmates attempted suicide within a few weeks of arriving at Sing-Sing. In 1839, a women's prison was built on a hill above the main cellblock at Sing-Sing and, for a short time, was overseen by a reform-oriented administrator, who was eventually fired. The women's prison closed in 1877. Also in 1877, a wall was built around the prison. By the 1880s, the stocks, flogging and the shower bath were replaced by confinement in a darkened cell as the principle form of punishment at Sing-Sing (The History Channel 1998a).

In 1891, the world's first electric chair, nicknamed "Old Sparky," replaced the gallows as the means of execution at Sing-Sing. Sing-Sing eventually became the "Death House" for the New York corrections system. Advertised as a painless, instantaneous form of execution, the electric chair transmitted 2,000 volts of electricity for three or four seconds, then 500 volts for three or four seconds, then 2,000 volts for three or four seconds to the condemned person. This resulted in body temperatures guaranteed to boil brain fluid. This form of execution featured burning flesh, foaming mouths and exploding eyeballs. The sides of the electric chair at Sing-Sing displayed deep grooves carved by the fingernails of the condemned (The History Channel 1998a). This was the context in which inmates were "reformed." From the inmate's perspective, Sing-Sing demonstrated that, if you have enough power, you can do anything you want to people.

The Louisiana State Penitentiary at Angola, nicknamed "The Farm" or "Angola" or "The Plantation," serves as a good example of another form of nineteenth-century American prison. Before the Civil War, The Farm had served as a slave plantation, populated by African Americans stolen from Angola in Africa. After the Civil War, it was turned into a state prison. The Farm is divided into six complexes, called camps, located on 18,000 acres, surrounded on three sides by the Mississippi River. The Farm, more than 30 miles from the nearest town, employs about 1,800 workers and holds over 5,000 inmates, making it one of the largest maximum-security prisons in America (Investigative Reports 1998). The camps are made up of long, one-story buildings. Because Louisiana metes out some of the harshest punishment in the United States, 85 percent of the inmates are serving life sentences, with little or no hope of parole. Almost 80 percent of the inmates are African American. The Farm is known as one of America's most dangerous and bloody prisons. Illicit drugs are everywhere on The Farm. Violence abounds. Rapes, stabbings and killings are commonplace.

The Farm is a multimillion-dollar agricultural enterprise. Just as they were in slave days, inmates assigned to the fields are awakened at 5:00 a.m. and are worked until sunset. Inmates are paid just a few cents per hour for their labor in the fields. In the 1800s, inmates were not compensated. Everybody at Angola has a job. Everybody goes to work, every day. The rate of pay for inmates at Angola tops out less than $1 per hour. Upon arrival at Angola, a new inmate is broken down through forced labor at some menial job. Inmates work long, hard hours. Most inmates work in the fields or on the levee crew. If you adjust to Angola quickly, you live. If you don't, you die. Inmates who attempt escape, if they are caught, are forced to do hard labor (Wikberg 1992).

Another infamous nineteenth-century penitentiary was the California State Prison at San Quentin, the first prison to be built in California. Built to accommodate Gold Rush–era law violators, San Quentin has a bloody history, featuring wholesale staff and inmate assaults. In July 1852, an abandoned ship was towed to Point San Quentin in the San Francisco bay. The ship was remodeled to accommodate 40 inmates but soon housed 150. Women and men were locked up together on the prison hulk. In 1853, construction of the new prison began on land, using convict laborers from the prison ship. Inmate-quarried rock and red brick were used to build San Quentin. In 1854, a single building was completed. The first building at San Quentin served as a lock-up, a dungeon and a hospital. By the end of the year, San Quentin housed 250 inmates, men and women alike. In the evenings, guards took female inmates to the saloons located on San Quentin's grounds. Guards and inmates were allowed to frequent the saloons, if they could afford drinks. Some female inmates worked as prostitutes, servicing guards and inmates. Female inmates also worked in the prison laundry (The History Channel 1998b). Until 1860, inmates wore civilian clothing. After 1860, inmates wore striped uniforms. Inmates who refused to work were locked up in the "sweat box," a small, windowless building.

The first cellblocks constructed were three story stone structures, designed to house 250 inmates. The cellblocks were soon nicknamed "the stones" by inmates. San Quentin cells were larger than those at Sing-Sing but had no windows and were equipped only with a cot, a chamber pot and a water bucket. Inmates nicknamed the most dangerous alley between cellblocks "blood alley." Another alley, where the chamber pots were emptied and cleaned, was nicknamed "the rose garden." In 1885, a free-standing hospital was built on San Quentin's grounds (The History Channel 1998b).

Punishment at San Quentin was brutal. Flogging was the most common form of punishment. In the 1850s, inmates who were insolent, who lied, or who gambled were given 12 lashes. Inmates who stole, fought or disobeyed were given 20 lashes. Inmates who attempted escape were shackled to a ball and chain and forced to carry the ball whenever they walked the prison grounds. "Showering" was used to punish assaults on guards and rioting. Showering at San Quentin involved an inmate being suspended in air, upside down, and having water, passing through a high-pressure nozzle, aimed at his mouth and genitals. Showering was finally outlawed, by the California state legislature, in 1913. Homemade weapons have always been common at San Quentin. In the 1880s, prison industries were started at San Quentin. A jute mill was constructed, featuring 200 looms used to make feed sacks, which were sold to farmers. Inmates provided labor for the mill, which operated around the clock until 1955, when it burned down (The History Channel 1998b).

California's second prison, Folsom, opened on July 26, 1880, when 44 inmates were transferred by boat and train from San Quentin. Folsom Prison, located near Represa, California, at the edge of the American River, was built of native stone. Designed to hold inmates serving long sentences, incorrigibles and habitual criminals, it was one of America's first maximum-security prisons. From its inception, Folsom State Prison was a violent and bloody place. The first escape from Folsom occurred in 1880, the same year that it opened (California Department of Corrections 2001a).

By the middle of the nineteenth century, it had become obvious that penitentiaries were failing to deter would-be criminals and to rehabilitate offenders. This should have surprised no one since penitentiaries were "overcrowded, understaffed, and minimally financed" (Clear & Cole 2000: 42). Prisons were also saturated with violence. In 1870, at the meetings of the National Prison Congress, an organization dominated by reform-minded prison administrators, a set of principles was developed to guide the operation of American prisons. It was suggested that: (1) The punishment of inmates should continue, but punishment should be augmented by expanded programs of education and industrial labor, resulting in a love of labor. (2) Sentences, rather than set at fixed terms, should be indeterminate, so that inmates who are successfully rehabilitated could be released back into the community on parole. (3) Education is of primary importance in prisons. (4) Prisoners and prisons should be classified by type. (5) Prison guards and prisoners must be committed to reform. (6) The prisoner's self-respect must be cultivated. (7) In the management of prisoners, moral force should be the primary tool, with physical force being used as little as possible (Fisher 2001).

As a result of these high-minded principles, and of the failure of the penitentiary, a new style of prison was born in the United States, called the "reformatory." The first reformatory, located at Elmira, New York, was opened in 1876 and was placed under the direction of Zebulon Brockway, who believed that inmates' problems should be diagnosed and then treated through a program of individualized education and industrial labor. For the most part, prisoners at reformatories were younger than most held in penitentiaries. Inmates at Elmira were given indeterminate sentences that offered the possibility of parole, if behavioral improvement was shown. In the next 30 years, reformatories were built by a number of states. However, reformatories proved to be no more successful at deterring crime and rehabilitating offenders than penitentiaries. Probable causes for the failure of reformatories were violence and overcrowding. At Elmira, for example, inmates were whipped and beaten with leather straps and rubber hoses in the dreaded Bathroom #4, often by Brockway himself. Others were chained for months in dungeons and fed bread and water. Inmates caught masturbating "had a metal ring surgically implanted in the foreskin of the penis" (Hallinan 2001: 71). Vocational training and formal education offered in the context of prison overcrowding and violence made rehabilitation difficult, if not impossible, for most prisoners. In spite of poor results at his prison, in 1898, Zebulon Brockway became president of the National Prison Congress.

Clearly, the American prison-building boom was well under way. New conventional prisons were being constructed everywhere in the United States. For example, adult prisons were built in Oregon (1871), Iowa (1873), Arizona (1875), Colorado (1876), Illinois (1878), California (1880), Kentucky (1883), North Dakota (1883), New Mexico (1884), Washington (1886), Michigan (1889), Montana (1889), North Carolina (1889), South Dakota (1891), Tennessee (1895) and Utah (1896) (Allen & Simonsen 1998: 42).

Federal prisons

Before the twentieth century, only a handful of federal prisons had been built in the United States. In 1776, the Continental Congress commandeered the Walnut Street Jail and used it as a prison for a number of years, before abandoning it and returning it to state control. In 1776, Congress authorized federal agents to use state and county prisons as places of confinement for persons found guilty of violating federal laws. In 1789, when the federal court system was begun, U.S. Marshals were given the responsibility of procuring prison space for federal offenders. U.S. Marshals placed federal offenders in a number of prisons including Connecticut's Simsbury; Pennsylvania's Eastern State Penitentiary; and New York's Sing-Sing, Auburn and Albany County penitentiaries. Federal inmates were placed in a number of Southern prisons where contract labor, a form of penal slavery, was commonly practiced. Contract prison labor was used in two ways. First, manufacturing facilities were built within the walls of some prisons and were operated by private, for-profit contractors, using inmate labor. The state was compensated for this arrangement, not inmates. Second, a prisoner for lease system was devised where inmates were sent out of prisons, usually in "gangs." Leased prisoners worked for private, for-profit contractors, at sites designated by the contractors. Once again, states were compensated for the leased labor, not inmates. Leased inmates were used to build roads, railroad tunnels and levees; to dig canals; and to quarry stone. Leased inmates were fed poorly, were frequently housed in cages and were subjected to whatever corporal punishment their profit-seeking masters saw fit to administer. For escape attempts, leased inmates could be tortured, maimed or killed. It is reported that most leased inmates died after a few years of such treatment. In 1831, a federal prison was opened in Washington, D.C., and operated until 1862, when it was closed in order to allow for the expansion of an adjacent military base (Keve 1991).

During early stages of the Civil War, both the North and South con-structed large holding pens for captives. For a short while, soldiers were exchanged and paroled from these holding pens. However, by late 1862, this system had broken down and exchange of war prisoners ended. Through-out the remainder of the Civil War, both sides operated approximately 150 prisons of many types (Speer 1997). The South converted a fort, called Cas-tle Pinckney, for use as a prison. The North converted Fort Warren, Fort Lafayette, Fort McHenry and Fort Delaware for use as Civil War prisons. The North converted penitentiaries in Alton, Illinois; Columbus, Ohio; and Michigan City, Indiana. Scores of buildings, in the North and South, were converted into Civil War prisons. In the North, enclosures for Civil War pris-oners were constructed near military barracks at Johnson's Island, Camp Morton, Camp Douglas, Camp Chase, Elmira and Rock Island. Tent prisons were built at Belle Isle in the South and at Union Point Lookout in the North. In the South, numerous open stockades held thousands of prisoners.

Andersonville Prison in south-central Georgia was the most notori-ous of the Southern Civil War prisons. Constructed in 1864 by slaves con-scripted from nearby farms, Andersonville was a stockade consisting of a 12-foot-high outer wooden fence that encircled thousands of tents, make-shift shacks and holes dug in the ground. Andersonville Prison sat on 16.5 acres and was designed to hold 10,000 prisoners. The first prison-ers arrived in February 1864, and by June, over 20,000 were confined at Andersonville. Using prisoners and slaves as workers, the holding fence was moved outward, encompassing an additional 10 acres. By August 1864, Andersonville held over 33,000 captive soldiers. Prison guards shot any inmate who passed beyond a wooden railing called the "deadline," stretching around the inner perimeter of the stockade. Severe overcrowd-ing created horrific health conditions. Food and clothing for inmates was scarce. By the end of the war, in 1865, an estimated 12,912 prisoners had died at Andersonville of malnutrition, exposure and diseases like scurvy, diarrhea, dysentery and gangrene. The rate of death during Andersonville's 13 months of operation approached 30 percent (Marvel 1994).

Libby Prison, located in Richmond, Virginia, was a set of three four-story-high tobacco warehouses before the Civil War. During the war, the warehouses were commandeered and accommodated over 125,000 captives, including Union officers, spies and slaves. Libby Prison had a capac-ity of 1,200 inmates, although it held many more on numerous occasions.

When, in 1865, the Union army captured Richmond, Libby Prison was taken over by the North and housed Confederate prisoners until 1868. The death rate at Libby Prison was much lower than at Andersonville. In 1888, Libby Prison was purchased, dismantled and reconstructed in Chicago, where it was operated as a tourist attraction until 1899. Other Civil War prisons in Richmond were called Castle Godwin (a converted jail), Castle Thunder (a converted tobacco warehouse) and Castle Lightning (another converted tobacco warehouse) (Speer 1997).

Bell Island Prison, which opened in 1861, consisted of a cluster of shacks and tents located on a small island in the James River, just west of Richmond. Bell Island Prison was configured to hold 3,000 inmates, but by 1863, almost 10,000 Union soldiers were held captive there. At Bell Island Prison, as many as 15 to 25 men died each day, some via drowning as they attempted escape through the river's rapids, others via gunshot wounds inflicted by guards, as they attempted escape. Others died at the hands of gangsters who preyed upon prisoners while guards stood by and watched (Speer 1997).

Elmira Prison, located at Elmira, New York, was a 40-acre stockade for Confederate soldiers, built around an abandoned army training camp. Elmira, which opened in June 1864, was the Andersonville of the North. The prison, a cluster of 35 barracks and countless tents, surrounded by a 12-foot-high fence, was designed to hold 5,000 inmates. The barracks at Elmira could hold only 1,750 captives. By August 1864, it held almost 10,000 captured soldiers. Many were forced to sleep outside, without bedding. Due to Union Army policy, food, clothing and bedding were scarce at Elmira. Fewer than 10 percent of the inmates had blankets. Many prisoners died suffering from exposure, starvation, pneumonia, smallpox, scurvy, dysentery and diarrhea. Inmates nicknamed the prison "Hellmira." Of the 12,123 soldiers imprisoned at Elmira, it is estimated that almost 3,000 died there. The death rate at Elmira Prison approximated that at Andersonville (Speer 1997).

Camp Douglas, located on the south side of Chicago, was another Andersonville of the North. In 1861, the federal government constructed a military training camp and prisoner-of-war camp on property formerly owned by Stephen A. Douglas. The prisoner-of-war camp consisted of barracks and tents surrounded by a 15-foot-high plank wall with a 3-foot walk on top for guards to use. There was a deadline along the interior of the wall. If inmates walked beyond the deadline, they were shot. Each barracks, measuring 70 feet by 25 feet, was designed to hold 125 inmates but held 200 or more. When the barracks filled up, tents were constructed. Camp Douglas, which soon earned the nickname "80 acres of hell," received its first 8,000 prisoners in February 1862. By 1864, Camp Douglas held over

12,000 captives. By July 5, 1865, when it closed, Camp Douglas had hosted over 18,000 Confederate soldiers (Levy 1994).

The monthly death rate at Camp Douglas was 10 percent, even higher than Andersonville's 9 percent. The camp weathered smallpox and cholera epidemics. Due to overcrowding, unhealthy living conditions prevailed. Rain washed sewage into the drinking water supply. Barracks walls and ceilings, tents and the earth were saturated with disease-causing contaminants. Food was scarce, forcing inmates to catch big, gray rats that became a main ingredient in "rat pies." Medical attention for prisoners was inadequate. Inmates died of starvation, exposure, cholera, smallpox, scurvy and brutality. Inmates were forced to sleep without blankets with the winter wind from Lake Michigan blowing over the camp. Chicago public health officials labeled Camp Douglas an "extermination" camp.

Punishments were varied and used frequently, even for minor offenses. Guards forced inmates to pull down their pants and to sit for hours in the snow or on frozen ground. Inmates were stretched over a barrel and whipped, sometimes with the metal buckle end of a belt. Inmates were forced to ride, often naked, "The Mule," a 15-foot-high wooden structure with a sharp saddle. Mule rides lasted 2 hours a day, for several days. To increase the level of torture, buckets of sand were tied to the ankles, and Mule riders were forced to hold large meat bones in their hands. Men would pass out from the pain and fall off of The Mule. After a Mule ride, most men could not walk for hours. Captives were placed into two forms of solitary confinement. A dark underground dungeon was used, as well as a 10-square-foot room with one 10-inch window for ventilation that might hold as many as 20 persons at a time (Levy 1994; Sword 1992). The North claimed that 3,775 died at Camp Douglas. The South set the figure at 4,275. An independent investigator estimated 6,129 persons died at Camp Douglas, approximately one-third of the Confederate soldiers held there (Levy 1994; Taylor 2000).

During the 1800s, the United States federal government also operated territorial prisons in the west, in Arizona, Colorado, Idaho, Montana, Utah, Washington and Wyoming (Keve 1991; The Marshals Monitor 2000). The Secretary of the Interior was responsible for site selection and construction of territorial prisons. The U.S. Marshal was responsible for operation of the prison in his territory. Although little is known today about nineteenth-century federal territorial prisons, experts assert that living conditions were terrible and security was often lax (Keve 1991). The Wyoming Territorial Prison opened in 1872 and operated as a federal prison until 1890 when it became a state prison. The Wyoming Territorial prison was nicknamed "The Big House across the River." The prison was located at the edge of the Big Laramie River. Inmates were forced to make brooms for resale, to chop wood and, in the winter, to cut blocks of ice from the frozen river.

The prison hosted such famous captives as Jesse James and Butch Cassidy as well as gamblers, thieves, cutthroats, prostitutes and highwaymen (The Marshals Monitor 2000). The Colorado Federal Territorial Prison in Canon City opened June 13, 1871, and was known as one of the "Hell Holes" of the Old West, a site of numerous hangings. The Colorado Federal Territorial Prison is perhaps most famous for hosting Alfred Packer, an inmate convicted of cannibalism. Another inmate at the Colorado Federal Territorial Prison was an 11-year-old murderer. Cells at the Arizona Federal Territorial Prison, in Yuma, were carved by inmates into a large stone mound protruding from the desert floor. One side of the prison was used to house inmates with tuberculosis, the other side hosted conventional criminals. The isolation cell was carved into the rock floor of the prison, a hole 3 feet deep, 3 feet wide and 8 feet long, fitted with an iron door featuring a small slit that served as a window. Summer temperatures in the isolation cell were sufficient to cook a human. Prisoners who escaped from the Arizona prison were pursued by Apache employees who were instructed to, upon capture of the inmates, torture them as they were brought back to the prison, but to keep them alive so that they could be shown to inmates who might be contemplating escape.

Privatized prisons

Privatization of certain prison functions was brought to the American colonies by English immigrants when businessmen transported convicted felons to Virginia and sold them into servitude (Ammon et al., 1992). Colonial-era American jailers were also businessmen who billed government agencies (usually counties) for services like removing inmate's chains, providing food and supplying clothing. Many jailers also sold meals, liquor and other privileges to inmates (Walker 1980). In the 1700s, jails and prisons were often operated by private contractors (Ethridge & Marquart 1993; McCrie 1992). Some inmates were paid exploitive wages to produce goods that were resold by businessmen.

In the 1800s, many private contractors were allowed to bring raw materials into prisons, to set up production facilities and to oversee inmates who produced goods that were then sold outside the prison by the contractor (Melossi & Pavarini 1981). At prisons like Auburn, Newgate and Sing-Sing, inmates were put to work in this fashion producing barrels, clothing, furniture, harnesses, nails, rugs and shoes. Other inmates built houses in nearby communities and quarried stone. Such privatized inmate industries helped pay prison expenses and sometimes generated sizable profits for prison authorities and state governments. Inmates were rarely paid for such work (Conley 1980; deBeaumont & deTocqueville 1833/1979; Gardner 1987; Lewis 1965; McKelvey 1936). This arrangement served legal officials and businessmen well. On the legal side, prisons could be subsidized or turned into profit-making factories. On the business side, inmates proved to be an attractive alternative to unionizing workers outside the walls, and production expenses were lower in prisons, yielding higher profits. The contract system of inmate labor was adopted by a number of prisons in the United States. By 1885, 13 states had contracts with privatized entities, both individuals and corporations, for the use of prison laborers (McCrie 1992).

In some states, businessmen actually took control of all prison functions. Such was the case at the Kentucky State Prison in Frankfort where an entrepreneur built and then leased the prison from the state for 5 years, turning it into a profitable factory (Sneed 1860). In Alabama and Louisiana, other penitentiaries were leased to companies (Ayers 1984; Carleton 1971). Texas ran a highly profitable textile manufacturing plant in one of its prisons (Ayers 1984). Missouri leased prisoners to a contractor who used them to build houses near the prison (Ayers 1984; Sellin 1976).

In the 1850s, California's first state prison, San Quentin, was constructed and operated under contract by two businessmen with political connections, on land that they owned. The first lease, signed in 1851, was for 10 years. From the construction phase onward, San Quentin, under private control, was plagued by corruption (Lamott 1961; McAfee 1987). The private contractors allowed some inmates to do work outside the prison, resulting in numerous escapes. Guards and inmates consumed liquor together at local bars. Both utilized the services of inmate prostitutes. Finally, in 1860, after a prolonged legal battle, state officials bought the private contractors out and took control of San Quentin (Lamott 1961).

In the late 1860s, Southern states leased masses of prisoners, most African American, to individuals and corporations. Inmates became a principle form of labor for many furniture, mining and railroad corporations. At the first of the year, state officials would sign contracts with corporate employers giving them a good idea of how many prisoners they needed to incarcerate in order to fulfill their commitments (Adamson 1983; Ayers 1984; Novak 1978; Sellin 1976). As a result, the numbers of African Americans sent to prison in the South increased dramatically. Whether American inmates were worked within the walls, or outside, they suffered from physical abuse, lack of food, an absence of medical care, overwork and unsafe working conditions often resulting in death (Ayers 1984; Sellin 1976; Walker 1988).

A number of reformers began to protest the brutal exploitation of inmate laborers. Labor unions and many businessmen began to complain about the unfair advantage gained by those who had access to cheap prison labor. By the 1890s, this resulted in a downturn in the use of inmate labor for private, profit-making purposes. Those against the use of inmate labor for profit lobbied for legislation prohibiting the practice. In 1905, President

Theodore Roosevelt signed an Executive Order making it unlawful to use convict labor on federally funded projects. In 1929, the U.S. Congress passed the Hawes-Cooper Act giving state governments permission to halt the movement of commodities manufactured by inmates into their states (Ammon et al., 1992). These actions effectively interrupted the use of inmate labor in profit-making activities, until later in the twentieth century.

Summary

In the preceding pages, we have seen the backbone of the American prison system take shape. We have seen the basic themes of imprisonment in the United States emerge. Isolation, overcrowding, physical violence, sexual violation and racism became the building blocks of the American prison movement. However, early imprisonment in America involved dual realities. On the one hand, there was the reality of those who created and managed the U.S. prison system. Legal officials and politicians asserted that imprisonment reforms, or rehabilitates, inmates by isolating them, by confining them, by forcing them into hard labor and by requiring that they contemplate the harsh consequences of their lawlessness. On the other hand, inmates experienced another reality, where severe overcrowding, rampant violence, brutal punishment and extreme deprivation defined their lives. In prison, inmates received an advanced education in the practice of inhumanity. Inmates learned that, if you have enough power, and if your actions are sufficiently hidden from public view, you can do almost anything you wish to others.

The United States was about to embark on a great experiment, wherein core social problems, like ethnic conflict and economic despair, would be managed by politicians through programs of mass imprisonment. In the next chapter, we view the second phase of prison building in the United States. As we move forward, it is important to keep in mind that while, in many ways, modern prisons are somewhat less violent, they are, nevertheless, built upon the themes of cruelty and inhumanity that were established from 1600 until 1900. In fact, a number of the U.S. prisons we've written about in this chapter are still in operation.

Chapter 3

The twentieth-century prison-building binge

Contents

State prisons

In the early part of the twentieth century, the reformatory movement continued its spread. By 1913, 16 states and the District of Columbia operated reformatories, the first having been built in New York (1876) and the last ones in Nebraska (1912–1913) and Connecticut (1913) (Allen & Simonsen 1998: 42). By 1920, however, the movement had ended, as reformatories were converted into conventional prisons (Hallinan 2001: 72). Similarly, in the South, the leasing of inmates to private entrepreneurs continued into the twentieth century. But inmate leasing ended around 1923, as Southern states brought on line their own prison farms and plantations (Murton 1976: 12).

Twentieth-century American corrections officials and, consequently, legislators, increasingly favored the industrial prison and farms or plantations as the most desirable models for imprisonment. The farm or plantation, favored in the South, was a prison built on a large tract of land where agricultural crops were grown, using unpaid inmate laborers. In the North, the industrial prison was favored. Industrial prisons consisted of several cellblocks, where inmates were housed. Industrial prisons also contained state-owned factories and shops where inmates were forced to work. Whether an industrial prison, a farm, or a plantation, the early twentieth-century prison operated by the same formula: start with an authoritarian warden who possessed almost total power to do with inmates as he pleased. Add paid guards, or trusty guards, and their supervisors, to whom wardens impart the authority to treat inmates as they choose. Then, add hard labor and rigid discipline, administered on prison grounds, largely hidden from public view.

The Louisiana State Prison at Angola, holding about 5,000 inmates, is a good example of a plantation, or farm-style, prison. San Quentin, which, by 1930, warehoused 6,000 inmates, became a prototype for the industrial prison (Hallinan 2001: 74). As a veneer, overlaying hard, exploitive labor, overcrowding and rampant violence, remnants of the reformatory movement, in the form of educational programs and counseling, were added. On some Southern plantation prisons, money was saved by using inmates as guards. Sometimes armed with rifles and pistols, other times with brass knuckles, whips and baseball bats, trusty guards were put in charge of enforcing Southern prison rules and of preventing escape. This practice set in motion a vast wave of corruption where trusty guards extorted money and sex from other inmates with little or no intervention from prison officials. Inmates who resisted were subjected to beatings, shootings and torture, often resulting in death. For example, in Arkansas, where, in the 1960s, Tom Murton worked as a prison warden, ground being excavated as part of a building project kept turning up the buried bodies of inmates killed by trusty guards. Murton was asked to stop the excavation, but he ordered that the digging continue. More dead bodies were found. Murton was eventually fired by the governor for allowing the digging to continue. But the holes Tom Murton had dug provided a rare glimpse into the world of prisons run by trusty guards and corrupt prison officials (Murton & Hyams 1967).

In 1906, the Mississippi legislature designated the Parchman Farm Prison Plantation as the state's primary prison. By 1917, the Parchman Farm Prison consisted of 13 agricultural camps where large cotton crops, and all food for the prison, were grown (Taylor 1993). Inmates were worked from sunrise to sunset, six days a week. In the fields, inmates who walked beyond a designated line were shot by trusty guards. Trusty guards were almost always selected from among the murderers serving time at the prison. At night, trusty guards watched over inmates in order to prevent escape. Trusty guards were used at the Parchman Farm Prison until 1972, when a federal court stepped in. The Parchman Farm Prison generated sizable profits, mostly from the sale of cotton. In the 1930s, canning and shoe factories, as well as a slaughterhouse, were opened at Parchman Farm Prison. In 1944, an elementary education program and a religious program were introduced. In the 1950s, high school classes were added to the education curriculum. In the late 1960s, however, inmates were still supervised by trusty guards, often called "trusty shooters." Inmates' lives at Parchman were defined by overwork, horrible food and harsh discipline featuring whippings and other types of torture (Taylor 1993).

Other movements were afoot in America's prisons. For example, in 1907, the Indiana legislature enacted a sterilization law that provided for the employment of two surgeons in each prison and for the examination of inmates by a committee in order to determine whether or not sterilization was necessary. By 1917, 16 states were legally sterilizing inmates. A 1942 U.S. Supreme Court ruling limited the use of sterilization on inmates. However, at the beginning of the twenty-first century, the practice was still legal in a few states, under certain circumstances (Hallinan 2001: 76–77). In 1910, the first psychiatrists began working in American prisons, making prescription drugs available for the control of inmates. By 1926, psychiatrists were working in 67 American prisons, and psychologists were employed at 45 prisons (77–78). In the early 1900s, medical experimentation on inmates accelerated. By 1906, Dr Harry Sharp at the Indiana Reformatory had performed 382 vasectomies on inmates, without using anesthesia, in order to "cure" masturbation. At San Quentin, from 1913 until 1940, Dr Leo Stanley performed autopsies of executed inmates, as well as plastic surgery and thousands of testicular implants on living prisoners (using a paste made from human, ram, goat, boar and deer testicles) (74–77).

By 1926, 99 prisons were operating throughout the United States. Between 1900 and 1944, the number of inmates in U.S. prisons had grown by 174 percent (Allen & Simonsen 1998: 44). By 1944, every state, and the federal government, had implemented some system of parole.

Federal laws soon curtailed the efficacy of the industrial prison as a money-making enterprise. The Hawes-Cooper Act of 1929 stipulated that inmate-made commodities were subject to the laws of any state where they were shipped. This meant that state legislatures could legally prohibit the movement into their state of inmate-made products made in another state. The Ahurst-Sumners Act of 1935 required that inmate-made products shipped out of state be labeled with the name of the prison where they were manufactured and that interstate shipment of inmate-made goods was illegal, where state laws prohibited it. In 1940, the Ahurst-Sumners Act was amended to completely prohibit the interstate shipment of inmate-manufactured products. These pieces of federal legislation killed most industrial activity in most state prisons, except for the production of goods that could be consumed by the prison system itself or by some other state agency. As a result, for the next four decades, masses of American inmates did prison maintenance work or sat idle (Irwin & Austin 1997). Without industrial labor to keep them busy, American inmates had more time to make prison brew, often called "pruno" or "apple jack"; to engage in sexual activity, all-too-often in the form of prostitution and rape; to extort other inmates; to steal, buy and sell contraband; and to beat, stab, shoot and bomb each other and prison guards. With most inmates sitting idle, the overlay of education and counseling had little effect. American prisons became warehouses, nicknamed "Big Houses," where punishment often took the form of inmate-on-inmate violence. American prisons expanded the practice of segregating "problem inmates" from other inmates in "the hole," a terrifying place for most humans, a place we later learned could bring on mental illness or could worsen already existing psychiatric abnormality (Grassian 1994). In spite of these dynamics, in the 1950s, many state prison officials and legislators started utilizing a rhetoric emphasizing rehabilitation. Prisons were renamed "correctional institutions," and guards were called "correctional officers." Perhaps the most telling indicator of the shallowness of the rehabilitation movement in American prisons is the fact that most correctional institutions offered educational and counseling programs that could accommodate fewer than 10 percent of the total inmate population. For example, a mid-1960s nationwide study of U.S. prisons revealed less than one psychiatrist, about 1.25 psychologists and approximately 1.25 counselors, on average, working with each 1,000 inmates in the United States (Hallinan 2001: 37).

During the first five decades of the twentieth century, state prison populations in the United States steadily marched upward. In 1904, there were 55,429 inmates in American state prisons, on the day they were counted. In 1930, the number had grown to 107,532 inmates. By 1950, there were 160,958 inmates warehoused in state prisons (Cahalan & Parsons 1986: 29). In many states, increases in inmates led to the building of additional prisons. In California, for example, new prisons were built in Tehachapi (1933), Chino (1941), Soledad (1946), Corona (1952), Tracy (1953), San Luis Obispo (1954) and Vacaville (1955) (California Department of Corrections 2001b). Unfortunately, as a new California prison was built, it would fill up, then overflow with inmates.

In the 1950s, New Jersey's Trenton State Prison served as a good example of a Big House, blending harsh custodial treatment and widespread violence with educational, vocational and counseling programs. Inmates found life inside Trenton's walls "depriving or frustrating in the extreme" (Sykes 1958/1966: 63). Life inside a Big House involved a fight to survive. Inmates found correctional officers, teachers and counselors to be of little help and, instead, depended upon other inmates for support. In turning to the "society of captives," inmates were forced to reject the larger society from which they came and into which they would eventually return. The society of captives embraced an upside-down value system where weak inmates could be justifiably exploited by the strong, where predators were tolerated and, hopefully, avoided. In spite of educational, vocational and counseling programs, "the Big House was a harsh and oppressive world of concrete and steel in which inmates were subject to chilling cold in the winter, oppressive heat and stench in the summer, and constant unnerving levels of noise" (Silverman & Vega 1996: 117). Regardless of its location, the dominant characteristics of a Big House prison are idleness, constant noise, overcrowding and incessant violence.

Prison subcultures

Inmate subcultures evolved within the walls of twentieth-century prisons. Inmates took on criminal identities that dictated their style of behavior, as well as the way other inmates would relate to them. *The thief* is an inmate who, usually through armed robberies or burglaries, made a "big score" involving large sums of money. Thieves often have money squirreled on the outside that they can access. Thieves are "cool." Thieves view American society as "corrupt and unjust." According to John Irwin, a sociologist and former inmate at Soledad Prison in California, thieves are a dying breed in American correctional institutions (1970: 11). *The hustler* displays "sharpness in language, intellectual skills" and "appearance" (12). The hustler constantly hustles. He is always on the lookout for a sucker who can be parted from his money. Hustlers trust no one. Believing everyone is dishonest, a hustler gets up on them before they can get down on him. *The dope fiend or junkie* is addicted to an opiate, like morphine or heroin. Drugs are the most important thing to a dope fiend. "The dope fiend believes that life is for the most part dull, mundane, routine, or just aggravating" (19). Dope fiends believe that the law discriminates against them, making drugs difficult and dangerous to acquire. *The head* uses psychedelic drugs like marijuana, peyote, methamphetamine, LSD or mescaline. Dope fiends and heads experience reality distortion and apathy (22). *Meth heads* are hyperactive. Today, to this list of drug-oriented inmates, we would add the *cocaine*, or *crack cocaine, user or dealer.* For increasing numbers of inmates, cocaine, or crack cocaine, has been the drug of choice, either as a way of making a living or for use as a pain killer. Like the thief, cocaine dealers often have access to sizable sums of money deposited outside the prison walls. *"Disorganized criminals,* who make up the bulk of convicted felons, pursue a chaotic, purposeless life, filled with unskilled, careless, and variegated criminal activity" (24). Disorganized criminals are "committed to 'doing wrong' – breaking rules, and getting into trouble" (24). Disorganized criminals, at least on the outside, often appear brave and carefree when facing trouble. Disorganized criminals are ready, at all times, to commit crimes. Disorganized criminals are impulsive and tend to view the world outside of prison as corrupt and exploitive. *State-raised convicts* have been in foster homes, orphanages and prisons since they were children. They are the new heroes of the prison yard (Abbott 1981). They are bitter, tough and violent. They "usually band together in ... cliques," in order to defend themselves from "the hostile, violence-prone prison world" (Irwin 1970: 27). State-raised convicts, since they have lived most of their lives in a world that allows little contact with women, are likely to practice one or another form of prison homosexuality. State-raised convicts can also be highly afraid of homosexual advances and can respond violently to such advances. State-raised convicts acquire a twisted set of sexual meanings. The "prison is their only world ... it is a dog-eat-dog world where force or threat of force prevails" (29). State-raised convicts are "easily provoked to violence by the stresses of prison life, and ... provoke the prison staff to use violence." They are "the most impulsive of the prison's ... hedonists, the most cunning and lethal of its jungle cats" (Johnson 1987: 86). The *square john* believes in property rights, in working for a living and in abiding by the law. Square johns do not think of themselves as criminals. Many square johns hold ethnic biases. Square johns, under certain circumstances, will "snitch" on other inmates (Irwin 1970: 34). Like thieves, square johns are a shrinking proportion of the American inmate population.

Johnson identifies two general types of inmates in modern prisons. First, "violence usually is the work of 'hard-core predators' who prowl the prison yard, making it a no-man's land for staff and inmate alike ... predatory prisoners are in the minority" (1987: 5). Second, *mature copers* do the best they can while in prison with what is rightfully theirs. Mature copers deal with problems without resorting to deception or violence. Mature copers find safe niches within prisons and reside as much as possible therein, in order to insulate themselves from stress, violence and other forms of predatory behavior (5 and 56–63). To these typologies we add other types of modern inmates, namely gang members, cartel or syndicate members, snitches or rats, weak inmates (punks, dings, or scapegoats), HIV-infected inmates, Hepatitis-C infected inmates, inmates over the age of 55, suicidal inmates (identified and unidentified) and death row inmates.

This diverse mix of types of inmates makes up the core of inmate sub-culture, where violence, distrust, alcohol and drugs, sexual predation and belief in corruption dominate. In the modern American correctional institution, state-raised convicts are on the increase. State-raised convicts are generally antagonistic towards prison administrators and correctional officers. In the modern American prison, toughness is the most important, the most highly respected attribute that an inmate can possess. Toughness in prison means two things: "being able to take care of oneself in the prison world where people will attack others with little or no provocation" and "having the guts to take from the weak" (Irwin 1980: 193).

Correctional officers, too, form a complex subculture. Correctional officers fall "into three general categories in terms of how they negotiate prison life" (Carter 1994: 45). Some correctional officers are *black and whiters*, strictly following the rules, allowing no extra privileges and keeping their distance from inmates. *Weatherpersons* are flexible, fair and establish cooperative relationships with inmates. Weatherpersons do not overreact to minor rule violations. *Easy lifers* have lost interest in their job. They find ways to meet work obligations while expending as little energy as possible. Easy lifers are often permissive in their dealings with inmates, believing this to be the least demanding strategy in most situations. To this list, we add *sadistic correctional officers*, who get pleasure from mistreating others. There exists a constant dynamic of tension between black and whiters, sadistic correctional officers, easy lifers and weatherpersons. Black and whiters and sadistic officers believe easy lifers and weatherpersons are "inmate huggers" and, thus, cause them a good deal of grief. Black and whiters frequently disapprove of rules violations committed by sadistic officers and easy lifers but must keep quiet in order not to break the code of silence that dominates the correctional officer subculture. In sum, the world of a correctional officer is stressful and dangerous. According to one analyst,

> [A] review of current research yields the distinct impression that correctional officers are alienated, cynical, burned out, stressed but unable to admit it, suffering from role conflict of every kind, and frustrated beyond imagining ... job turnover is high, salaries are low, and correctional officers often fear for their lives.
>
> (Philliber 1987: 9)

Manufacturing and marketing fear of crime

The twentieth-century prison-building binge accelerated in the 1970s, as a result of a number of intersecting forces. First, some critics of the American criminal justice system began to argue that indeterminate sentences and coercive rehabilitation programs forced lower-class, minority inmates to serve unduly long sentences (American Friends Service Committee 1971). Other critics, based upon their examination of highly questionable data, asserted that rehabilitation does not work and, thus, should be abandoned in favor of an "isolate and punish" policy in American prisons (Martinson 1974; Wilson 1975). A few years earlier, politicians discovered that "law and order" was the ideal theme upon which to base an election campaign. Barry Goldwater, in 1964, and Richard Nixon, in 1968, were the first to run for the presidency as "law and order" candidates, as has every successful presidential candidate since then (Beiser 2001; Schlosser 1998). Fixed prison terms and longer sentences became important parts of the "law and order" package politicians offered in exchange for voter support.

Between 1940 and 1970, 5 million African Americans moved from Southern cities to Northern cities (Mauer 1999: 51–53). In the 1960s, 1970s and 1980s, epidemics of heroin, cocaine and crack cocaine use hit American cities. Inmate riots broke out at infamous prisons like San Quentin, Attica and the New Mexico State Penitentiary. The media, especially television, covered these events extensively, creating a heightened fear of crime and a distaste for criminals and convicts, among American voters. Politicians quickly took advantage of the situation. In 1973, the New York state legislature enacted the "Rockefeller drug laws" which imposed mandatory prison sentences for a number of drug offenses and set strict limits on plea bargaining (57). In fact, the penalty in New York for possessing small amounts of narcotics became a 15-year mandatory sentence (Beiser 2001: 3). In 1976, the California state legislature passed a law that eliminated parole and identified the role of prisons as punishment. Soon thereafter, Indiana and Maine followed suit. A number of other states, including Arkansas, Delaware, Colorado, Hawaii, Ohio and Pennsylvania, passed legislation lengthening most prison sentences. Many other states enacted laws that replaced indeterminate sentences with fixed sentences. Most of these harsh, new laws focused on drug and gun-related offenses. Then, in 1980, Ronald Reagan was elected President of the United States, and the U.S. Congress moved even farther to the right.

"Throughout the 1980s lawmakers competed with one another to introduce ever-harsher penalties" (Beiser 2001: 3). President Reagan stacked the U.S. Supreme Court with justices who were hostile towards persons charged with crimes and towards inmates. Reagan and his operatives, though soft on middle-class and elite crime, adopted the punishment of downscale offenders as their overarching crime policy. Taking the advice of his paid political consultants, Reagan, his wife, Nancy, and the Attorney General declared a War on Drugs (Beiser 2001). Congress funded the War on Drugs with hundreds of millions of dollars in new allocations for federal police officers. Congress allocated money used to encourage state governments to follow suit. Between 1982 and 1988, federal drug prosecutions increased by 99 percent, while all other federal criminal prosecutions rose by only 4 percent (Mauer 1999: 61). The federal War on Drugs became a model for state legislatures and legal officials. By 1986, 37 states had passed new fixed sentence laws (Hallinan 2001: 37–38). In 1988, President Reagan pushed for, and Congress enacted, the Anti-Drug Abuse Act, which required long, mandatory sentences for a number of drug offenses. This piece of legislation was intended to result in a drug-free America by 1995 (Mauer 1999: 62). In 1987, a U.S. Department of Justice statistician, grossly misinterpreting the data he examined, wrote a widely circulated report that concluded every incarcerated offender saved taxpayers $405,000. This incorrect conclusion became a buzz phrase repeated again-and-again by conservative politicians throughout the United States (64). In the last year of Reagan's second term as President, Assistant Attorney General William Bradford Reynolds, in a widely circulated memo titled "A Strategy for the Remaining Months," declared "[O]verall, of course, we must make the case that public safety demands more prisons" (quoted in Mauer 1999: 63).

During his 1988 presidential campaign, George Bush picked up where Reagan and his operatives had left off. Bush claimed the release from prison on furlough of convicted murderer, Willie Horton, who proceeded to commit rape, proved that his opponent, Michael Dukakis, was "soft on crime" (Beiser 2001: 4). Taking the advice of paid political consultants, in televised debates, Bush portrayed himself as a big backer of the death penalty, while Dukakis equivocated. Bush played the crime card and won the election. Major themes of the Bush administration were increasing mandatory minimum sentences for criminal offenders, especially drug law violators, and constructing more prisons. By the end of Bush's term in office, the drug war was in full force and the prison building binge had accelerated beyond precedent. From 1980 until 1993, the Reagan-Bush years, the federal corrections budget increased by 521 percent. State governments followed this lead (Mauer 1999: 68).

In 1992, during his campaign for the presidency, Bill Clinton and his paid political consultants resolved that they would be more robust "crime fighters" than any of their Republican competitors. In fact, Clinton, during the primaries, rushed back to Arkansas in order to reject clemency for Ricky Ray Rector, an African American with developmental disabilities, who was to be executed (Beiser 2001: 4; Mauer 1999: 68–69). Major policies favored by the Clinton administration were "three-strikes" laws, hiring an additional 100,000 police officers and increased funding for prisons and boot camps (Mauer 1999: 74).

Washington state passed the first three-strikes law in 1993. California's three-strikes law, enacted in 1994, was the broadest in the nation. It stipulated that persons convicted of any three felonies be sentenced to prison for 25 years to life and that persons convicted of any two felonies be given a doubled sentence. As of May 2001, 6,721 inmates were serving sentences under California's three-strikes law, and another 43,800 had been sentenced under the two-strikes provision (King & Mauer 2001: 3). By 2026, it is estimated that 30,000 California inmates will be serving sentences under the three-strikes law "at a cost of at least $750 million – and more than 80 percent of them will be 40 or older" (Lewin 2001: 1). As of 2014, approximately 8,800 California inmates are serving life sentences under "three-strikes" convictions. Most California three-strikes convictions are for property, drug or other nonviolent offenses. Three-strikes laws worsen the ethnic imbalances that characterize American prison inmate populations. In California, African Americans make up 7.5 percent of the general population. However, 37 percent of the persons sentenced under California two-strikes provision are African American, and 44 percent of the persons sentenced under California three-strikes laws are African American. In Washington state, African Americans make up 4 percent of the general population and 37 percent of those sentenced under the three-strikes law (King & Mauer 2001: 13). Currently, about one-half of all state governments have passed some form of three-strikes legislation.

Recently, voters in some states are approving modifications to three-strikes laws that should reduce the numbers of criminals going to prison for life. In California, for example, voters in 2012 approved Proposition 36, a piece of legislation that authorizes life sentences only when felony convictions are "serious or violent" and that authorizes resentencing of inmates, if a third strike conviction "was not serious or violent."

In 2000, when George W. Bush was elected President of the United States, the White House became occupied by a man whose father had been a pioneer in the "fear of crime" and prison-building movements. As Governor of Texas, George W. Bush had presided over one of the two largest prison systems in the country, a system that hosted the nation's busiest lethal injection chamber, located at Huntsville. George W. Bush's tax reform policies, his energy extraction policies and his missile defense policies failed to win him a sufficient level of popularity with American voters. Consequently, as re-election time approached, President Bush took the advice of paid political consultants. He agreed to be marketed as a "super crime fighter/drug warrior." As history records, with a little help from his friends in Florida as well as on the Supreme Court, George W. Bush won a second term as U.S. President. According to a study by Jacobs and Helms (2001), which looked at data for the past 52 years, the number of persons imprisoned in the United States increases more when Republicans occupy the presidency than when Democrats hold the nation's highest office. The only exception to this pattern were the terms served by Democratic President Bill Clinton who, perhaps, became the most super of all crime-fighters.

In spite of the War on Drugs,

[C]ocaine has become the "all-American drug" and a $30 to $50 billion-a-year industry. It permeates all levels of society, from Park Avenue to the ghetto. Lawyers and executives use cocaine. Baby boomers and yuppies use cocaine. Police officers, prosecutors and prisoners use cocaine. Politicians use cocaine.

(Inciardi 1986: 79)

However, the War on Drugs resulted in the long-term incarceration of disproportionate numbers of African Americans. Research indicates that approximately 13 percent of regular drug users in the United States are African American. However, 62.7 percent of all drug offenders admitted to prison are African American (Schiraldi et al., 2000: 1). The Human Rights Watch conducted an examination, in 37 states, of the role ethnicity and drugs play in prison admissions. In the states with the greatest ethnic disparities – Illinois, Wisconsin, Minnesota, Maine, Iowa, Maryland, Ohio, New Jersey, North Carolina and West Virginia – African American men are sent to prison at a rate 27 to 57 times greater than that for European American men. All 37 states showed higher incarceration rates for African American men than for European American men. In the 1980s, over 500,000 men were sent to prison on drug convictions. In the 1990s, more than 1,000,000 men were admitted to prison on drug charges (Human Rights Watch 2000). In 1980, 8 percent of U.S. prisoners were incarcerated for drug offenses. In 1998, 23 percent of U.S. prisoners were incarcerated for drug offenses (Mother Jones 2001: 2). On June 30, 2000, the incarceration rate for male inmates in state or federal prisons and local jails was 4,777 per 100,000 for African Americans, 1,715 per 100,000 for Hispanics and 683 per 100,000 for European Americans (Beck & Karberg 2001: 9). By 2012, about 12 percent of American men could expect to be incarcerated at some point during their lifetime. By 2012, almost 3,000 per 100,000 African American men, about 1,200 per 100,000 Hispanic men and a little over 450 per 100,000 European American men were incarcerated in the United States. The United States ranks number one, in terms of having the world's highest incarceration rate (Mother Jones 2001: 1; The Sentencing Project 2012a: 2).

Politicians have been helped by the media, especially television and motion pictures, in their efforts to profit from manufacturing and marketing fear of crime. The media profits from convincing the public that crime is out of control. Why? Because fear of crime compels viewers to watch crime programming and, thus, increases television ratings and movie attendance. "From 1990 to 1998, ... homicide stories on the three major networks rose almost fourfold" (Beiser 2001: 5). Between 1990 and 1998, while the homicide rate dropped 33 percent, news coverage of homicides increased by

473 percent. Some argue that 40–50 percent of all local news air time is "devoted to violent topics" (Stamoulis 2001: 2). Most Americans use television and movies as a basic source of information about what is happening in the world around them. "Television has literally become a centralized system that creates a shared consciousness" (Dyer 2000: 85). And television alone provides 7 hours of violent programming on an average day (83). Cop and crime shows dominate television and the movies. For the last several years, "sensational violent crimes make up a disproportionately large part of the content that we see on the television news" (87). A recent public opinion survey revealed that eight out of ten respondents believed news features about violent crimes heightened their fear of becoming victims (Beiser 2001: 5). In short, violent television and movie programming manufactures a fear of crime in most Americans, a fear that politicians manipulate in order to gain and retain positions of power. Thus, a symmetry between the media and the polity has been achieved. The media generates large sums of money, and politicians gain and retain office, all by manufacturing and marketing fear of crime.

Recent expansion of the prison-industrial complex

Between 1990 and 2000, approximately 3,300 new prisons were built in the United States, at a cost approaching $27 billion. Another 268 prisons were either in the planning stages or under construction, adding $2.4 billion to the cost of the American prison building binge (Beiser 2001: 4).

As Table 3.1 illustrates, largely due to the War on Drugs, building and operating state prisons has become an increasingly costly enterprise. In 1974, U.S. taxpayers spent almost $2 billion on state corrections. By 1980, the tab had more than doubled. Between 1980 and 1996, the cost of state corrections systems increased by 645 percent, to a little over $29 billion. By 2010, the costs of operating state corrections systems had mushroomed to well over $48 billion per year. It is noteworthy that states spent about 75 percent of their corrections budget on correctional institutions (U.S. Department of Justice 2012).

Table 3.2 presents information about corresponding growth in the numbers of state corrections employees. Between 1971 and 1980, growth

Table 3.1 State corrections expenditures (in billions), 1974, 1980, 1996 and 2010

	1974	1980	1996	2010
Expenditures in billions	1.9	4.5	29.3	48.5

Sources: 2010 – U.S. Department of Justice 2012 (Revised April 30, 2014): 1; 1996 – U.S. Department of Justice 2000a: 4; 1980 – U.S. Department of Justice 1995: 3; 1974 – U.S. Department of Justice 1977: 44.

Table 3.2 State corrections employees, 1971, 1980, 1995 and 2012

	1971	1980	1995	2012
State corrections employees	107,317	163,670	413,271	440,724

Sources: 2012 – Governing the States and Localities 2016: 2; 1995 – U.S. Department of Justice 2000a: 18; 1980 – U.S. Department of Justice 1995: 33; 1971 – U.S. Department of Justice 1977: 72.

in corrections employees was modest. However, between 1980 and 1995, the number of state corrections employees increased by 252 percent. As the data for 2012 show, growth in state corrections employees has slowed considerably, largely due to economic strictures imposed by the Great Recession of 2008 (Maciag 2014: 2).

Table 3.3 shows increases in the numbers of inmates held in state prisons. Between 1970 and 1980, the population in state prisons increased by almost 90,000 inmates. Between 1980 and 1999, there was a 471 percent increase in state prisoners, moving from 261,292 to 1,231,475 inmates. The Great Recession of 2008, and the shrinking tax dollars it brought about, set off a spate of prison closings throughout the United States, as well as significant tightening of state corrections budgets. All of this resulted in a slowed rate of increase in state prison inmates, between 1999 and 2013, the most recent year for which data are available. However, as the United States economy began to recover, state spending on prisons was again on the rise. For example, in California, between 1980 and 2011, spending on corrections grew from $622 million to $9.2 billion, a 1,300 percent increase (Anand 2012: 7). In fact, "[A]fter adjusting for inflation, [California] higher education in 2011 received 13% less state funding than it did in 1980. Corrections, on the other hand, expanded its share of the state's general fund by 436%" (5).

In the largest industrial states, growth in the number of prisoners, and in the number of prisons, has been unprecedented. California, for example, in 1900, needed two prisons, San Quentin and Folsom, to accommodate its inmate population. In the 1980s, as the inmate population exploded, California prisons became "dangerously overcrowded" (Schlosser 1998: 1). Folsom Prison, for example, was the site of six or seven stabbings per

Table 3.3 Persons present in state prisons on the day of survey, 1970, 1980, 1999 and 2013

	1970	1980	1999	2013
State prisons	177,737	261,292	1,231,475	1,358,875

Sources: 1970 and 1980 – Cahalan & Parsons 1986: 29; 1999 – U.S. Department of Justice August 2000b: 1; 2013 – U.S. Department of Justice September 2014a: 2.

week. Plagued by overcrowded conditions and poor sight lines in the cell-blocks, correctional officers at Folsom feared for their lives. In order to alleviate the problem, between 1984 and 1994, California taxpayers financed the construction of eight new maximum-security prisons (Schlosser 1998: 1). Folsom Prison was converted to a medium-security facility, which houses about 3,800 inmates, including murderers, rapists, child molesters, armed robbers, drug dealers, burglars and petty thieves. Nearby, a new maximum-security facility, called the California State Prison at Sacramento (nicknamed "New Folsom") was built. New Folsom welcomed inmates in 1987. New Folsom holds around 3,000 inmates and features a "death-wire electrified fence," set around the prison's outer boundary between two chain link fences. The "death-wire electrified fence," metes out a lethal shock of 5,100 volts to anyone who touches it, more than twice the voltage administered by Florida's electric chair. According to Larry Cothran, Executive Officer of the California Department of Corrections Technology Transfer Program, the death-wire electrified fence is "killer": "It is very basic, but it is built to kill" (Glave 1997: 4). About one-third of the inmates at New Folsom are serving life sentences. New Folsom holds around 1,000 murderers and 500 armed robbers (Schlosser 1998: 2). As the twenty-first century approached, 28 California prisons employed death-wire electrified fences around their outer perimeters (Glave 1997: 4). At Salinas Valley State Prison, another new California prison, the death-wire electrified fence "is so effective that 11 of 13 guard towers can be left unoccupied, saving Salinas Valley $1 million a year in staffing costs" (Rendon 1998: 2). By 2001, the California Department of Corrections had become the largest prison system in the U.S. (in terms of the number of inmates incarcerated), operating 33 adult facilities (California Department of Corrections 2001b: 1–6). On June 30, 1991, California prisons held almost 102,000 inmates. By June 30, 2000, California's prisons were stuffed with 162,000 inmates (California Department of Corrections 2001c: 1). By 2001, most California prisons were operating at 150 percent to over 200 percent of design capacity, in spite of the many new prisons that were built in the 1980s and 1990s.

Severe overcrowding suggests that the prison-building boom will continue in California and that many outdated prisons will stay open. San Quentin, for example, has been in operation for 149 years. At the turn of the century, it was operating at over 175 percent of design capacity, housing approximately 6,000 inmates, including about 550 on death row (California Department of Corrections 2001d: 2). In early 2015, San Quentin's inmate population had shrunk considerably, down to 4,260 inmates. However, San Quentin was designed to house no more than 3,088 inmates (California Department of Corrections and Rehabilitation 2015). The old prison is one of the most dangerous for inmates and correctional officers in the

California system. San Quentin costs more to operate than most new prisons with its holding capacity. If San Quentin's 432 acres were redeveloped, as a site for new homes, the land is estimated to be worth about $665 million. However, it would cost California taxpayers about $800 million to build two new prisons in which to house San Quentin's inmates, since all other prisons in the state are perpetually overcrowded (Locke 2001: 5B). Thus, in spite of its high operating costs, and its high level of danger, San Quentin will likely continue to operate well into this century. In fact, in spite of California's recent financial problems, its prison system is likely to grow. For example, the California Department of Corrections and Rehabilitation estimates that, between 2014 and 2019, about 4,000 additional new beds will have to be added to the system, in order to accommodate the projected influx of new prisoners (Beard et al., 2014: 37).

Similar growth occurred in Texas, which operates the second-largest prison system in the United States. In 1849, Texas built its first prison to house three inmates. By 1989, Texas had built 35 prison facilities. Between 1990 and 1999, Texas built 70 additional prison facilities. In 1990, 48,320 inmates were held in Texas prisons. By 1999, the Texas inmate population had swollen to 146,930. Between 1988 and 1997, Texas taxpayers spent almost $2.3 billion on prison construction. Between 1990 and 1999, the operating budget for Texas prisons increased by 282 percent (Texas Department of Criminal Justice 2000: 1–12). Texas inmates are awakened at 3:30 a.m. They eat breakfast at 6:00 a.m., and each inmate who is physically able then goes to work. They are not paid for their labor. Most inmates "work in prison support jobs – cooking, cleaning, laundry and maintenance of the system's 107 prison units" (Texas Department of Criminal Justice 2001a: 3). Around 10,000 Texas inmates labor in the system's vast agricultural complex, which generates about $50 million worth of crops and livestock each year. Another 8,000 Texas prisoners work in 46 factories, which produce about $100 million of goods each year. Prisoners who refuse to work are placed in their cells 24 hours a day (4). By 2012, Texas prisons held approximately 152,000 inmates (Texas Department of Criminal Justice, 2013: 1). Similar prison growth has occurred in other states. New York, for example built 38 new prisons between 1982 and the turn of the century (Rohde 2001: 3).

By 2000, the United States, which represents about 5 percent of the planet's population, accounted for 25 percent of its prisoners. In the 1990s, the United States spent more money building prisons than it did building colleges and universities. The United States spent six times more to incarcerate nonviolent offenders than the federal government spent on child care and 50 percent more incarcerating nonviolent offenders than federal welfare programs spend on families in need (Ziedenberg & Schiraldi 2000: 4–5).

There is some evidence that growth in U.S. imprisonment rates may be slowing down, or perhaps even grinding to a halt. In 2000, the number of American state and federal prison inmates grew by only 1.3 percent, a much smaller rate of growth than the annual average of 6 percent for the 1990s. In 2000, 13 states saw the number of inmates in their prison systems decline. States with the largest inmate population declines in 2000 were Massachusetts (5.6 percent), New Jersey (5.4 percent), New York (3.7 percent) and Texas (3.2 percent) (Butterfield 2001a: 1–2). Recent drops in imprisonment rates may be the result of a number of factors, including: declines in annual arrest rates dating back to 1992; an emerging movement to treat first-time, nonviolent drug offenders rather than imprison them; a slowdown in parole revocation actions; and deteriorating morale in a number of big-city police departments that may be resulting in fewer arrests.

In November 2000, California voters approved Proposition 36, which went into effect on July 1, 2001. Proposition 36 makes approximately 20,000 nonviolent drug offenders, each year, eligible for treatment programs rather than imprisonment. Proposition 36 could lessen the number of drug offenders going to prison in California. However, it will most likely only postpone the movement of a number of offenders into prison, since "the state may lack the rehabilitation facilities to make the program work" and since drug testing of offenders diverted into the program could turn up a large number of new offenses (Lichtblau 2001: A8). Legislatures in Connecticut, Indiana, Louisiana, Mississippi and North Dakota recently eliminated some sentencing laws originally passed in the 1990s that required persons convicted to serve long prison terms without the possibility of parole. Legislatures in other states, including Alabama, Colorado, Georgia, Idaho, New Mexico and New York, are re-examining their criminal laws, looking for ways to reduce the numbers of inmates in their state prison systems (Butterfield 2001b: 1; Martinez 2001: 1A). New York State's Chief Judge, Judith S. Kaye, is leading a movement to replace prison terms with court-ordered treatment for 10,000 drug law offenders. If successfully implemented, the drug treatment program could save New York taxpayers as much as $500 million per year (Schiraldi et al., 2000: 14). However, mandated treatment for drug addiction is plagued with significant problems and might only delay the movement into prison of drug law violators (Szalavitz 2001). In Mississippi, where between 1994 and 2001, 15 new prisons were built, "the state found itself with 2,000 more prison beds than prisoners," setting off a fight for prisoners between "private prison companies and their lobbyists, legislators with (state-run) prisons in their districts, counties that operate their own prisons and sheriffs who covet convicts for local jails" (Gruley 2001: A1). This kind of fight is likely in any industry where vendors compete for shrinking numbers of consumers.

It is difficult to tell whether the American prison-building boom has peaked or whether the system has reached a plateau and will soon burst into a new growth phase. Forces favoring a new growth phase include ever-increasing numbers of police officers and judges in American society, the penchant politicians have for winning and retaining office through posturing as crime fighters and the media's manipulation of crime for profit making. Also, some states house large numbers of sentenced prisoners in county jails and will, sooner or later, have to move them into conventional prisons. Other states operate old prisons like San Quentin that, because of high operating costs and employee safety concerns, will have to be replaced. And the federal prison system continues to project significant growth well into the future. Forces favoring a slowdown, or halt, to prison growth involve the exorbitant cost of building and operating American prisons. In the 1990s, state governments built accommodations for 528,000 new prison beds at an average cost of $50,000 per bed. Today, American taxpayers contribute over $30 billion annually to operate state and federal prisons. In sum, we believe that the American prison-building binge will continue after a brief respite to gather new momentum. There is some evidence to support our belief. As the economy has improved, America's collective appetite for incarceration seems to have again come alive. For example, between late 2013 and late 2014 the U.S. prison population increased by an additional 4,300 inmates (U.S. Department of Justice 2014b: 1). At the state level, we see a similar pattern of inmate growth in the Commonwealth of Virginia where, between 1970 and 2014, the state experienced a 735 percent increase in its prison population and opened 14 new prisons. Since the 1980s, Virginia prison spending increased by 288 percent. The American Recession of 2008 put a halt to inmate population growth, for a few years. However, in 2013, Virginia's prison population again began to grow. Consequently, Virginia's 2015 corrections budget will for the first time go over the $1 billion mark (Justice Policy Institute 2014: 2–4).

Control units

American prisons have always had segregation or isolation cells, where misbehaving and highly dangerous inmates could be held, for short periods, separate from the general population. A common nickname for isolation or segregation cells is "The Hole." In fact, forced-isolation prisons date back to the Western Penitentiary, built near Pittsburgh, Pennsylvania, in 1829 and the Eastern Penitentiary, built in Philadelphia in 1836. However, in the 1970s and 1980s, as U.S. prisons became more and more overcrowded, and as concentrations of state-raised inmates increased, violence against inmates and correctional officers escalated (Annin 1998: 35). Prison administrators responded by embracing the tight management policies endorsed by John Dilulio's "control model" that emphasizes total control over the prison population at all times (Stohr et al. 1994). Prison officials devised "control units," which are sections of prisons, or whole prisons, designed to isolate inmates for long periods. Control units operate "on a total lockdown basis as a normal routine" (Riveland 1999: 5). Control units go by many names, including "Security Housing Units" (SHUs), "Boxcar Cells" (cells having solid doors), "Adjustment Center," "Maximum Control Complex," "Administrative Maximum" (Ad-Max), "Violence Control Unit," "Special Management Unit," "Intensive Management Unit," "Super-Maximum Security" prisons and "Maxi-Maxi" prisons. The United States leads the world's nations in the use of boxcar cells, "prefabricated, high-tech cellblocks, operated from a central console station" (Grondahl 2000: 5). In the United States, there are over 20,000 inmates housed in about 57 supermax prisons or control units in 42 states (Stryker 2001: 10). Control units differ somewhat from state to state. But they also share a number of common qualities:

1   Most inmates are kept in solitary confinement, although California, Oklahoma, New York and Texas house two inmates in a number of control unit cells.
2   Inmates are kept in cells that average from 6 feet by 8 feet (for one inmate) to 14 feet by 8 feet (for two inmates).
3   Inmates are locked in their cells 22 to 23 hours per day and are allowed little or no contact with other prisoners. They eat, sleep, shower, urinate and defecate in, or very near, their cells.
4   Inmates are allowed to exercise in isolation at most 1 hour per day in a small cage near their cells.
5   Educational, vocational and religious programs are either not allowed or are highly limited.
6   Placement in a control unit is for administrative purposes, rather than for punishment. Consequently, inmates can be held in control units for as long as prison administrators choose, sometimes lasting for years.
7   Staff–inmate interaction is kept to a minimum.

Control units and supermax prisons are supposed to "isolate inmates who through behavior – or threat of such behavior – are dangerous or chronically violent, have escaped or attempted to escape from a high-security correctional facility, or have incited or attempted to incite disruption in a correctional facility" (Riveland 1999: 22). "Unfortunately, in most jurisdictions, the criteria for determining entry to and exit from supermax confinement are so vague that arbitrariness and unfairness are inevitable" (Fellner 2000: 5). For most of the twentieth century, highly violent and dangerous inmates were dispersed throughout a prison system. With the advent of control units, American prison policy changed towards concentrating dangerous inmates in special sections of prisons or in special "end-of-the-line prisons."

The Pelican Bay State Prison, located close to the Oregon border, near Crescent City, California, is one of the most notorious, modern and secure penal facilities in the United States. Pelican Bay employs cutting-edge technology and security devices. Pelican Bay, referred to as California's new Alcatraz, opened in December 1989 and houses over 3,000 inmates. The prison is divided into a minimum-security unit, a maximum-security congregate housing unit and the Security Housing Unit (SHU) where as many as 1,600 inmates are held. Inside the SHU is a 50-cell "Violence Control Unit." Since its opening, Pelican Bay has been steeped in violence and litigation. Pelican Bay, like all California prisons, is severely overcrowded. Inmates are crammed into 10-foot by 12-foot, two-man cells. For every 7 inmates who leave, 13 new inmates arrive (MSNBC 2000). Pelican Bay is, for the most part, escape-proof. Around its outer perimeter stand three fences. On the outside are 12-foot high chain link fences topped with razor wire. Between the chain link fences stands a "death wall" fence capable of administering a lethal shock to anyone who touches it. Coaxial cables and microwave detection systems tell correctional officers if anyone penetrates the three-fence barrier. The fence is also patrolled constantly by guards (Hallinan 2001: 116). A federal judge described the use of violence by Pelican Bay guards as "staggering" (*Madrid v. Gomez* 1995: 1181). Guards at Pelican Bay have been accused of having inmates beaten and shot (Arax & Gladstone 1998: A1).

Inmates at Pelican Bay are deeply divided into ethnic and prison gang factions. Inmates in the maximum-security congregate housing unit consider themselves in a state of war. They must be ready for anything. Over 900 violent assaults occur at Pelican Bay each year. It is a population "besieged by violence, incinerated by hatred." According to one inmate, "some guys are going to get their heads blown off; some guys are going to get stabbed real good" (MSNBC 2000). Fights, stabbings, beatings, getting "rat packed" (one inmate getting jumped by five or six others) and episodes of mass violence are common. Most of the violence occurs in the exercise yards, where inmates bury weapons underground, to be used at a later time. The most dangerous place is the main exercise yard of Facility A, nicknamed the "gladiator arena" by inmates. On January 28, 2000, all of the Southern Hispanics attacked all of the African Americans in the exercise yard with homemade knives, called "shanks." Guards launched tear gas canisters into the yard. Pepper spray was used. But the fighting went on for over 30 minutes. Finally, rifles were fired into the yard, and the combatants were subdued. One inmate died, and 40 others were wounded. Eighty-nine weapons were confiscated. The maximum-security congregate housing unit was placed on long-term lock down. Inmates were allowed out of their cells every second day for 2 hours of exercise in the yard and were segregated by ethnicity (MSNBC 2000). Pelican Bay remains a cauldron of hatred, waiting to erupt again.

The Security Housing Unit at Pelican Bay was designed to hold 1,056 inmates (California Department of Corrections 2001e: 2). By the turn of the century, the SHUs at Pelican Bay held over 1,600 prisoners. Due to overcrowding, some SHU cells are shared by two inmates. Inmates in Pelican Bay SHUs are kept in tiny 80 square foot cells, behind three locked doors, for 22.5 hours per day. They are allowed to exercise outside their cells for no more than 90 minutes per day in a 28-foot by 12-foot cage, nicknamed the "dog-walk." Before and after exercise periods, inmates are strip searched. SHU cells are designed to impair visual stimulation. When outside their cells and the exercise yard, inmates are shackled at the waist and ankles. Except for double-celled prisoners, inmates cannot see other inmates or the outside world. Inmates are exposed only to artificial, muted light. They are watched by correctional officers via video cameras. Cell and corridor doors are operated electronically. Nothing can be put on cell walls. All consumer items allowed in cells are first taken from their containers by guards and placed in paper cups. All cells are equipped with microphones and speakers that allow guards to communicate from a distance with prisoners and to listen to whatever inmates say. When inmates are removed from their cells, they are handcuffed, chained and escorted by two armed guards. Inmates are fed twice a day in their cells and are allowed three showers per week. No educational or vocational programs are allowed. Cell doors are constructed of thick, perforated metal sheets, designed to prevent inmates' throwing urine/feces mixtures at correctional officers (Romano 1996: 5–6).

On July 1, 2001, over 900 inmates at Pelican Bay and Corcoran State Prison (California's other supermax prison) began a hunger strike to protest their being held indefinitely in SHUs. They claimed California prison officials use a vague gang policy to determine who is placed in SHUs. One of the leaders of the strike, Steve Castillo, an inmate at Pelican Bay, contends that extended incarceration in a SHU drives some inmates insane. He reports seeing an SHU inmate "playing a game of chess with pieces made out of his own feces." Other SHU prisoners smear "their bodies and cells with their feces." On July 6, 2001, the inmates agreed to suspend their strike "after California state Senator Richard Polanco (D – Los Angeles), chairman of the Joint Committee on Prison Construction and Operations, promised to probe the situation expeditiously" (Cockburn 2001: 12).

As a result of numerous lawsuits filed by Pelican Bay prisoners, federal judges from the Northern District of California have had the prison under scrutiny since 1991. In one class action lawsuit (*Madrid v. Gomez*), Pelican Bay inmates claimed that their rights under First, Sixth, Eighth and Fourteenth Amendments to the U.S. Constitution had been violated. Deliberate use of excessive force, failure to provide adequate medical and mental healthcare, isolation and sensory deprivation and violations of due process in segregation decisions were among the harms protested in the lawsuit. The court focused only on a small group of Pelican Bay SHU inmates with pre-existing mental conditions, rather than on all Pelican Bay SHU prisoners. After a lengthy trial, Chief U.S. District Judge Thelton Henderson ruled in favor of the inmates on a number of counts. Judge Henderson concurred that Pelican Bay officials had failed to provide adequate medical and mental healthcare for SHU inmates. Judge Henderson agreed that Pelican Bay officials had permitted and condoned a pattern of excessive force and that incarceration in SHUs of mentally ill inmates, as well as persons with "borderline personality disorders, brain damage or mental retardation, impulse-ridden personalities, or a history of prior psychiatric problems or chronic depression" crosses the constitutional line (in Romano 1996: 6–7). Stuart Grassian, a Board Certified Psychiatrist, who since 1974 has been on the faculty of the Harvard Medical School and who is an expert on solitary confinement, was asked to study the situation at Pelican Bay. In a declaration to the U.S. District Court, he offered the following conclusions: "the prisoners I interviewed in Pelican Bay SHU, by and large, were not the tough, tightly controlled 'James Cagney' types but, instead, mentally impoverished, illiterate, impulse-ridden, and, quite often, severely mentally ill" (1994: 165). "Many of the inmates placed in Pelican Bay's SHU are thus likely to be among the *least* capable of tolerating the experience and among the *most* likely to suffer behavioral deterioration in the SHU" (1994: 198). Doctor Grassian warned that incarceration in the SHU could make worse existing mental illness and could induce mental illness in inmates who had not previously been afflicted. A special master was appointed by Judge Henderson, to monitor treatment of mentally ill inmates confined in Pelican Bay's SHU. Pelican Bay's major response to these problems was to build a new SHU called the Psychiatric Security Unit (Hallinan 2001: 122). Two chief psychiatrists at Pelican Bay resigned their positions, complaining that prison officials would not allow them to provide adequate mental health services for inmates (123).

Located near Westville, Indiana, the Maximum Control Facility represents a supermax prison built on a much smaller scale than Pelican Bay. In 2000, the authors toured the Westville Maximum Control Facility, as guests of Superintendent Daniel McBride. The Maximum Control Facility was established in 1991 and houses approximately 170 adult males who have been identified by prison officials as highly violent, as escape prone or as members of prison gangs. The Maximum Control Facility was built adjacent to a medium-security prison that houses almost 3,000 inmates (Indiana Department of Correction 2001). Conditions at the Maximum Control Facility are described as among the harshest in the country (The Learning Channel 1999). All inmates come to the Maximum Control Facility from other Indiana prisons. Inmates are kept in their cells 23 hours per day. They shower in a hallway outside their cells and are allowed to exercise in a large cage near their cells for about an hour each day. Whenever out of their cells, inmates are shackled at the waist and ankles. Inmates have little contact with each other or with staff. When inmates are moved about in the prison, lights flash in the hallways, signaling employees and visitors to evacuate areas where inmates travel, thus minimizing contact. There are more guards than inmates at the Maximum Control Facility. As is the case at most supermax prisons, on-duty guards wear combat fatigues. As a security measure, guards are searched as they arrive for work and as they leave after work.

Cells are small and are lighted 24 hours a day. All personal belongings must be kept in a box, so that inmates can be moved about the prison with little notice. A small space on the cell's front wall is designated for objects, like photographs, inmates might wish to hang up. An official explained to us that a space on the front wall was selected so that prison employees would not have to look at the stuff. Inmate possessions are severely limited. Most inmates are allowed to keep a couple of books, a radio, a few personal hygiene items and a few items of personal clothing in their cells. After three months of good behavior, inmates are allowed to purchase a television set, if they can afford to do so.

Cell shakedowns are common, and guards have been accused of routinely abusing inmates. A 1992 lawsuit filed by inmates at the Maximum Control Facility alleged physical and mental abuse. As a result of the lawsuit, prison operations are now monitored by outside authorities (The Learning Channel 1999). During our tour, we asked Superintendent McBride what rehabilitation programs were offered at the Maximum Control Facility. He responded that there was very little emphasis on rehabilitation. He assumed that rehabilitation would be provided at the prisons from which his inmates came and to which they could be returned. After our visit, we concluded that the Maximum Control Facility was not a healthy place for inmates or employees.

H-Unit was opened in 1991, on the grounds of the Oklahoma State Prison at McAlester, a maximum-security prison built in the early 1900s. H-Unit is Oklahoma's supermax. It was built in response to a riot in 1985 at the Oklahoma State Prison by over a hundred inmates who went on a rampage, stabbing three guards and holding seven others hostage for 17 hours (The Discovery Channel 2001). About 4,000 extremely violent inmates, escape-prone inmates, gang members and those on death row are housed at H-Unit. H-Unit is a cement and hardened iron structure, buried on two sides, giving it the appearance of an underground bunker. There are no windows. There is no natural light and no fresh air, in H-Unit.

Due to overcrowding, a number of inmates, including death row inmates, are double-celled. For 23 hours per day, inmates are kept in cells measuring 15.5 feet by 7.5 feet. Three times per week, inmates are allowed out of their cells to shower. Five times per week, inmates are taken to exercise cages, with as many as five other inmates (Farrell 2000: 1). Exercise periods often result in vicious arguments and fights (The Discovery Channel 2001). Whenever inmates are taken from their cells, they are strip searched and then shackled at the waist and ankles. H-Unit is a "noncontact unit", where guards are almost always separated from inmates by bars. All doors are controlled electronically. There are no educational or job training programs on H-Unit.

Inmates describe H-Unit as "barbaric and heinous" (The Discovery Channel 2001). Inmates describe going insane as one of their biggest fears. Inmates describe the guards in H-Unit as disrespectful and physically violent (Farrell 2000: 4). Cell extractions are brutal, sometimes involving an electronic shield that administers a severe and potentially dangerous shock. Death row inmates are allowed to attend "church" in handcuffs and leg chains, always separated from the minister by bars (The Discovery Channel 2001). Fights between cellmates are common and sometimes result in murder (Farrell 2000: 4). Amnesty International contends that the prisoners held in H-Unit are living "in conditions which have been found to be inhumane both by Amnesty International and the United Nations Human Rights Commission" but not by federal judges in the United States (Amnesty International 2001:1). According to Amnesty International, a Nobel Peace Prize-winning organization, confinement in SHUs equates with torture under international law (Grondahl 2000: 5). The first author, in 2012, while working as an expert on the appeal of a death sentence and while interviewing the appellant on H-Unit, listened as another inmate was beaten in an adjoining room. We could hear the blows as they landed on the inmate. We could hear the inmate begging that the beating stop. He then fell silent, and the sound of fists landing on flesh ended.

The New York Department of Corrections leads the country in the use of SHUs. New York corrections officials hold approximately 8 percent of their 72,000 inmates, almost 5,700 persons, in SHUs. The national average is 2 percent (Rhode, 2001: 6). Since 1997, due to overcrowding, New York has allowed the placement of two inmates in SHU cells. About 2,800 New York inmates have been held in SHUs for more than 1 year, and over 150 have been incarcerated in SHUs for over 5 years (Grondahl 2000: 9). In fact, New York Department of Corrections officials sentenced one inmate to 17 years in a SHU for his alleged role in a prison riot (Quirini 2000: 1). SHU cells for 2 inmates in New York are 14 feet by 8 feet and offer about 60 square feet of open floor space, less than federal law requires for pigs used in scientific research projects. New York SHU inmates are allowed to exercise for

1 hour per day in a 9-foot by 7-foot cage (Grondahl 2000: 7; Quirini 2000: 1). Religious leaders representing the Capital Region Ecumenical Organization have protested New York's overuse of SHUs, contending that such incarceration treats inmates like animals, has negative consequences for their mental health and impedes their readjustment to society when they are released (Quirini 2000: 1).

A better way to configure control units currently exists. For example, Oak Park Heights in Minnesota is a supermax prison where over 60 percent of the inmates have been convicted of murder. In fact, Oak Park Heights houses the most dangerous criminals in Minnesota. Oak Park Heights boasts the security cameras and centrally controlled electronic doors of other modern supermax prisons. The entire prison can be locked down at any time. But inmates are given a choice. If they are cooperative and remain nonviolent, they are allowed to remain in the general population where they have access to a wide array of vocational, educational and spiritual activities. They are allowed to be out of their cells from 7 a.m. until 10 p.m.

If inmates are violent, or if they choose not to participate in educational and vocational programs, they are then placed in the special housing unit, or the segregation unit, where they are locked in their cells for 21 to 23 hours per day. According to Warden Jim Bruton, "good behavior will get you good rewards, bad behavior will get you severe penalties" (The Discovery Channel 2001). Most inmates at Oak Park Heights choose educational and vocational opportunities over isolation and deprivation. No escapes have occurred from Oak Park Heights, and policies there have kept violence to a minimum. In an ironic twist, some inmates use prison rules, and prescribed punishments for infractions, to manipulate their way *into* solitary confinement. For example, a supermax inmate recently told a federal judge that "he makes dangerous threats so that he'll be placed in solitary confinement," a place in prison he believes to be safer than daily exposure to the general inmate population (Mitchell 2015: 8A).

Summary

Largely due to politicians' election and re-election strategies, and to media profit seeking, the United States went on a binge of prison building in the last 50 years of the twentieth century. Placing people in prison became the principal way to resolve a number of America's major social ills, especially those related to ethnic conflict and to the use and sale of illicit drugs. As we arrived at the twenty-first century, the United States had created the largest prison system of any country. The United States imprisons a larger proportion of its population than any other major country. Unfortunately, these policies failed to abate illicit drug use and sales as well as a number of other social ills, like high rates of poverty and widespread unemployment in inner-city neighborhoods. In spite of the unprecedented American prison building binge, most correctional institutions today are severely overcrowded and highly dangerous, for inmates and for corrections employees alike. In turn, severe overcrowding has forced corrections officials to employ "tight control" policies.

The use of control units has spread rapidly in American prisons. Some corrections officials and politicians justify the widespread use of control units, arguing that this is the best way to prevent violence and escapes elsewhere in their prison systems, by concentrating "the worst of the worst" and by holding them in SHUs and supermax facilities (Grondahl 2000: 9). However, critics argue that the building of control units encourages prison officials to place inmates therein who do not require such restrictive controls and to ignore, possibly even encourage, abusive actions towards prisoners (Fellner 1999: 7). Common abuses of control unit inmates include forcing male inmates to strip for the purposes of highly intrusive searches and showers in front of female employees, the excessive and punitive use of pepper spray, unwarranted use of electronic stun devices and electronic shields and the improper use of firearms (Fellner 1999: 23–31; Timberg 2001: B01). A 1999 report, sponsored by the National Institute of Corrections, on supermax prisons, warns,

> [L]ittle is known about the impact of locking an inmate in an isolated cell for an average of 23 hours per day with limited human interaction, little constructive activity, and an environment that assures maximum control over the individual.... Generally, the overall constitutionality of these programs is unclear.... Caution in expanding the types and number of inmates placed in these facilities will serve all parties well.
>
> (Riveland 1999: 2)

Most inmates are eventually released from control unit incarceration and from prison. After their release from prison, damage done to inmates in control units might become a liability, not only for ex-cons, but for their spouses and children, for their neighbors, as well as for other members of the communities in which they live.

Chapter 4

Federal prisons in the twentieth and twenty-first centuries

Contents

Early federal prisons

Before the twentieth century, the federal government had briefly operated the Walnut Street Jail in Philadelphia and had run a prison in Washington, D.C., for a short time. The military ran prisons for court-martialed soldiers. The only other federal prisons were out West in the territories, run by U.S. Marshals. For the most part, eighteenth and nineteenth-century federal offenders were housed in state and local prisons on a contract basis (Bates 1936; Bennett 1970; Keve 1994). Federal inmates were held at the Albany County Penitentiary in New York, at the Auburn State Prison in New York, at the Detroit House of Correction, at the Eastern State Penitentiary in Philadelphia, at the Georgia State Penitentiary in Milledgeville, at San Quentin in California and at the Walnut Street Jail (Keve 1994: 26–27). But, as the twentieth century approached, the number of federal inmates in state and local prisons increased, as did the cost of keeping them in state and local prisons. Questions were raised about the way federal inmates were being treated. In response, in 1887, the U.S. Congress passed a bill prohibiting the use of federal inmates as contract laborers. Shortly thereafter, Congress began putting in place a legal structure for creation of a federal prison system.

Leavenworth

In 1891, Congress passed the Three Prisons Act, stipulating that federal prisons should be built in the Southeast, in the Northeast and west of the Rocky Mountains. In 1895, the Department of Justice inherited a U.S. Army prison at Fort Leavenworth, Kansas, and began operating it as a federal prison. The military prison consisted of steel cages housed inside an old supply depot building. In 1896, federal inmates began construction of a new 1,200-bed prison at a site 2 miles away from the military prison. The prison, when completed, would have two large cellblocks and two smaller cellblocks. It would be relatively self-sufficient, containing a farm, power plant, bakery, slaughterhouse and school. Also in 1896, several female prisoners arrived at the new Leavenworth Prison, including a 15-year-old girl serving a sentence for arson (The History Channel 1998c). In 1903, a small number of inmates moved into the new prison, and in 1906, larger numbers of inmates were moved into what was still an only partially completed prison. That same year, control of the military prison was transferred back to the Army (Keve 1994: 30–31). Strict discipline was imposed. Guards carried batons. No talking was allowed. All inmate movement was in march formation (The History Channel 1998c). Construction of the new federal penitentiary at Leavenworth, Kansas, was not completed until 1926.

Atlanta

Construction of the second federal prison, at a site near Atlanta, Georgia, began in 1901. For the first year, the Atlanta prison was built by paid laborers, since inmates were not readily available. When completed, the Atlanta prison was to be a 4-cellblock facility with 1,200 beds. In 1902, the first prisoners were moved in and replaced the paid laborers as construction workers (Keve 1991: 64–65). By 1903, the Atlanta prison held 350 inmates, although construction would not be completed for another 20 years. Both the Leavenworth and Atlanta prisons were operated on minimal budget allocations, experienced shortages of guards and were overcrowded. Built to accommodate 1,200 inmates each, by the 1920s, the maximum-security federal prisons at Atlanta and Leavenworth each held over 2,000 convicts, with more arriving daily (Christianson 1998: 218; Keve 1991: 53). By 1925, Leavenworth held 3,262 inmates (Keve 1991: 56). It was a common practice to segregate inmates by ethnicity (54, 63).

McNeil Island

The third federal prison was at McNeil Island, Washington, an isolated place on Puget Sound, where a territorial prison was already in operation. Construction of the territorial prison's first cellblock had actually begun in 1871. It opened in 1875 and consisted of 42 8-foot by 6-foot cells. In 1909, the McNeil Island prison was formally recognized as a federal penitentiary and, by default, became the third prison authorized by the 1891 Three Prisons Act (Keve 1991: 50). In 1909, there were 1,796 federal prisoners in the newly created system (Bates 1936: 128).

Notable early federal inmates

In its early years, the federal prisons hosted a number of notable inmates. Karl Panzram, who committed at least 20 murders and who sodomized over 1,000 men, was incarcerated at Leavenworth. Panzram also enjoyed burning down churches, preferably with their ministers inside. Panzram was eventually hanged by federal officials for his numerous offenses. Famous gangsters like George "Machine Gun" Kelly, Frank Nitti and George "Bugs" Moran were imprisoned at Leavenworth (The History Channel 1998c). In 1909, a 13-year-old boy arrived at Leavenworth. He had been convicted of manslaughter (The History Channel 1998c). In 1909, 19-year-old Robert Stroud killed a man who had assaulted a female friend of Stroud's who was alleged to be a prostitute working for him. Stroud was given a 12-year sentence to be served at McNeil Island Penitentiary. In prison at McNeil Island, while fighting, Stroud stabbed another inmate and was transferred to the Leavenworth Federal Penitentiary. At Leavenworth, Stroud stabbed a guard, killing him. For this offense, Stroud received a death sentence, which was later commuted to life in prison by President Woodrow Wilson, with the stipulation, imposed by federal prison officials, that he be held in solitary confinement (Christianson 1998: 242). Stroud should have been nicknamed "The Birdman of Leavenworth" since he was allowed to raise, and trade in, birds at Leavenworth, not at Alcatraz, where he was later incarcerated.

Around 1918, 97 members of a labor union called the International Workers of the World (Wobblies) were sent to Leavenworth for violating the Espionage and Sedition Act, which prohibited citizens from speaking out against the war (Christianson 1998: 215). Most of the Wobblies served 10- to 20-year sentences (The History Channel 1998c). In 1920, Jack Johnson, the African American heavy-weight prize fighting champion, arrived at Leavenworth to serve a term for violating the Mann Act, which prohibited consorting with European American women (The History Channel 1998c). In 1919, political activist, Eugene Debs, was convicted of violating the 1918 Espionage and Sedition Act. He had been accused of encouraging young men to burn their draft cards. Debs was sent to the federal penitentiary at Atlanta, where he shared a cell with five other inmates. In 1920, while still in prison, Debs received 919,000 votes as the presidential candidate for the Socialist Party. President Warren Harding eventually pardoned Debs and 23 other political prisoners. On the day of his release, all 2,300 of Atlanta's inmates were reportedly allowed out of their cells in order to say goodbye to Debs. Walking away from the prison, with tears in his eyes, Debs tipped his cap and raised his cane as the inmates cheered (Christianson 1998: 217–218). Life at the Atlanta prison was harsh. Guards carried clubs, a practice that would be allowed in federal prisons until 1938. There is evidence of an inmate being punished for picking his teeth. Another was punished for dragging his feet while exercising. Yet another was thrown in "the hole" for throwing a bible out of his cell. An inmate was "handcuffed to his cell door for sixteen hours for laughing loudly on his way out of the mess hall after supper" (Bennett 1970: 81).

The building boom begins

In 1910, a second cellblock was opened at McNeil Island. Ten years later, a kitchen, a dining room and an administration building were added. In the 1930s, running water finally arrived at McNeil Island (Keve 1991: 72). In 1930, the McNeil Island penitentiary housed over 1,300 inmates, making it as overcrowded as the two bigger federal penitentiaries at Leavenworth and Atlanta (73). In 1925, a federal women's prison was opened in Alderson, West Virginia. One year later, a federal reformatory for young men opened in Chillicothe, Ohio, bringing the number of prisons in the federal system to five (Keve 1994: 32).

In 1929, Sanford Bates was appointed superintendent of federal prisons. In September 1929, the War Department once again turned over its disciplinary barracks at Fort Leavenworth so that it could be used to house federal prisoners. Shortly thereafter, the prison at Fort Leavenworth held 1,800 federal inmates (Bates 1936: 133). In 1930, the U.S. Congress passed legislation creating the Federal Bureau of Prisons, and Bates was made its first director (Dilulio 1994: 161). The three original federal prisons were bursting at their seams with inmates, so unused pieces of property were transferred by the War Department to the Federal Bureau of Prisons, and six temporary prison camps for federal inmates were quickly set up adjacent to army facilities at Fort Bragg, North Carolina; Fort Meade, Maryland; Camp Dix, New Jersey; Camp Wadsworth, New York; Fort Riley, Kansas; Camp Eustis, Virginia; Maxwell Field, Alabama; and Fort Lewis, Washington. A large, permanent federal prison camp was built near Petersburg, Virginia (Bates 1936: 133). At the end of 1930, the Federal Bureau of Prisons operated 14 institutions and housed over 13,000 inmates.

The Federal Bureau of Prisons acquired 950 acres near Lewisburg, Pennsylvania, and set about building a new prison designed to hold 1,000 inmates. When the Northeastern Penitentiary at Lewisburg, Pennsylvania, opened on November 11, 1932, it was considered the most modern prison in the world (Home Box Office 1991). It consisted of 88 steel cells, 450 guarded rooms for inmates and a number of prisoner dormitories. Lewisburg also featured a library, classrooms, a hospital, a mess hall and a chapel (Bates 1936: 136). Lewisburg filled up quickly and has held as many as 1,500 inmates. Among the thousands of inmates held at Lewisburg was Harry J. Patton, museum curator, puppeteer, photographer and Smithsonian Institution specialist in the history of photography. Patton, loyal to his Quaker heritage, was a conscientious objector during World War II. Imprisoned at Lewisburg, he worked at the dairy farm, tending the institution's three bulls and operating the dairy truck. Harry Patton was paroled in 1945 and was later pardoned by President Harry S. Truman. On his application to a retirement community, Patton described himself as a graduate of the "Federal Crime School" at Lewisburg (Rasmussen 2000: 5B). On October 4, 2001, there were 1,313 prisoners at the Lewisburg Federal Penitentiary. In terms of ethnicity, 45 percent of Lewisburg's inmates are African American, 35 percent are European American and 20 percent are Hispanic American. The control unit at Lewisburg holds inmates in their cells 23 hours each day. For about an hour each day, they are allowed to exercise alone in a fenced yard. The 6-foot by 8-foot cells were designed for one inmate but currently hold two per cell. The outside windows in control unit cells have been sealed. Consequently, air can only enter through small openings, called "wickets," in the closed cell doors. This situation makes breathing difficult. Lewisburg has earned the reputation as one of the most dangerous of the federal prisons. Homemade knives, called "shanks," are a common possession of inmates. Inmates carry shanks in order to aggress on others and in order to defend themselves. According to Lieutenant Clark, a supervising officer at Lewisburg, "there is no fistfighting at Lewisburg. If you are going to fight in a penitentiary, it's not to be bullshitting around, it's gonna be to injure somebody, or to incapacitate him" (Home Box Office 1991).

Alcatraz

In the 1930s, Attorney General Homer Cummings and FBI Director J. Edgar Hoover lobbied Sanford Bates, Director of the Federal Bureau of Prisons, to build a prison where difficult-to-manage inmates could be concentrated into a single institution (National Park Service 2001: 1–2). The Federal Bureau of Prisons considered land in Alaska but decided, instead, to remodel a military prison on Alcatraz Island, located in California's scenic San Francisco Bay. Alcatraz Island, nicknamed "The Rock," was an ideal place for a federal prison where inmates could be isolated and where communication with persons outside the prison walls could be kept to a minimum. In 1853, the U.S. Army began construction of a fort on Alcatraz Island, to protect the Bay. Work on the fort was completed in 1859. By the late 1850s, military prisoners were housed on the island. In 1861, the fort on Alcatraz Island was designated as the Army's main prison west of the Mississippi River. In the ensuing years, it held as many as 600 inmates. During the Indian Wars, many famous Native American chiefs were incarcerated on Alcatraz Island (Bates 1936: 43). In 1909, the fort was torn down, and its basement served as the foundation for a new military prison built by inmates. The new military prison consisted of a cell house containing three-story cellblocks. In all, there were 600 5-foot by 9-foot cells. The Pacific Branch, U.S. Disciplinary Barracks was finished in 1911. In the 1920s, the military prison held an average of 400 men (The History Channel 1998d).

In 1933, ownership of the 12-acre Alcatraz Island military prison was transferred to the U.S. Department of Justice to be used as a federal prison (Federal Bureau of Prisons 2001f: 1). The Federal Bureau of Prisons removed soft-steel fronts from the 600 Army disciplinary barracks cells and replaced them with 336 cells featuring hardened steel fronts and windows. Cell doors were equipped with automatic locking devices. Gun galleries and stairways were constructed at the ends of each cellblock. Metal detectors were placed in doorways and at the boat dock where inmates, visitors and staff entered and exited the island. Gun towers and flood lights were placed around the outer boundaries of the island, and barriers were built around the 75-foot cliffs hovering above San Francisco Bay. Tear gas canisters were installed throughout the prison (Bates 1936: 145). All building materials had to be shipped to the island via barge or boat (The History Channel 1998d). The new federal prison in San Francisco Bay was supposed to be escape-proof. The Bay's frigid, shark-infested waters, and the powerful undercurrent that pulled floating objects out towards the Pacific Ocean, purportedly posed insurmountable problems for inmates who might escape from the island. However, this was largely a myth. On October 17, 1933, a 17-year-old girl swam, followed by a rescue boat, from the mainland to Alcatraz Island in 43 minutes. A few days later, two women, one 20 years old, the other, 18 years old, followed by two boats full of news reporters, swam from the mainland to Alcatraz Island. When they arrived at the island, the 18-year-old stopped, but the 20-year-old swam around the island and then swam back to the mainland (Keve 1991: 176).

On August 11, 1934, the United States Penitentiary, Alcatraz Island received its first 14 inmates from the federal prison at McNeil Island. Later in August, 53 inmates arrived from the federal prison in Atlanta. Federal authorities sent 8 inmates to Alcatraz from a reformatory in Washington, D.C. A few weeks later, 103 prisoners arrived from Leavenworth (Keve 1991: 177–178). Soon thereafter, Alcatraz housed over 200 men who had been transferred mostly from Leavenworth, Atlanta and McNeil Island. One inmate was kept in each cell. The U.S. Penitentiary at Alcatraz Island had 336 cells in B and C Blocks and 42 in D Block. The inmate population at Alcatraz peaked at 302. The fewest inmates held there was 222, and the average inmate population was about 260. Ninety guards were employed at Alcatraz. About 60 of the guards and their families lived on the island. The others lived in the San Francisco area. The warden and his family lived in a large house near the cellblocks. The associate warden, a captain and their families lived in duplexes on the island. Other employees and their families were housed in Building 64, four houses and three apartment buildings (National Park Service 2001: 14–15). Industrial shops, using inmate laborers, were operated on the island, including a wood shop, a shoe shop, a tailor shop, a dry cleaning facility and a large laundry. Eventually, a furniture reconditioning shop and a shop that manufactured cargo nets for the Navy were added (Keve 1991: 180). The profusion of industrial shops on Alcatraz Island, of course, made weapons production and procurement an easy matter for inmates.

A few of the men incarcerated at Alcatraz were famous. Al Capone arrived as part of the first shipment of inmates. Capone, "the most prominent gangster of all time," was serving an 11-year sentence for income tax evasion (Bennett 1970: 99). He had been at the federal prison in Atlanta. Capone's family had taken up residence in a nearby hotel, and through them, he continued to direct mob activities in Chicago. At Atlanta, Capone had corrupted guards and recruited bodyguards and servants from among the inmates (National Park Service 2001: 3). For recreation, Capone played tennis with partners and opponents selected by him. In the Atlanta prison, Capone purportedly carried thousands of dollars with him in the hollowed-out handle of a tennis racket. After arriving at Alcatraz, Capone was given the job of mopping floors and was soon nicknamed "The Man With The Mop" (Bennett 1970: 100). One day, after arriving at Alcatraz, Capone forced himself into the front of the line of men awaiting haircuts at the barber shop. At the Atlanta prison, Capone had been allowed to step to the front of any line of men. At Alcatraz, a fearless ship hijacker named Jimmy Lucas told Capone to get to the back of the line. When Capone refused to do so, Lucas grabbed a pair of scissors from the barber and stabbed Capone. After this incident, Capone lost a good deal of standing among inmates (100). Capone was interviewed at Alcatraz by James V. Bennett, the second Director of the Federal Bureau of Prisons. Throughout the interview, a guard stood behind Bennett and aimed a rifle at Capone's heart. This was a standard practice when Bennett was interviewing inmates at Alcatraz. During the interview, Capone reportedly offered to bribe Bennett in exchange for a more favorable work assignment or for transfer to another prison (101). In 1939, Capone, suffering from advanced syphilis, was transferred to a federal prison on Terminal Island and then on to the federal prison at Lewisburg, Pennsylvania. In November 1939, he was released from prison. His family took him to Florida, where he died at the age of 48 (Keve 1991: 181; National Park Service 2001: 3).

George "Machine Gun" Kelly arrived at Alcatraz in 1934, as part of the second official shipment of inmates to Alcatraz from other federal prisons. Kelly had started as a bootlegger and had served a 3-year term at Leavenworth for that offense. When he got out of Leavenworth, Kelly, with associates, robbed banks. In 1933, Kelly kidnapped a wealthy Oklahoma oil man and for that offense was sentenced to life in prison, first at Leavenworth, then at Alcatraz. Kelly was, by all accounts, a model prisoner. However, largely due to the influence of J. Edgar Hoover, he served 17 years on Alcatraz Island. In 1954, Kelly suffered a heart attack and was transferred back to Leavenworth. Kelly was released on parole in 1954. In 1959, a final heart attack took his life (National Park Service 2001: 4).

The most famous Alcatraz resident was Robert Stroud. At Leavenworth, Stroud had raised birds and had studied their diseases. Stroud published on the subject and, from Leavenworth, sold birds and medicines for avian diseases. Stroud had originally been sentenced to 12 years for manslaughter. He served 3 years at McNeil Island and was transferred to Leavenworth. After about 4 years at Leavenworth, Stroud fatally stabbed a guard in front of about 2,000 inmates. He was convicted of murder and sentenced to death. Stroud's mother appealed to President Woodrow Wilson, and his sentence was commuted to life in prison without parole. Federal prison officials decided that "The Bird-man" would be kept in segregation for the rest of his life. Stroud was sent to Alcatraz in 1942 and was not allowed to keep birds during his 17-year stay on the island. At first, Stroud was mixed into the general inmate population at Alcatraz. But when Ed Swope took over as warden, Stroud was isolated in a prison hospital room. In 1959, his health failing badly, Stroud was transferred to the federal medical prison in Springfield, Missouri. In 1963, one day before President John F. Kennedy was assassinated, Stroud passed away, with little public notice.

Stroud was found dead by another infamous Alcatraz alumnus, Morton Sobel who, along with Julius and Ethel Rosenberg, was convicted of conspiracy to commit treason. In 1953, the Rosenbergs were electrocuted at Sing-Sing Prison in New York. Sobel received a 30-year sentence and, largely due to the influence of J. Edgar Hoover, was incarcerated at Alcatraz from 1952 until 1957. Sobel served 18 and a half years of his sentence and, after his parole, resided in San Francisco (National Park Service 2001: 5–6).

Capone, Kelly and Stroud certainly fit the image of the vicious and irredeemable type of criminal that Attorney General Homer Cummings and FBI Director J. Edgar Hoover had in mind when they lobbied for a Devil's Island prison on American soil. However, even Alcatraz housed mostly unknown, redeemable men. In the words of Sanford Bates, the first Director of the Federal Bureau of Prisons, "there are but very few of the prisoners of the type of "Machine Gun" Kelly. Most of them are more of [a] reformable type and our work should really be judged by what we can do for these men" (quoted in Ward 1994: 83). This situation exposes an irony common of supermax prisons. It is more cost effective to build a several-hundred bed facility than it is to build a prison with 100 or fewer beds. In time, given the overcrowded nature of prison systems, the extra supermax beds are filled with men who pose no special threats to security and who are not likely to escape, but who nevertheless must endure the harsh and damaging conditions of the supermax facility (King 1999: 177).

Life on Alcatraz Island was truly harsh. After the prison opened, news reporters were not allowed to visit the island (Ward 1994: 86). Upon arrival, inmates were stripped and meticulously searched. All body cavities were examined. Inmates called part of this examination "the finger wave." In its early years, Alcatraz offered no educational programs, no counseling programs and no religious programs. There was no commissary. Inmates were not allowed to possess magazines, newspapers or radios. Recreation was limited to the weekends in the big, dangerous outdoor exercise yard. Meals were restricted to 20 minutes, and the code of silence was imposed (The History Channel 1998d). Alcatraz inmates were entitled to food, clothing and shelter. Anything else they received was considered a privilege that had to be earned (Keve 1991: 179). Consequently, receiving visitors and letters were "privileges" rather than rights that could be taken away as punishment for rule infractions. There were 12 inmate counts per day, and each guard was expected to count the inmates under his supervision every 15 minutes. Until 1939, the old military prison dungeon was used for solitary confinement. Eventually, six isolation cells were built on D Block. Men thrown in "the hole" stayed there for 19 days with no light, no baths, no tooth brushing and no clothing changes. At night, their blankets and mattresses were taken away. Air was piped into the isolation cells from the frigid Bay. Over the years, many of these restrictions were eased. But all inmates not in isolation cells endured the psychological torture of looking out over the Bay at San Francisco and of listening to sounds from the city drifting over the island. Except for the rampant inmate violence, mental brutality rather than physical punishment was the norm at Alcatraz. Monotony ruled. Inmates nicknamed Alcatraz "The Island of the Living Dead" and "Hellcatraz" (The History Channel 1998d; Ward 1994: 88). By 1963, the sea air had weakened the walls of Alcatraz and repairs would have been costly. In light of this situation, Attorney General Robert Kennedy ordered that the prison be closed. On March 21, 1963, the last 27 inmates were removed. USP Alcatraz closed after 29 years of operation (National Park Service 2001: 8). Alcatraz inmates were transferred to McNeil Island, Leavenworth and the federal prison in Atlanta.

Marion

Just a few months after Alcatraz closed, a new high maximum-security prison was opened in southern Illinois near a town called Marion. In 1963, the United States Prison at Marion located on 1,200 acres transferred from the Fish and Wildlife Service to the Federal Bureau of Prisons was "fully operational" (Keve 1991: 187). Marion was designed to house 500 adult male inmates who were difficult to control (Committee to End the Marion Lockdown 1992: 2). Although Marion had been identified as the successor to Alcatraz, during its first year of operation less formidable prisoners were held there. But in 1964, ten former Alcatraz inmates arrived at Marion (King 1999: 166). By the late 1960s, Marion had received a large number of former Alcatraz residents (Ward 1994: 89). Over the next several decades, federal prison officials concentrated "high-risk" and "troublesome" inmates at Marion. Marion's workshops provided inmates with an unending supply of weapons (King 1999: 168). Assaults, escape attempts and escapes were frequent events (Keve 1991: 191).

In 1968, federal prison officials at Marion inaugurated a behavior modification program named the Control and Rehabilitation Effort (CARE). Inmates put into the CARE program were placed in solitary confinement and were coerced into participating in "group therapy" sessions where they were psychologically attacked, broken down and brought under the control of staff. Inmates in the CARE program were encouraged to betray other inmates and to turn against them. In July 1972, a group of inmates initiated a work stoppage in order to protest the beating of a prisoner by a guard. In response, all prisoners were locked in their cells for six days. After the lockdown, seven prisoners suspected of leading the strike were placed in solitary confinement. The strike stopped for a short time and then began again. In response, 60 additional inmates were placed in H-Unit under solitary confinement and were enrolled in the CARE program. This action gave birth to Marion's first control unit: "In 1973, H-Unit at Marion was officially designated the Long-Term Control Unit" (Committee to End the Marion Lockdown 1992: 2).

Inmates in the control units were considered by prison officials to be in administrative segregation rather than disciplinary segregation and, thus, were not being punished. Consequently, inmates in administrative segregation could be held there indefinitely. H-Unit was divided into four sections, three with 18 one-man cells each and one with 16 one-man cells, providing accommodations for a maximum of 70 prisoners. Each cell was 6 feet, 6 inches by 8 feet. Each cell offered 42 square feet of living space, far less than the minimum of 80 square feet required by American Correctional Association standards. Each cell was made up of three concrete walls and a steel grille front. Forty-six cells were fitted with an additional front section featuring a solid steel door equipped with a small Plexiglas window. These units earned the nickname "boxcar cells." In 1979, Marion Penitentiary was given the task of providing long-term segregation in a highly controlled setting for federal prisoners who "threatened other inmates or staff, possessed deadly weapons or dangerous drugs, disrupted the orderly operation of a prison, escaped or attempted to escape in those instances in which the escape involved injury, threat of life or use of deadly weapons" (King 1999: 167). The provision regarding disrupting the orderly operation of a prison was sufficiently vague that it allowed prison officials to place any prisoner they chose at Marion or in other control units spread throughout the federal prison system.

On October 22, 1983, two Marion guards, in separate incidents, were fatally stabbed by control unit inmates. In each incident, an inmate was being escorted outside his cell by three guards. That day, officers Merle Clutts and Robert Hoffman were killed. Two other guards were injured. In the next few days, a number of other violent incidents occurred (Keve 1991: 194). A state of emergency was declared, and the federal prison at Marion was placed on permanent lockdown (King 1999: 168). New policies were implemented. Most industrial shops were closed. Inmates were locked in their cells 23 hours per day and allowed to exercise, alone, in a yard an hour each day. Inmates could only walk, do calisthenics and chin themselves on a stationary bar. No other exercise equipment was allowed. When out of their cells, inmates were handcuffed behind their backs, were forced to wear leg shackles and were escorted by at least two guards. When there was reasonable suspicion, or whenever inmates left their cells or returned, they were forced to undergo digital rectal examinations (Committee to End the Marion Lockdown 1992: 5; Keve 1991: 194–195).

Over time, some restrictions have been lessened. As many as 18 inmates in B- and C-Units are allowed to use the gymnasium and outside recreation area at the same time. B-Unit inmates are allowed out of their cells without handcuffs and leg shackles in order to work at the few remaining shops and to eat in the dining hall (198). D-, E- and F-Units are more restrictive. Prisoners there spend 22 and a half hours per day in their cells. Most of their recreation time is spent in the hallway in front of their cells. In winter, they are allowed to exercise in an outside yard 1 hour per week. In summer, they are allowed to exercise outside 3 hours per week. On a more restrictive note, showers must be taken during inmate exercise periods. Rings at the four corners of bunks allow guards to strap inmates down, "spread eagle," for days at a time, if it is deemed necessary. Each inmate has a small television in his cell and, through this medium, can take one correspondence course at a time. G-, H- and I-Units are even more restrictive. There, prisoners spend 23 hours per day in their stark cells. They are strip searched before and after each exercise period. They are allowed one telephone call per month and three showers per week. Inmates in boxcar cells, with solid second outer cell doors, on I- and H-Units suffer from sound deprivation and have trouble breathing (Committee to End the Marion Lockdown 1992: 5–6). Because the tactics used at Marion lessened inmate violence and injuries to guards, control units and boxcar cells proliferated throughout the federal prison system and into state prisons as well.

Officer Merle Clutts had been stabbed 20 times by a Marion inmate named Thomas Silverstein, a leader of the Aryan Brotherhood, one of the most powerful gangs in the U.S. prison system. Silverstein, who was serving a sentence for armed robbery, had previously fatally stabbed two other inmates. For killing Clutts, Silverstein was sentenced to life in prison without parole and was placed on "no human contact" status. Silverstein was sent to the federal prison in Atlanta, Georgia, where he was held in a special cell. In 1987, he was freed for a short time during a riot by Cuban detainees but was recaptured and traded back to prison officials by the Cubans. Since 1987, Silverstein was held in a special isolation cell, lighted 24 hours a day, at the federal penitentiary at Leavenworth, Kansas. Out of respect for officer Clutts, guards refused to talk to Silverstein. More recently, Silverstein has been held, in isolation, at a super maximum-security facility located near Florence, Colorado. Silverstein once told an interviewer "I didn't come in here a killer, but in here you learn to hate. The insanity in here is cultivated by the guards. They feed the beast that lingers within us all" (Summers 2001: 3–4).

Marion's most famous inhabitant was John Gotti, boss of the Gambino crime family. Gotti was once considered America's number one gangster. Nicknamed the "Teflon Don" for his many evasions of prosecution and conviction, or the "Dapper Don" for his style of dress, Gotti was convicted in a 1992 case involving multiple murders, extortion and a number of other crimes. Gotti was sentenced to life in prison. He was held in a 6-foot by 6-foot solitary confinement cell at the Marion federal penitentiary for 7 years, far longer than most inmates stay at Marion. About his life in prison, Gotti said, "[Y]ou know where I am? I'm in G Unit, the most secure unit on this planet. No contact, no nothing that ain't monitored" (ABCNews. com 1999: 4). In 1998, Gotti was diagnosed with throat cancer. In 2000, his health failing badly, Gotti was transferred to the U.S. Medical Center for Federal Prisoners in Springfield Missouri (Organized Crime About 2001: 2). Gotti died in custody on June 10, 2002.

The building boom accelerates

By 1940, the federal prison system had grown to 24 institutions and housed over 24,000 inmates. By 1980, there were 44 federal prisons. But, as Table 4.1 indicates, the inmate population was just over 24,000 inmates, about the same as in 1940 (Federal Bureau of Prisons 2001a: 2; 2001b: 5). By 2001, largely due to increased prosecution of illicit drug offenders and illegal immigrants, the federal prison system had expanded to 99 institutions holding a total population of 129,406 inmates in Bureau of Prison institutions. Another 12,454 federal inmates were held in privatized prisons, and 13,440 other federal inmates were incarcerated in other non–Bureau of Prisons facilities (Federal Bureau of Prisons 2001b: 1).

The Federal Bureau of Prisons was "projecting dramatic population increases for the next several years because it appears that current Federal law enforcement efforts will continue," (Federal Bureau of Prisons 2001a: 2) and because, "in 1997, Congress passed a law requiring the Bureau of Prisons to assume responsibility for incarcerating the District of Columbia's

Table 4.1 Persons present in federal prisons on the day of survey, 1970, 1980, 2001 and 2015

	1970	1980	2001	2015
Federal prisons	21,094	24,252	129,406	169,279

Sources: 1970 – Cahalan & Parsons 1986: 29; 1980 – Federal Bureau of Prisons 2001b: 5; 2001 – Federal Bureau of Prisons 2001b: 1; 2015 – Federal Bureau of Prisons 2015a: 1–2.

sentenced inmate population by the end of 2001" (Federal Bureau of Prisons 2001c: 1). President Bush's proposed fiscal budget for fiscal year 2002 requested $4.7 billion for prisons, largely for new prison construction and activations, as well as for additional contract bed space (NDAA 2001: 1–2). Between 2001 and 2003, 16 new federal prisons were scheduled to open (The November Coalition 1999: 1–2). In fact, "the Bush administration announced 30 new federal prisons are now or soon will be in the siting process" (Urban/Rural Coalition Against Prisons 2001: 1). Consequently, by 2015, the number of Federal Bureau of Prisons institutions had grown to 121. By 2015, the number of inmates held in federal prisons had grown to 169,279 inmates. Another 24,092 federal inmates were held in privately managed facilities, and another 15,151 federal inmates were incarcerated in "other facilities" (Federal Bureau of Prisons 2015a: 1–2). In its expanded form, the Federal Bureau of Prisons operates institutions at five security levels: minimum, low, medium, high and maximum (Federal Bureau of Prisons 2001c: 1).

The precipitous increase in federal inmates has resulted in corresponding increases in the numbers of federal corrections employees. Table 4.2 shows that in the 1970s and 1980s there were fewer than 10,000 federal corrections employees. However, between 1980 and 2001, the number of persons employed in federal corrections jobs increased 344 percent. By 2015, the Federal Bureau of Prisons was employing 39,463 persons. This is another significant increase in the number of persons needed in order to keep incarcerated an ever-growing federal inmate population.

Costs of operating the federal prison system have gone up. Between 1980 and 2002, according to the data presented in Table 4.3, there was a tenfold increase in the cost of federal corrections. Given the fact that in 2000 the Federal Bureau of Prisons had 20 new prisons "funded and in

Table 4.2 Federal corrections employment, 1971, 1980, 2001 and 2015

	1971	1980	2001	2015
Federal corrections employees	7,223	9,636	33,172	39,463

Sources: 2015 – Federal Bureau of Prisons 2015b: 6; 2001 – Federal Bureau of Prisons 2001b: 6; 1980 – U.S. Department of Justice 1995: 33; 1971 – U.S. Department of Justice 1977: 72.

Table 4.3 Federal corrections expenditures, 1974, 1980, 2002 and 2013

	1974	1980	2002	2013
Federal corrections expenditures	$237,300	$408,000	$4,700,000	$6,700,000

Sources: 2013 – Pew Charitable Trusts 2015: 1; 2002 – NDAA 2001: 2; 1980 – U.S. Department of Justice 1995: 3; 1974 – U.S. Department of Justice 1977: 44.
Note: Dollar amounts are in thousands.

Prisons in the 20th and 21st centuries

some stage of planning or construction; and we have asked for money for nine more prisons in our Fiscal year 2000 budget," significant increases in federal corrections expenditures were inevitable. For example, in the first three months of 2001, the Federal Bureau of prisons awarded contracts for the construction of five new prisons in California (two prisons), South Carolina, Mississippi and Arkansas. The construction cost for these new prisons was estimated to be over $491,000,000 (Federal Bureau of Prisons 2001g: 1–2). The Federal Bureau of prisons also began contracting with for-profit corporations to build prisons where medium- and high-security federal inmates could be housed. The first such facility opened in California in 1997 (Sawyer 2000: 1). Such growth in the federal prison system resulted in an annual budget for 2013 approaching $7 billion.

UNICOR

In 1934, the U.S. Congress and President Franklin D. Roosevelt created the Federal Prison Industries, Incorporated (Federal Bureau of Prisons 2001d: 1; Federal Prison Industries, Inc. 2001: 2). Federal Prison Industries, Inc., renamed UNICOR in 1978, is a wholly owned government corporation that operates industrial programs using low-paid inmate laborers. While the pay rate varies from job to job and can vary from $.23 to $1.15 per hour, UNICOR is known to pay inmates $10 per week for 40 hours of labor (Macias Rojas 1998). Federal law requires that 50 percent of an inmate's UNICOR income go to pay any debt they have been assessed. UNICOR's original mission was to manufacture goods to be sold to other federal agencies. In most cases, federal agencies are obligated to buy UNICOR-produced goods if they are available, without allowing private sector businesses to compete for the contracts (Friel 1999: 3). UNICOR employs approximately 21,000 federal inmates, in virtually all of its prisons, in 100 manufacturing and service industries ranging from furniture to clothing to map-making to recy-cling to textiles to electronics to fleet and vehicular management to data entry (Daniels 2001: 1; Friel 1999: 1). As the numbers of federal inmates increase, UNICOR is looking for ways to expand its operation. According to a U.S. Department of Justice ruling, UNICOR is free to market its ser-vices to the private sector. Consequently, UNICOR is seeking work, like data entry, that has been performed outside the United States (Friel 1999: 1). In so doing, UNICOR administrators hope to avoid direct competition with businesses operating inside the United States. However, some UNICOR activities may expose inmates and correctional workers to extreme health risks. For example, in some federal prisons, UNICOR recycles computers, televisions and other electronic devices containing valuable materials that can be reclaimed. However, such electronic devices also contain "a cocktail of hazardous materials such as lead, mercury, polyvinyl chloride (PVC), and cadmium" (Jackson et al., 2006: 4). Workers and inmates exposed to toxic "E-waste" can experience brain swelling and other forms of brain damage, cancer, harm to the heart, liver and spleen, respiratory failure and reproductive impairment.

ADX

In 1994, as part of a federal corrections complex in Florence, Colorado, the Federal Bureau of Prisons opened a new supermax penitentiary intended to replace Marion. This new facility featured state-of-the-art architecture for extreme control. Formally titled the U.S. Penitentiary Administrative Maximum Facility (ADX), the prison has already earned a number of nicknames including, the "Alcatraz of the Rockies," the "Big One" and the "Hellhole of the Rockies" (Annin 1998: 35). ADX is one of four federal prisons in Florence, Colorado. It was designed to hold 490 inmates (The November Coalition 2001: 4) and, at the turn of the century, hosted 387 (Federal Bureau of Prisons 2001e: 2). The high-technology prison is designed so that a single guard can control the movement of a number of inmates in several cell-blocks by using electronically controlled doors, cameras and audio equipment. By moving inmates through a series of sliding doors, opening one in front and closing one behind, contact with guards can be minimized. ADX has gained a reputation for being more restrictive than Marion. The entrance to ADX is underground. Cell doors are solid, and there are no exterior cell windows (Committee to End the Marion Lockdown 1992: 6). ADX has taken on the responsibility of housing the "worst of the worst" in federal prisons, including "high-risk" and "troublesome" inmates. Cells are 8 feet, 8 inches by 12 feet, 3 inches. Cell doors are solid and contain a 5-by-42-inch window, with only a view of an outer cell door. Cells are equipped with a 12-inch black-and-white television with headphones. Each cell is equipped with a concrete bed, desk and stool, all permanently fastened to the floor. Mirrors, toilets and sinks are made of steel. Thirty-three percent of the inmates at ADX are locked in their cells 23 hours per day. Another 40 percent spend 22 hours per day in their cells. All inmates in solitary confinement get to exercise in an enclosed cage, alone, for an hour per day. Before inmates are allowed out of their cells, they are handcuffed behind their backs through a portal. Inmates out of their cells wear leg shackles and are accompanied by three guards, one always walking behind the prisoner holding a leash attached to him.

ADX has held some of the most notorious criminals of the modern age. Oklahoma City bomber Timothy McVeigh was held there before his execution. Near where McVeigh was kept, in the same cellblock, Ted Kaczynski, The Unabomber, sits in a cell watching his life waste away. Elsewhere in ADX, Ramzi Yousef, convicted of the World Trade Center bombing, and Luis

Felipe, leader of New York's Latin Kings gang, are warehoused. One inmate at ADX, serving a 45-year sentence, says "lock yourself in your bathroom for the next four years and tell me how it affects your mind. It begins to erode the five senses. It's dehumanizing" (Annin 1998: 35). Oscar Lopez Rivera, a Puerto Rican nationalist and a purported leader of the Fuerzas Armadas de Liberacion Nacional (FALN), was imprisoned for five months at ADX while serving a 55-year sentence for seditious conspiracy that began in 1981. Rivera's group has been accused of over a hundred bombings in the 1970s, resulting in at least five deaths. While at ADX, Rivera was kept among the 27 percent of inmates allowed out of their cells to eat and work and to visit the commissary. Rivera was returned to Marion where he is locked in his cell 22 hours per day (Prendergast 1996: 1–2).

In a 2013 lawsuit, an attorney who interviewed 140 ADX prisoners over a 2-year period claimed that as many as one-half of the 425 inmates held at ADX were severely mentally ill and that correctional workers were failing to provide adequate care and treatment for severely mentally ill inmates. Examples cited include guards blocking the exit of odor from cells where inmates eat and otherwise manipulate their own feces, an inmate who has mutilated his body 100 times and, finally, a head-banging inmate who has removed his own pinky fingers, both earlobes, his scrotum and a testicle from his body (Mitchell, 2013: 4A). Reacting to the lawsuit, the Bureau of Prisons transferred as many as 30 of the severely mentally ill inmates from ADX to a special unit at the Atlanta federal prison. This case has turned into the largest lawsuit ever filed against the Federal Bureau of Prisons (Binelli 2015: 36–41).

Summary

The federal prison system began modestly, with the construction of maximum-security facilities at Leavenworth, Atlanta and McNeil Island. However, by 1930, the federal prison building boom had produced 14 institutions. By 1940, the federal prison system had grown to 24 institutions. By 1980, the Federal Bureau of Prisons operated 44 long-term lock-ups. By 2001, the federal prison system had expanded to 99 institutions. By 2015, the Federal Bureau of Prisons was operating 121 institutions and was housing tens of thousands of other federal inmates, mostly in privately owned and managed prisons. The federal prison system continues to grow at unprecedented rates. The number of federal inmates, and the cost of federal corrections, has spiraled upward at alarming rates, supported by American politicians' "war on crime" and by a penchant among American police officers, criminal court judges and voters for "getting tough on criminals." Unfortunately, the war is far from over, and the supply of criminals available to be imprisoned seems endless.

There is a broader political economic perspective into which federal prison growth should be placed. In its early years, the United States federal government, like its prison system, was small. The federal government possessed little power to wield in its relations with state governments and with other sovereign nations. However, World War II changed everything. The United States came out of the war with an economy running on all cylinders. Until the beginning of its military blunders in Vietnam and, later, elsewhere, the American economy had grown and grown and grown again. By the 1970s, the United States was well along in its development as a corporate state, a civilization in which power comes under the control of a small number of "supercorporations" based in the United States but operating around the world (Fusfeld, 1972: 1). United States supercorporations and the federal government formed an increasingly powerful alliance that continues to the present. As United States supercorporations grew in power and wealth, so did the power, wealth and influence of the federal government. As a consequence, throughout the last one-half of the twentieth century and on into the twenty-first century, the size of federal police forces and of the federal court system expanded again and again. With such expansion came the need for a significantly larger federal prison system, a need that continues at least for the near future. In a United States dominated by supercorporations, it is no surprise that the federal prison system, given its thirst for new prison space, brought corporations that own and manage prisons into its fold.

Chapter 5

Profiting from punishment: corporations and American prisons

Introduction

Corporations profit from American prisons in four general ways (Shichor 1995). First, vendors provide products and services for prisons. The following is a partial list of services and products sold to prison systems by for-profit vendors (Federal Bureau of Prisons 2001h; Macias Rojas 1998; Schlosser 1998):

- architectural/engineering services
- ADP equipment (including maintenance, software, and supplies)
- automotive supplies
- building materials and building renovation equipment
- camera equipment
- community-based halfway house services
- construction services
- dental equipment and supplies
- dictating/transcribing machines
- door and window frames
- electrical supplies
- equipment and chemicals used for executions
- fence wire
- fire sprinkler systems
- food items
- fork lifts and lift trucks
- fuel oil
- garbage collection services
- heating and air-conditioning services, hot water heaters
- laundry and dry cleaning services
- lumber
- medical services and supplies
- metal-detecting devices and other security equipment
- office supplies
- plumbing supplies
- protective clothing
- roofing materials
- steel
- telephone equipment and services for inmate use
- word processing equipment and services
- X-ray equipment and other health service equipment.

Second, corporations provide private financing for prisons. By utilizing private financing to build prisons, either in the form of funds secured from banks and investors or through the sale of bonds, politicians and private prison operators have been able to continue their prison-building binge without being required to seek the approval of voters (Dyer 2000; Mattera et al., 2001). Third, corporations contract with prison administrators to use inmate laborers to manufacture goods and to provide services like telemarketing, booking airline telephone reservations and performing data entry tasks (Abramsky 1998; Johnson 2001). Fourth, corporations contract with corrections officials to manage and operate prisons and jails (Bates 1997).

Selling products and services

In the past few decades, local, state and federal spending on products and services for jails and prisons has grown into "a multibillion-dollar industry with its own trade shows and conventions, its own Web sites, mail-order catalogues, and direct marketing campaigns.... A directory called the *Corrections Yellow Pages* lists more than a thousand vendors" (Schlosser 1998: 16). Products and services marketed for prison consumption range from the mundane, such as food, clothing, plumbing supplies, fencing, razor wire, bullet-proof surveillance cameras and healthcare, to the exotic, such as padded cells in a variety of colors, electrified fences, violent prisoner chairs, less-than-lethal handheld electronic immobilization weapons and body orifice security scanners, to the highly expensive like prison architectural services and construction.

Corporations like DMJM, the DLR Group and KMD Architects profit from the design of prisons. Similarly, companies like Brown & Root, CRSS and Turner Construction build prisons for a profit. The American Correctional Association (ACA) organizes two conventions per year that bring prison administrators and vendors together. Through mail-outs to its membership and through its Web site, ACA solicits buyer and seller attendance at its conventions. The ACA also sells buyer contact information to vendors for marketing purposes. It is estimated that over 80 percent of sales to prisons occur at conventions like those organized by the ACA (Johnson 2001).

The prison telephone business

Before the 1990s, inmates in American prisons were able to call family members and their attorneys for approximately the same telephone rates that were assessed people making calls who were not in prison. Then, the corporations came calling. Corporate representatives successfully lobbied legislators and prison officials to take over prison and jail telephone services. In turn, the corporation would pay the prison or jail system "concession fees" or "commissions" on calls made by inmates. By 2013, total "concession fees" paid by telephone corporations was approaching

$500 million per year. From modest beginnings, the prison inmate telephone industry has grown into a $1.2 billion-a-year money-maker. AT&T, BellSouth and MCI, three large American telephone service providers, have operated prison telephone services. More recently, private equity firms came calling, buying up and consolidating prison telephone providers. Today, equity firms operate Global Tel-Link Corporation and Securus Technologies. Global Tel-Link Corporation controls about 70 percent of the American prison telephone business. Securus Technologies has secured another 20 percent (Williams 2015: 2–3).

Telephones are one of the few ways that inmates can keep in contact with relatives and friends in the free world. Most calls from prisons and jails must be made collect. Some inmate calls can be made using a debit card number. Thus, the burden of payment for prison telephone calls is transferred from inmates to relatives and friends. A great deal of money has been made from the prison telephone business. In 1995, inmates in Louisiana prisons "made 2.7 million calls ... for an average annual bill of $605 per inmate (Hallinan 2001: 146). In one Washington prison, during December 1997, "inmates spent an astonishing $458,581 calling home for Christmas – an average bill, per inmate, of more than $200" (146). Prison telephones for inmates can make as much as $15,000 per year, approximately five times the income of a conventional pay telephone. Prisoner telephone calls "generate a billion dollars or more in revenues each year" (Schlosser 1998: 15). AT&T, Sprint and MCI have been known to charge inmates "6 times the normal cost of a long-distance call within the U.S." (Macias Rojas 1998: 1). "MCI imposes a $3.00 surcharge on all inmate telephone calls.... MCI Maximum Security and North American Intelecom have both been caught overcharging for calls made by inmates; in one state, MCI was adding an additional minute to every call" (Schlosser 1998: 16). In California, MCI installed pay telephones throughout the California prison system at no cost to the Department of Corrections. MCI gave the Department of Corrections a 32 percent share of the income generated from California inmate telephone calls. In 2001, the California Public Utilities Commission ordered MCI to refund more than $500,000 in overcharges on collect telephone calls made by prisoners to their families (Prisoners' Advocacy Network-Ohio 2001). In 2013, after 12 years, AT&T agreed to settle a class action lawsuit, by paying $45 million to as many as 70,000 to 120,000 persons who, between 1996 and 2000, were overcharged for a telephone call made from Washington state prisons (Martin 2013: 1).

In 2013, the Federal Communications Commission (FCC) stepped in and capped *interstate* telephone calls to 25 cents per minute (plus whatever surcharge is imposed by the provider). Twenty-five cents per minute was a considerable improvement over rates that had been assessed in the past. There was an expectation that prison telephone rates would go down by as much as 25 percent to 50 percent (Gustin 2014: 1). Unfortunately, the expected drop in rates did not come about. Somehow, members of the Federal Communications Commission failed to realize that most telephone calls made by prison inmates are *intrastate* in nature. Major corporate prison telephone players adapted to the new cap on *interstate* telephone calls by raising their fees and rates on *intrastate* telephone calls, thus securing and extending their profitability. In late October 2015, the Federal Communications Commission revisited their 2013 decision, extending its caps to *intrastate* telephone calls made by inmates. The new cap on charges for intrastate telephone calls made by inmates was supposed to be implemented in 2016 (Denver Post 2015c: 14A).

In sum, no competition for telephone customers exists inside American prisons. Unlike other American consumers, inmates cannot switch to another telephone company. Simply put, state corrections departments have been partners in the exploitation of inmates. For example, in 2014, the Colorado Department of Corrections realized a $1.53 million profit from its prison telephone partnership. In Colorado, the corporate provider charged inmates as much as four times more to make an intrastate call than it charged some inmates in other states for making a similar call (Denver Post 2015c: 17A). The burden of excessive telephone costs has fallen disproportionately on the families of inmates, for the most part on low income people who committed no crimes. Hopefully, the 2015 FCC ruling, if fully implemented, will bring to an end this form of punishment for inmates and their loved ones. It is noteworthy that the explosion of inmate cellular telephone possession and use occurred within the context of exploitation of inmates when they used the legitimate, prescribed telephone system provided by corrections systems and their corporate partners.

Transporting inmates for profit

Throughout most of American history, sheriff's deputies and U.S. Marshals transported inmates from criminal court to jail, from jail to prison, and from prison to prison. In the 1980s, private companies began transporting inmates, often across state lines. Private companies replaced sheriff's deputies and U.S. Marshals by offering to transport prisoners for about 50 percent of what this service had cost before. Many prisoner transport companies are small. They are usually paid standard fees and expenses by government agencies based upon mileage. However, some prisoner transport companies are quite large. For example, TransCor America, a Corrections Corporation of America (CCA) subsidiary, moves inmates about the nation using over a hundred vehicles (Friedmann 1997b; TransCor America, LLC, 2015). Private companies cut costs by employing nonunion guards, by providing minimal training, by making multiple pickups and deliveries per trip, and by sometimes using poorly maintained, high mileage vehicles. This system of transfer can take as long as a month, leaving inmates locked day after day in vehicles, while spending nights in a series of county jails. Transport guards and drivers are often poorly trained and suffer the stress of overseeing captives who see their journey between lock-ups as an opportunity to escape. Transport guards and drivers also endure the wear-and-tear of driving long distances on America's highways. It is not surprising that private transport guard turnover is high.

Very little legal oversight is in place for private prisoner transportation firms. Vans and passenger cars used by private transport firms are not bound by federal laws that regulate the use of commercial vehicles. Prisoner transportation companies are only required to carry liability insurance. Transport drivers do not need commercial licenses. No rest requirements are imposed on drivers. Commercial vehicle maintenance regulations do not apply to vans and automobiles. In fact, the interstate movement of cattle is better regulated (Schlosser 1998). Unless the jail is used as a "prisoner motel," local legal officials will likely not know that private transport personnel and multiple inmates visited their communities, unless something goes wrong.

In 1997, six inmates and two guards were traveling on I-40 near Dickson, Tennessee, in a van owned by Federal Extradition Agency, a private vendor with headquarters in Memphis. An inmate who had been dropped off earlier reported that the van was making "knocking noises" and that the guards would not stop to inspect the vehicle. The drive shaft broke free of its housing, forcing the van off of the highway. The gas tank was pierced, and a fire broke out, trapping the six inmates inside. The driver and guard received only minor injuries, but all six inmates perished. Fire damage to the inmates was so extensive that two were incorrectly identified and turned over to the wrong families. The van had been driven over 260,000 miles. Its universal joint malfunctioned as a result of excessive wear, causing the drive shaft to break free (Friedmann 1997b: 1). Two months later, another van owned by Federal Extradition Agency crashed in Kansas killing one guard and injuring five prisoners (2).

Even what might seem like minor mechanical problems in a prisoner transport vehicle can result in tragedy. For example, in 2009, a TransCor America van was moving a federal inmate who was serving a 5-year sentence from a prison in Kansas to another in Indiana. His transport involved a number of stops in order to pick up and deliver other prisoners. According to a recitation of facts issued by a U.S. District Court in Illinois, the van's air conditioner had ceased working. Temperatures that day reached 95 degrees. After a call to company headquarters, the van driver was told to complete his scheduled inmate transfers. The 66-year-old federal inmate "died in the unairconditioned TransCor van due to heat stroke" (Zoukis, 2013: 34). In 2014, a 54-year-old female inmate, with a history of physical and mental illness, while being transported approximately a thousand miles, from Kentucky to Florida and while shackled with ten other inmates in a Prisoner Transportation Services of America van, was found "slumped over dead inside the van during a stop for food at Taco Bell" (Ovalle 2014: 1). Other travelers in the van reported that the victim had been having hallucinations throughout their journey, that she had drunk little water, and that she had refused a meal at an earlier stop. After finding her unresponsive, the first telephone call the transport driver and guard allegedly made was to their employer. They reportedly then tried to revive the prisoner. Only after that attempt proved ineffective, did the driver and guard dial 911 in order to ask for local help (2).

In 1994, the owners of Fugitive One Transport were arrested and charged with the rape of a female prisoner they were moving from Connecticut to Texas (2). In 1999, the American Civil Liberties Union (ACLU) of Colorado filed a suit on behalf of a 43-year-old female inmate, alleging that she had been sexually assaulted by a TransCor America guard while she was being transported from Texas to Colorado. This prisoner alleged that she was sexually assaulted while still in shackles. The 43-year-old inmate alleged that she was threatened with retaliation if she reported the assault and that she was not allowed to use the toilet at rest stops during her 5-day trip from Texas to Colorado. The ACLU alleged that she was suffering from post-traumatic stress disorder (American Civil Liberties Union 1999). This case was settled in 2001, when the victim received a "substantial settlement" from TransCor America (Private Corrections Working Group, 2015: 2). According to TransCor lawyers, at least five other similar lawsuits have been filed against the inmate transport corporation (2).

In a variation on the same theme, in 2010, a prison transport driver in Kentucky was arrested by the FBI and eventually was sentenced to 5 years in prison for having sex with a female prisoner after supplying her with alcohol and illicit drugs (Curtis 2015: 1). In 2015, a 54-year-old prison transport driver was sentenced to 12 years in federal prison for fraud, while operating a prisoner transport service under false pretenses. The fraud charge was for his hiding a prior felony offense, for his using an alias and for his sexual use of female inmates. While working for United States Prisoner Extradition Services and Interstate Criminal Extraditions, the driver, a veteran of the prison transport industry, used "female prisoners for his own sexual gratification" (1). For select female passengers, he would forgo the use of handcuffs and shackles. He would supply them with alcohol and illicit drugs. In turn, he would engage in sex with the women either in his van or in a motel.

Escapes from private transport vehicles are common. During a move from Iowa to New Mexico in 1996, six prisoners (five murderers and a rapist) jumped the unarmed husband-and-wife co-owners of R & S Prisoner Transport while at a rest stop in Texas. The prisoners seized the van and took the couple hostage before being captured after a high-speed police chase, thanks to a motorist who saw the event and called for help. In 1997, a rapist serving two life sentences, while being moved from Utah to Arkansas, seized a Federal Extradition Agency van and a gun, taking seven other prisoners hostage. The inmate stole two additional vehicles and a horse and took one more hostage before his capture a day later. In 1997, while being moved from New Mexico to Massachusetts, a man charged with murder and armed robbery seized a shotgun and took over a TransCor America van while stopped at a Colorado gas station. The van was surrounded by police and, at the urging of other prisoners in the van, the man surrendered. Four days later in Minnesota, an inmate escaped from the same TransCor America van, while being moved from Kansas to Florida. He took a couple hostage and spent the night in their home. He was later taken into custody in Chicago (Friedmann 1997b: 2; Schlosser 1998: 23). In 2005, an 18-year-old inmate escaped from a TransCor America van in Florida. While chasing the escapee, the driver left the back door open and the keys in the van's ignition, creating an opportunity for the 12 other inmate passengers to escape. Luckily, no other inmate took advantage of the situation (Private Corrections Working Group 2015: 1). In 2009, Prisoner Transport Services lost two prisoners to escape in separate incidents about six months apart. One prisoner simply disappeared from a transport van while it traveled from Florida to Pennsylvania. Six months later, another prisoner, while in transport custody at an airport, escaped (Ovalle 2014: 2).

In sum, movement of corporations into prisoner transport created yet another profitable element of the burgeoning American prison industry. Corporations relieved local, state and federal governments of the burdensome, never-ending, responsibility of moving prisoners about the nation. Savings were promised and, perhaps, some were realized. However, this corporate aspect of American prisons operates out of sight of most of the citizenry and appears to be lightly regulated. While operating in the shadows of American criminal law, prison transport corporations have accumulated an impressive history of criminal misconduct and safety indiscretions.

Profiting from prison healthcare

Medical care and other health expenses can account for as much as one-third of a prison's budget. Only security costs more (Cannon 2015: 1). Prison systems in at least 20 states contract with for-profit entities for some, or all, inmate medical care (Dober 2014: 1). The drive for profit, when combined with a traditional skepticism among prison medical practitioners about the validity of inmate requests for health services, can become a formula for death and disaster. Corizon Health (CH) and its major competitors, namely Wexford Health Services, Armor Correctional Health Services, NaphCare, Correct Care Solutions and Centurion Managed Care, have been assuming the responsibilities of providing healthcare for American jail and prison inmates. Corizon Health is the nation's largest for-profit provider of healthcare and management services for prisons. CH was formed in 2011, when Correctional Medical Services (CMS), the former largest provider, merged with Prison Health Services. Headquartered in St Louis, Missouri, CMS provided healthcare services to more than 270,000 inmates held in over 330 prisons spread over 29 states (Berkowitz 2001). Corizon Health is owned by Valitas Health Services, which is majority-owned by Beecken Petty O'Keefe & Company, a large Chicago-based private equity corporation. In 2015, Corizon Health served almost 350,000 inmates held at over 500 facilities in 27 states (Corizon Health 2015). Corizon Health generates annual income approaching $1.5 billion (Dober 2014: 2).

While perhaps saving prison systems some money, privatized prison health providers have a long history of impropriety. For example, the *St. Louis Post-Dispatch* reported in 1998 that CMS, Corizon's predecessor, was also involved in "more than 20 cases in which inmates allegedly died as a result of negligence, indifference, understaffing, inadequate training or overzealous cost-cutting" (quoted in Berkowitz 2001: 2). Listed among those inmates receiving medical death sentences is an Alabama prisoner whose condition was ignored by medical personnel as his weight dropped 50 pounds, as he displayed symptoms of mental disorder and as he became dehydrated. Another 46-year-old inmate died after medical personnel failed to provide her with heart medicine prescribed by her doctor. An Oklahoma prisoner died after nurses allegedly ignored his complaints of abdominal pain that resulted from a perforated ulcer (4). Others who died while being cared for by CMS include a Nevada inmate whose diabetes went untreated, an Alabama prisoner whose kidney dialysis machine was loaded with the wrong chemical and a Virginia convict who died of a heart attack after medical providers failed to conduct the tests ordered by his doctor (Allen and Bell 1998: 1). According to criminologist Michael Vaughn, an expert on jail and prison healthcare, "[F]or every death there are hundreds of cases of inmates in these correctional facilities who are receiving substandard care" (quoted in Allen and Bell 1998: 4).

Since its formation, Corizon Health has been in litigation about numerous situations involving inmates held in prisons throughout the United States where litigants allege improper healthcare was provided (Dober 2014). Herein, we have space only for representative examples. For example, in 2011, a Special Master appointed by a U.S. District Court judge issued a report about healthcare provided by Corizon Health at an

Idaho prison. The master found serious problems with healthcare at the prison, problems so serious that they either had resulted or could result in serious harm to inmates. The master concluded that persons responsible for healthcare at the prison were "deliberately indifferent to the serious healthcare needs of their charges" (7). In 2013, a federal appeals court confirmed a $1.2 million award to a Florida convict who had sued Corizon Health. This ruling confirmed that Corizon Health had a set of practices in place that denied inmates access to hospitalization, even in some extreme cases of need (5).

For-profit prison medical care corporations are not alone in providing substandard services. They are joined by a number of state departments of correction. For example, in Washington state, at the Washington Corrections Center for Women, an inmate died as a result of infection brought on by a perforated chronic gastric ulcer with acute peritonitis. She had sought help from the prison's medical practitioners who treated her disrespectfully, failed to conduct proper diagnostics, and failed to prescribe appropriate hospitalization and medication. After the inmate's death, consultants hired by the Department of Corrections concluded that she had been treated largely by a physician's assistant without proper oversight by the prison doctor. It was learned that the prison doctor, one physician's assistant and one contract doctor were responsible for the medical needs of 540 inmates and tended to 40 to 60 sick prisoners per day, making it impossible for them to undertake appropriate diagnostics. This situation was described as "a recipe for continued, potentially life-threatening, yet preventable problems" (quoted in Wright 1998: 79).

At the Monroe Washington State Reformatory, a male inmate died of a heart attack. Before his death, the inmate had sought help from prison medical personnel. An electrocardiogram (EKG) was done, and the results were read by a computer with a history of producing faulty diagnoses. The computer deemed the test normal. After the inmate's death, an investigation by the Washington Department of Health revealed that some of the prison medical practitioners did not have current licenses on file, that three of the four attending medical professionals did not have current documentation of CPR/first aid training and that the prison medical facility did not have in place appropriate procedures and protocols for the assessment, care and transfer of inmates at risk of heart attack (82).

In California, by 2006, conditions had grown so bad that federal judges took over the state prison inmate medical care system (Marois 2013: 1). In order to escape federal judicial control, among a number of initiatives, the California Department of Correction and Rehabilitation spent $900 million on a new medical and mental health prison (4). Unfortunately, California state prisons are still running at about 150 percent of capacity.

In sum, substandard inmate medical care is one of the most serious problems woven into the expansive American prison system. In America, medical care is expensive. Competent, thorough and respectful medical care is extremely expensive. In this broader cultural context, prison officials and politicians have been eager to "outsource" this expensive responsibility to a willing corporation for, say, $28 million or $48 million per year, depending upon the number of inmates and the number of facilities to be served. In turn, since their annual income is set, prison healthcare providers have significant incentives to minimize costs in all possible areas, including diagnosis, treatment, hospitalization, aftercare and provision of prescription drugs. Substandard prison medical care has the potential to become a national disaster as the numbers of inmates increase who are suffering from a wide range of infectious diseases like tuberculosis, HIV/AIDS, and hepatitis C.

Private financing for prisons

In the 1980s and 1990s, corporate representatives lured politicians with the promise of quickly providing additional prison bed space through methods that could bypass voter approval. Giants of the industry like Corrections Corporation of America (CCA) and Wackenhut Corrections, as well as smaller private corrections companies like Privatization Corporation (Pricor Inc.); Avalon Enterprises; Esmor Correctional Services, Inc. (renamed Correctional Services, Inc.); and Cornell Cox (renamed Cornell Corrections and then renamed Cornell Companies, Inc.), raised money to build privatized prisons via the equity and debt markets.

Corrections Corporation of America raised start-up funds by selling Massey Burch Investment Group a 22 percent share in the corporation. In 1986, CCA went public, with the help of influential underwriters like Donaldson, Lufkin and Jenrette and Prudential-Bache Securities, raising $18 million. In 1991, General Electric Capital Corporation bought preferred stock in CCA for $5 million. In 1988, Sovran Bank, First Union Bank and Southeast Banking Corporation loaned CCA $24 million. In 1989, the 1988 loan was replaced with a $30 million line of credit from First Union Bank, Southeast Banking Corporation and AmSouth Bank. Later in 1989, CCA borrowed $9 million from a subsidiary of Toronto Dominion Bank. Late in 1996, CCA arranged a revolving credit account with First Union Corporation for $117 million. In all, CCA's long-term debt grew from $9.5 million in 1965 to $57.8 million in 1991 to $117 million in 1996 (Mattera et al., 2001: 13–14).

Pricor Incorporated received $3.3 million in start-up funds from Massey Burch Investment Group. In 1987, with the help of influential underwriters like J.C. Bradford & Company, and a subsidiary of PaineWebber named Rotan Mosle Incorporated, Pricor Incorporated went public, raising $6.7 million. In 1986, Pricor set up a $9 million line of revolving credit with Signet Bank of Richmond, Virginia, and Sovran Bank/Central South of

Nashville, Tennessee, which it used to pay off Massey Burch. In 1987, Pricor arranged a new $24 million term loan and a $6 million revolving loan from Signet Bank (13).

In 1988, Wackenhut Corrections, a subsidiary of Wackenhut Corporation, used funds provided by the parent company to get started. In 1994, Wackenhut Corrections, with the help of underwriter Prudential Securities, went public. That same year, Wackenhut Corrections opened a $15 million line of credit with Barnett Bank of South Florida. Two years later, Wackenhut Corrections, through underwriters Prudential Securities and Lazard Freres, raised $52 million by selling 4.6 million shares of stock (14). In 2002, Group 4 Falck, a Danish corporation, acquired Wackenhut Corporation. Group 4 Falck presently owns 57 percent of Wackenhut Corrections but will most likely sell it to another entity (Hoover's Online 2002b: 1).

A number of smaller corrections corporations raised money by issuing stock. Avalon Enterprises issued stock in 1991 and then went through name changes to Avalon Community Services to Avalon Correctional Services. In 1994, Esmor Correctional Services Incorporated (today called Correctional Services Corporation) issued $5.2 million of stock through underwriter Janney Montgomery Scott, a subsidiary of Penn Mutual Life Insurance. In 1996, Cornell Corrections, raised $37 million on the American Stock Exchange, through underwriters Dillon Read & Company, Equitable Securities and ING Barings. In 1997, Cornell Corrections raised another $41 million by issuing 2.25 million shares of common stock with the help of underwriters SBC Warburg Dillon Read, Equitable Securities and Wasserstein Perella Securities (Mattera et al., 2001: 14).

Lease-revenue bonds: public money goes to corrections corporations

In the 1980s, as voters increasingly refused to approve new financing for prison construction, prison corporations, their politician allies (including state treasurers), creative lawyers and investment bankers devised new ways to finance the prison-building boom (Anderson 2008: 1). They quickly turned to lease-revenue bonds. The idea to use lease-revenue bonds to build prisons originated within the offices of a California law firm (Prison Legal News 2013: 1). Lease-revenue bonds had originally been used to finance the building of entities that would generate income, like toll roads, universities, bridges, stadia and hospitals. The process is simple. A state government creates an agency charged with the building of prisons. The state agency issues bonds and builds prisons. The agency leases the prisons to the state department of correction, which, in turn, makes lease payments. Lease payments are then used over time to pay off the bonds. No step in this process requires voter approval (1). Because there is some risk of default, lease-revenue bonds pay a higher rate of interest than do traditional revenue bonds, which require voter approval and which were the traditional means for raising money to build prisons (Anderson 2008: 1).

In 1989, the proceeds from tax-exempt lease-revenue bonds issued by six Texas counties were used by N-Group Securities, Incorporated, to build six private prisons that were to be operated by Pricor Incorporated. The tax-exempt bonds raised $74 million. When a newly elected governor refused to approve contracts for the housing of inmates in the new prisons, and failing to meet court-ordered standards, the six prisons went unfilled. After extended litigation, the prisons were eventually sold to the state of Texas and were merged into its corrections system. This series of transactions marked the beginning of the use of lease-revenue bonds to circumvent tax-payer approval for new prisons (Mattera et al., 2001: 14; Justice Strategies 2010: 1).

CCA induced various governmental agencies to issue industrial revenue bonds to fund early prison-building projects. In 1989, the Industrial Development Board of Jefferson County, Tennessee, issued $9 million in industrial revenue bonds for CCA so that it could build a juvenile detention center. Later that year, Grants, New Mexico, issued $12 million in industrial revenue bonds for CCA so that it could build a prison for women (Mattera et al., 2001: 18). But the industry soon turned to lease-revenue bonds as the most lucrative way to build private prisons with public funds. Lease-revenue bonds are an especially attractive way to finance prison-building, because they do not require voter approval. Lease-revenue bonds, some-times called "lease-payment bonds," had been used by government agen-cies to build revenue producing facilities like convention centers, athletic stadia and toll roads. Because the facilities would produce income that could be used to repay investors, the issuance of such bonds did not require voter approval. Sometimes, governments would lease prisons from the cor-porations that owned them, thus creating the revenue stream necessary for lease-revenue bonds to be used to generate prison construction funds. In other cases, governments created public building authorities or non-profit corporations that functioned as landlords, leasing the new prisons to pri-vate corporations. In either case, the requirement of voter approval of new governmental debt was circumvented (18–19).

In 1985, California borrowed $105 million via high-interest, costly lease-revenue bonds for the construction of new corporate prisons. In the 1980s and 1990s, the state of New York issued $7 billion in lease-revenue bonds, through the Urban Development Corporation originally created to build low-cost housing, to build and buy prisons (Dyer 2000: 250). In the end, lease-revenue bonds are a bad investment for taxpayers since they are issued at a higher rate of interest than more traditional voter-approved state general obligation bonds and since their underwriting and issuing costs are much higher than voter-approved state general obligation bonds. For example, in 1991, the New York Department of Corrections sold the Attica prison to the Urban Development Corporation for $200 million. The Urban Development Corporation paid for the prison using money from the sale of bonds that did not require voter approval. New York taxpayers will pay, over time, $700 million to retire the bonds that were used to buy Attica. This is ironic since, in 1981, New York voters had defeated a $500 million general obligation bond issue proposal to be used to build new prisons (250–253).

California has been the most aggressive in using lease-revenue bonds to build prisons. Other states utilizing this tactic in order to avoid voter approval of new prison building are Alaska, Florida, Michigan and Texas (Anderson 2008: 1). In Florida, the Correctional Privatization Commission (CPC) was created in 1995, in order to facilitate building new prisons by issuing Certificates of Participation (COP), a form of lease-revenue bond. In turn, the CPC created the Florida Correctional Finance Corporation to issue and sell COPs. By 1996, five new privatized Florida prisons had been built using COPs as a source of funding. Between 2006 and 2010, Florida spent almost $717 million on prison construction and expansion. That figure includes the costs of prisons built using money generated by traditional, voter-approved bonds, and the rental costs of prisons built using money generated by COPs (Prison Legal News 2013: 2).

Politicians in California, in 2007, in order to satisfy a federal judge's order to reduce prison overcrowding, agreed to spend $7.4 billion to build prisons that could hold over 50,000 inmates (Californians United for a Responsible Budget 2008). At that time, the California prison system was operating at almost 200 percent of capacity. By 2013, only about $1.5 billion had been spent (Marois 2013: 1). In 2006, with federal court control looming, the California governor, a movie actor, suggested that $11 billion in lease-revenue bonds should be issued in order to build new prisons and jails. As the governor's proposal met resistance among state legislators, the sum to be borrowed was reduced to $7.4 billion. However, due to the effects of a recession, as well as ongoing resistance on the part of some state legislators, only $1.6 billion of the bonds had been issued by mid-2013 (3). It is noteworthy that, in 2013, when the California Department of Corrections and Rehabilitation issued $310 million in lease-revenue bonds, in order to build prisons, Moody's Investor Service gave the bonds an A2 rating. According to Moody's, "the A2 rating reflects strong legal mechanisms for lease payments" (2013: 1).

It has become apparent that lease-revenue bonds are proving to be a blessing for bankers, lawyers, underwriters, architects, contractors, investors, corrections corporations and crime-fighting politicians. These entities have formed an alliance to build more prisons without consulting voters.

Not quite as apparent is the fact that prisons built with money generated from lease-revenue bonds prove to be considerably more expensive than prisons built with money generated by issuing traditional general obligation bonds, the type of bonds that require voter approval. Prisons built via lease-revenue bonds are more expensive because the interest paid to investors is higher, by as much as 30 percent or more (Ashton & Petteruti 2011: 32). In sum, there is only one compelling reason to build prisons with money secured through lease-revenue bonds. That reason is to avoid the need for voter approval.

Profiting from inmate labor

Use of inmate labor has always been a staple of American prisons. However, in the 1930s, Congress, via passage of the Hawes-Cooper Act and the Ashurst-Sumner Act, eliminated the use of prison labor for profit-making purposes. In particular, the Ashurst-Sumner Act made it a crime to transport prison-made products across state lines. These laws applied only to profit-making. Consequently, throughout the twentieth century and on into the twenty-first, inmates in the United States have worked in a wide variety of prison jobs, including as appliance repair persons, assembly line workers, cooks, dish washers, farm and ranch workers, laundry workers, opticians, plumbers, electricians, carpenters, gardeners, medical aides, office helpers, painters and x-ray technicians. Inmates also provide labor for prison industries that manufacture goods and services earmarked for consumption by other governmental agencies. Today, over 40 states operate prison industries programs. California, Florida, North Carolina and Texas operate the largest prison industries programs.

By the 1980s, for-profit work began creeping back inside the walls of American prisons. For example, the Prison Rehabilitative Industries and Diversified Enterprises (PRIDE) program was created in 1981 by the Florida state legislature. PRIDE is a private, non-profit corporation. By the mid-1990s, PRIDE was grossing almost $80 million in annual sales. Some of PRIDE's profits are spent helping Florida parolees when they are released from prison. By the mid-1990s, the North Carolina prison industries program had exceeded $50 million in annual sales. The Texas Industries Division (TID) was created in 1963. By the mid-1990s, TID boasted a work force of over 7,000 inmates (Wisely 1998: 140).

California's inmates have been manufacturing goods for state agencies since the mid-1900s. "In 1944, the Prison Reorganization Act created the California Correctional Industries Program to oversee all prison manufacturing programs" (Browne 1996: 66). In 1982, the California Correctional Industries Program was renamed the Prison Industry Authority (PIA).

In California, inmates manufacture over a hundred types of products. PIA sells approximately 2,000 items through a catalogue sent to all state agencies. State agencies in California are required to buy from PIA if the item they need is listed in the catalogue. By the mid-1990s, California state agencies were spending approximately $135 million each year buying PIA products. In 2010, PIA generated almost $180 million in revenue. Between 2004 and 2010, PIA actually shrank a bit, losing 441 inmate jobs (California State Auditor 2011: 1).

Many prison industries programs generate millions of dollars in annual profits, in large part by paying inmates low wages or no wages at all. For example, in Washington state, inmates were paid 38 to 42 cents per hour for working as prison kitchen, laundry and janitorial laborers (Wright 1997: 3). By 1998, "nearly 60,000 inmates at the local and state levels, and about 20,000 at the federal level were employed in traditional correctional industries" (National Correctional Industries Association 2002: 2). Some states, like Georgia and Texas, pay inmate workers nothing for their labor. In 2009, many other states paid inmates around a dollar per day for prison labor. Maximum wages for inmate labor paid by state prison systems hovers around five dollars per day (Prison Policy Initiative 2015: 2). The federal government saves millions of dollars each year by forcing thousands of immigrants who have been arrested to do most of the menial labor performed at federal detention centers. These inmates, for the most part, have been convicted of no crimes. Most, after appearing in court, will be allowed to remain in the United States, because they were in the country legally. Yet immigrant detainees are forced to work, for around $1 per day, mopping floors, cleaning toilets and emptying trash (Urbina 2014: 1).

For-profit corporations and inmate labor

In the 1970s, U.S. Supreme Court Chief Justice Warren Burger lobbied for a remake of prisons in the United States into "factories with fences" (Pens 1996: 2). Wardens would become "marketers of prison labor," and prisons "little more than industrial parks with bars" (Hallinan 2001: 147). In 1979, the U.S. Congress passed an amendment to the Justice System Improvement Act creating seven Prison Industry Enhancement Certification Program (PIECP) pilot projects. PIECP pilot projects authorize state and local departments of correction to allow businesses to use inmate labor and prison facilities to manufacture goods that can be sold on an interstate basis or to provide services like telemarketing and airline reservations for a profit. The amendment also permits the sale of prisoner-made goods to the federal government in unlimited quantities.

PIECP was expanded by the Justice Assistance Act of 1984, and the Crime Control Act of 1990 extended operation of the program indefinitely (Pens 1996: 2; Abramsky 1998: 3; National Correctional Industries

Association 2002: 2). PIECP is authorized to certify 50 jurisdictions. At the beginning of 2001, PIECP had certified 39 jurisdictions – 34 state correctional agencies, 4 county agencies, and 1 jail industries board (National Correctional Industries Association 2001: 5). In 1979, a little more than 1,700 inmates were employed in PIECP programs, involving work in about 80 industries (Smith et al. 2006: 6). At the beginning of 2001, almost 4,000 inmates were employed in PIECP jobs (National Correctional Industries Association 2001: 5). By 2004, PIECP was functioning in 36 state prison systems, employing over 5,000 inmates in jobs involving about 200 industries. In 2004, inmates in PIECP prison jobs earned over $276 million. From that collective income, over $162 million was taken back, in the form of charges for room and board, taxes, family support and victim's compensation, a deduction of about 58 percent (Smith et al., 2006: 6). PIECP employers are supposed to pay inmates wages no lower than those made by private sector employees doing the same, or similar, work in the same locality. This requirement usually translates to paying inmate laborers minimum wage. Most state legislatures have passed laws requiring that employed inmates must pay for the cost of incarceration (room and board), for victim compensation and for support of their families. Consequently, corrections agencies holding PIECP certification are allowed to deduct as much as 80 percent of gross wages for taxes, room and board, family support and contributions to victims' programs (National Correctional Industries Association 2002: 4). If the full 80 percent is deducted, this means that a PIECP inmate being paid $7.00 per hour, for a 40-hour work week, will get to keep $56 from his or her gross pay. Collectively, for the fourth quarter of 2014, PIECP inmate workers grossed a little over $11 million in wages. From that figure, a little over $6.6 million was deducted (about 60 percent of gross pay), leaving net "take-home" wages of a little more than $4.6 million (National Corrections Industries Association 2015: 3).

Most PIECP-certified jobs are for laborers and other low-skilled workers (Hallinan 2001: 149). Work at a PIECP job is supposed to be voluntary, although some departments of corrections use coercive methods to induce inmate participation, like loss of "good time," canteen privileges and visitation privileges for noncompliance (Browne 1996: 65–66; Pens 1998b). PIECP-certified employers are required to provide worker's compensation for inmate laborers but not health insurance, retirement benefits, sick leave or vacations. When the demand for products or services turns downward, or when a surplus of stock on hand develops, inmates can simply be left in their cells, until the PIECP employer once again needs them. Departments of correction provide low-cost or no-cost factory, office or warehouse space and some supervisory personnel, as well as subsidized water and electricity (Pens 1996: 2). Inmate laborers are not allowed to join, or form, unions (Wright 1997).

The list of corporations employing inmate laborers is seemingly end-less. For example, in Washington, MicroJet has employed inmates to make aircraft components, some of which were sold to Boeing Corporation, paying them $7 per hour instead of the $30 per hour a Boeing employee would make for the same work. MicroJet was given a rent-free factory by the Department of Corrections. Other corporations utilizing Washington inmate laborers include blinds maker A&I Manufacturing, telemarketer Washington Marketing Group, garment maker Redwood Outdoors, prod-uct packager Exmark, nautical lift builder Nyman Marine, and crab pot maker Elliot Bay Metal Fabrication (Pens 1996: 1–3; Wright 1997: 2). Wash-ington inmates package products sold by Microsoft. Dell, Jansport and Costco reportedly use Washington inmate labor (Winter 2008: 1). Lucent Technologies, IBM and Intel, often through subcontractors, have reportedly employed South Dakota inmates.

In California, more than 70 prison factories were operational by the turn of the century (Abramsky 1998: 4). At the Richard J. Donovan Correctional Facility, near San Diego, California, inmates alleged that they were paid less than minimum wage to sew into imported cloth-ing "Made in U.S.A." labels (Blumberg 1999: 1). In 2011, the California Department of Corrections and Rehabilitation launched a new web-based Joint Venture Program for companies, worldwide, who want to "lower their cost of production" (California Department of Corrections 2011: 1). According to a press release, the promised savings will come from the absence of "employment benefit costs." By 2015, the Cali-fornia inmate PIECP work program, called "CALPIA," employed about 7,000 inmates at 24 prisons, producing over 1,400 goods and services across 57 industries (Prison Industry Authority 2015: 1). The CALPIA corporate recruitment plan has been quite successful, even attracting some business from Third World countries. For example, a corporation that owned and operated a *maquiladora* in Mexico, near the border, shuttered the factory and moved to a new manufacturing facility at San Quentin Prison in California (Pelaez 2014: 3).

In Oregon, inmates are employed to make a line of clothing called Prison Blues (Correction Connection 2016: 1–3). In South Carolina, South African furniture maker, Kwalu, Inc., relocated its factory to a prison in Ridgeland. At another prison in South Carolina, female inmates used to make Victoria's Secret lingerie for a subcontractor. But, after losing the con-tract, switched to making reservations for Omega World Travel. In Iowa, the Boomsma Chicken Farm used inmates to process and package eggs and to clean chicken houses. Heartland Communications Group employed Iowa inmates to sell magazine subscriptions via the telephone. Female inmates packaged products for Diamond Crystal Foods (Winter 2008: 1–3; Hallinan

2001: 144–153). Elsewhere in the nation, inmates have been used by Chevron and TWA, for data entry and telephone reservation work respectively (Macias Rojas 1998: 1; Parenti 1999: 2).

Proponents of turning prisons into factories with bars argue that privately employed inmates are able to pay for the costs of imprisonment, saving taxpayer dollars, and that privately employed prisoners are taught job skills that will serve them well when they are released (Washington State Institute for Public Policy 2005: 1–2). Proponents point out that privately employed inmates are able to help support their families and contribute to victim compensation programs. They argue that prison idleness is reduced. In 2011, a Nevada Senator introduced a bill that would require all inmates in low-security prisons to work at least 50 hours per week (Brown & Severson 2011: 2). His goal is to create a national labor force of prisoners, eliminating idleness in prisons and supplying corporations with an endless supply of laborers who cannot organize and who, therefore, are in a compromised position when negotiating wages and working conditions.

Critics of turning prisons into factories with bars assert that the recaptured costs of imprisonment are more than offset by the loss of business and jobs that workers and employers outside of prison experience and that many prison laborers are being turned into twenty-first century slaves (Khalek 2011:1–7). In other words, "the wages and jobs of employees on the outside are undermined by the abundance of cheap prison workers" (Abramsky 1998: 3). Welders, telemarketers and metal fabricators who are unemployed might have to go to prison in order to get a job (Pens 1996: 3). Another criticism of for-profit prison factories is that, like Third-World workers, employers treat inmates poorly, knowing that their only alternative source of employment is traditional prison industries that pay far less than the take-home pay earned in a PIECP job (Wright 1997: 3). Finally, since most PIECP jobs are menial and since many for-profit employers insist that inmates possess required job skills before they are hired, the argument that inmates learn new marketable job skills through PIECP employment is weakened considerably.

Inmates employed by for-profit corporations who are sent out-of-state to serve their sentences, frequently earn no benefits for the taxpayers of their states, for victims, or for their families. Privatized prisons contract with for-profit employers to provide inmate laborers, usually charging the corporation $5 to $7 per hour per inmate, but pay the inmate as little as 23 cents to $1.15 per hour, keeping the difference. Only six states have passed legislation closing this corporate loophole (Dyer 2000: 232–233; Black 2015).

Privatized prisons

The most recent chapter in the history of privatized prisons was actually begun in juvenile facilities when, in 1976, the state of Pennsylvania contracted with a private company, RCA Services, to assume control of its Weaversville Intensive Treatment Unit, a high-security facility housing male juvenile offenders. In 1982, the state of Florida contracted with the Eckerd Foundation to assume control of its Okeechobee School for Boys. By the turn of the century, more than 40,000 juveniles were housed in prisons operated by private organizations, some not-for-profit and many for-profit (Austin & Coventry 2001: 12). In the 1980s, state legislatures enacted laws permitting privatized organizations to operate jails and prisons. Corrections Corporation of America (CCA) was founded in 1983 by Thomas Beasley, who had political connections in Tennessee, and was financed by Jack Massey, a principal in the Kentucky Fried Chicken and Hospital Corporation of America empires. Beasley had been chairman of the Tennessee Republican Party (Friedmann 1997a: 1). A CCA board member unsuccessfully ran as the Democratic candidate for Tennessee governor in 1994 (1). In 1984, Hamilton County, Tennessee, contracted with CCA to operate its jail (Mattera et al., 2001: 1–2). That same year, the U.S. Immigration and Naturalization Service (INS) contracted with two private companies to operate detention centers for illegal aliens (Austin & Coventry 2001: 12). In 1985, CCA won a contract in Bay County, Florida, to operate a 400-bed jail. Also in 1985, CCA submitted a proposal, eventually turned down by the state legislature, to take over operation of the entire Tennessee prison system. At the time the proposal was submitted, the governor's wife, Honey Alexander, was a stockholder in CCA (Friedmann 1997a: 1). In 1986, U.S. Corrections Corporation was given a contract to operate a Kentucky prison located at the site of a closed college. In 1987, CCA won contracts to operate a Tennessee prison and two prisons in Texas (Mattera et al., 2001: 2). By 1988, the Immigration and Naturalization Service had awarded eight contracts to private corporations for the operation of detention centers housing illegal aliens (Austin & Coventry 2001: 12). In the late 1990s, CCA "identified California as its 'new frontier'" (Davis 1998: 2). Thus, in little more than a decade, the modern era of privatized prisons was reborn, with little notice and with even less legal oversight.

By the turn of the century, 28 states had passed laws authorizing private organizations to operate prisons. Ten other states had determined that existing corrections law allowed private organizations to operate prisons. The federal government had authorized private organizations to operate prisons on behalf of the federal prison system, the U.S. Marshals Service and the Immigration and Naturalization Service (INS). Similarly, privatized prisons were allowed in Puerto Rico and Washington, D.C. Growth in privatized prisons happened quickly. By 2000, there were "158 secure adult correctional facilities either in operation or under construction in the United States" (Thomas 2000: 1). Privatized prisons were located in 30 states, Washington, D.C., and Puerto Rico. No privatized prisons had been built in Alaska, Hawaii and Wisconsin. However, these states were sending inmates elsewhere in the United States to be held in privatized facilities (2). Texas led the nation, boasting 43 privatized jails, detention centers and prisons, followed by California with 22. Florida, New Mexico and Oklahoma each had eight private prisons. Colorado, Mississippi and Tennessee each hosted six privatized prisons (Thomas 2001: 3, 14). These figures include not only privatized prisons under contract with state departments of corrections but also privatized prisons under contract with federal agencies and county governments.

Texas serves as a good example of how prison privatization gets started at the state level. In 1987, the Texas state legislature gave the Texas Department of Criminal Justice (TDCJ) authority to contract with Wackenhut Corrections Corporation, and Corrections Corporation of America to design, locate, construct, manage and operate two 500-bed prisons. In 1991, the legislature gave TDCJ authority to contract with US Corrections Corporation, Concept, Inc., Wackenhut Corrections Corporation and Corrections Corporation of America to construct and operate three new 500-bed prisons and to add 500 beds to a prison already in operation. One TDCJ employee was assigned to each privatized prison and served as a monitor, representing the state's interests (Texas Department of Criminal Justice 2001b: 1–2). It is noteworthy that a "Bobby Ross Group prison in Texas, the Newton County Correctional Center, was Hawaii's third largest prison" (Johnson 2001: 4). In contrast, Illinois and New York still had laws in place that prohibited their departments of corrections from establishing contracts with privatized organizations to manage prisons (16).

As of July, 2002, CCA's 61 U.S. jails and prisons held over 54,000 inmates, making it the sixth largest prison system in the country behind only Texas, California, the Federal Bureau of Prisons, New York and Florida (Corrections Corporation of America 2002: 1): "The Federal Bureau of Prisons is its largest customer; the Bureau, the U.S. Marshals Services, and INS together account for almost 30% of the firm's sales" (Hoover's Online 2002a: 1). In terms of U.S. market share, CCA led with 52.23 percent, followed by Wackenhut Corrections Corporation with 22.34 percent, Management and Training Corporation with 8.67 percent and Cornell Companies, Incorporated, with 7.47 percent. Nine other corrections corporations shared the remaining 9.29 percent of total U.S. market share (Thomas 2001: 7–8).

By 2010, the private prison industry had consolidated considerably, mostly through acquisitions. Corrections Corporation of America and Geo

Group combined controlled over one-half of the contracts in place with departments of correction. In order to enhance their tax advantages, both prison corporations are set up as real estate trusts. Their combined revenue was estimated at almost $3 billion per year. Geo Group was created through the acquisition of a number of private prison corporations, including Cornell Companies and the large Wackenhut Corrections Corporation. In 2010, CCA operated 66 facilities holding about 75,000 inmates. Geo Group had become almost as large as CCA (Mason 2012: 2; Ashton & Petteruti 2011: 5–8). By 2015, CCA had become the nation's fifth largest correctional system. By 2015, Geo Group had grown to 106 facilities capable of accommodating about 85,000 inmates (The Geo Group, Inc., 2015: 1). Around 15 percent of Geo Group's operations are outside the United States. CCA has apparently stopped providing information to the public about the total number of its facilities and about the total number of inmates it is housing. In mid-2014, when thousands of Central American refugee families arrived at the Southern U.S. border and began crossing, the Obama Administration had to act quickly. CCA was retained to operate a 2,400-bed detention center for refugees, located in Texas. In all, the Administration asked for funds to provide well over 6,000 beds for the newly arriving refugee families. CCA seemed like an unlikely choice for the new refugee detention center contracts since, in 2009, the Obama Administration had stopped sending refugee families to a huge CCA-operated detention center, also located in Texas, amid accusations of human rights violations (Parker et al., 2014: 4).

CCA's formula for success has been to contribute generously to the campaigns of politicians who might help them and to hire former high-ranking federal government employees (Friedmann 1997a: 1–2; American Civil Liberties Union 2011; Rasor 2012; Krugman 2012). For example, in the mid-1990s, CCA principals were major donors to Tennessee lawmakers' campaigns. At one time, the Speaker of the House in Tennessee's General Assembly was married to a CCA political lobbyist (1): "In recent years CCA's CEO has distributed more campaign money to Tennessee politicians than any other individual. The company also operates a robust lobbying operation in DC and in several states where it has operations" (Parenti 1999: 3). CCA employs a number of former Federal Bureau of Prisons administrators, as well as the brother of a member of the U.S. House of Representatives (Friedmann 1997a: 2). In a 5-year period, CCA reportedly donated at least $43,000 to Colorado politicians who were in positions to influence prison policy (Tankersly 2005: 5A). Between 1999 and 2014, CCA reportedly spent $18 million on federal lobbying efforts (Takei 2014a: 2).

Wackenhut Corrections, a subsidiary of Wackenhut Corporation, was named after its founder, former FBI agent George Wackenhut. Wackenhut's three original partners had also been FBI agents. Fifty-seven percent of Wackenhut Corrections was purchased in 2002 by the Danish corporation Group4 Falck. In 2002, Wackenhut Corrections operated approximately 50 lock-ups with more than 40,000 beds. Most facilities were located in the United States. However, Wackenhut also operated prisons in Australia, New Zealand, Puerto Rico, South Africa and the UK (Hoover's Online 2002b: 1). Before getting into the prisons-for-profit business, Wackenhut Corporation had acquired "contracts to guard America's nuclear waste dumps and testing installations" (Parenti 1999: 3). Wackenhutt also reportedly did some contract spying: "By the late sixties the corporation had dossiers on three million American 'potential subversives.' By the 1970s and 1980s the company had expanded into strikebreaking and guarding U.S. embassies" (3).

The U.S. Congress mandated that increasing numbers of federal inmates be placed in privatized prisons (Sawyer 2000). Prison authorities quickly responded. For example, in 1998, the Federal Bureau of Prisons (FBOP) awarded a 10-year contract to CCA for the operation and management of a contractor-owned prison in Eloy, Arizona. The prison would hold 500 FBOP sentenced inmates and 750 to 1,000 non-sentenced INS detainees. The contract price for the 10-year period was almost $315 million (Federal Bureau of Prisons 1998). In 1999, FBOP awarded a 10-year contract to Cornell Corrections, Incorporated, for the operation and management of a contractor-owned prison in Philipsburg, Pennsylvania. The prison would hold 350 minimum-security male offenders, 350 various security male offenders and 350 various security female offenders. The contract price for the 10-year period was almost $343 million (Federal Bureau of Prisons 1999). In 2000, FBOP awarded a 10-year contract to CCA for the operation and management of contractor-owned prisons in California City, California, and Milan, New Mexico. These prisons would hold non–U.S. citizen criminal alien inmates. The contract price for the 10-year period was over $529 million for the California City facility and almost $231 million for the Milan, New Mexico, facility (Federal Bureau of Prisons 2000a). Finally, also in 2000, FBOP awarded a 10-year contract to Wackenhut Corrections Corporation for the operation and management of a contractor-owned prison in Winton, North Carolina. The 1,200-bed facility would hold sentenced felons from the District of Columbia. The contract price for the 10-year period was almost $327 million (Federal Bureau of Prisons 2000b).

In 2006, Geo Group, then conducting business as Wackenhut Corrections Corporation, began operating refugee detention centers for the U.S. federal government. Denial of medical services, the overuse of isolation cells (called SHUs) and deaths while in custody have been recurring issues in lawsuits filed against Geo Group's handling of detained immigrant families in recent years (Parker et al., 2014: 4). In 2015, nine former or current immigrant detainees filed suit in U.S. District Court, alleging that Geo Group employees forced them to do menial labor, like janitorial and food service work, for $1 per day. They contend that they were threatened with placement in solitary confinement if they did not work. In their reply to the lawsuit, Geo Group lawyers pointed out that the $1 per day pay rate for inmates was set by the federal government in 1950 (Moreno 2015: 6A).

Inmate escapes, inmate-on-inmate violence and guard violence

Inmate escapes, inmate-on-inmate violence and violence perpetrated by guards have plagued CCA. For example, in 1998, six inmates, including five murderers, sentenced in Washington, D.C., escaped from a CCA prison located in Youngstown, Ohio. In the aftermath of that event, it was discovered that in its first year of operation the Youngstown CCA prison had been the site of 2 murders and 20 inmate-on-inmate assaults involving stabbing. A U.S. Department of Justice report on the Youngstown escapes, murders and assaults identified problems with operational deficiencies, security procedures and classification of prisoners (Greene 2000: 1). The U.S. Department of Justice found "substantial staff turnover problems" at a CCA prison in Chattanooga, Tennessee. Understaffing is a major contributor to prison violence. A constant flow of new employees into a prison keeps administrative personnel in a perpetual training mode (Bates 1997: 7). A few months after the U.S. Department of Justice finding, a woman died "from an undiagnosed complication during pregnancy" after waiting in extreme pain "at least twelve hours before CCA officials allowed her to be taken to a hospital" (4). Representatives of the British Prison Officers Association "saw evidence of inmates being cruelly treated" at the Chattanooga facility. At a CCA prison in Texas, "they found inmates confined to warehouse-like dormitories for twenty-three hours a day" living in "possibly the worst conditions we have ever witnessed in terms of inmate care and supervision" (4). In Texas, two CCA prisons were run by wardens who, as employees of the state, had been punished for beating inmates (5). At a 750-inmate CCA prison in Lawrenceville, Virginia, the corporation used a high-tech control room and other observation technologies to reduce the number of guards it employed to five during the day and two at night (5).

A CCA-run prison in Idaho, known among inmates as a "gladiator school," has earned the reputation as the state's most violent prison. For example, for a 1-year period in 2007–2008, a comparable state-run Idaho prison recorded 42 inmate-on-inmate assaults while the CCA-run prison recorded 132. In 2010, both prisons had grown somewhat larger. But in spite of lawsuits, media scrutiny and some probing by governmental agencies, the pattern of violence had not changed. In 2010, the state-run prison recorded 38 inmate-on-inmate assaults. The comparable CCA-run prison recorded 118 inmate-on-inmate assaults. (Boone 2011: 1). Two years after an

Ohio prison had been sold to CCA, the inmate-on-inmate violence rate had increased 187 percent. The inmate-on-staff violence rate had increased by 300 percent. Two previous audits at the prison had identified widespread problems at the prison, including high turnover rates among guards. Apparently, CCA management and guards had allowed gangs to take effective control of the prison. Illicit drug use had grown rampant. Inmates reported frequent extortion and theft. (American Civil Liberties Union of Tennessee 2015: 1; Kirkham 2013: 1).

Wackenhut Corrections has also had its share of problems. In 1994, at a Texas juvenile facility for girls, Wackenhut faced a class action suit alleging that girls had been "degraded, humiliated, assaulted, harassed, and emotionally abused." It was also alleged that the prison "was deficient in medical care, counseling, and vocational training." Wackenhut settled the suit out of court, and two employees pleaded guilty to charges of sexual assault (Greene 2000: 2). Texas legal officials removed the girls but allowed Wackenhut to continue operating the institution as a prison for boys. At another prison in Texas, one suffering from chronic staff shortages, Wackenhut employees faced allegations of "sexual misconduct and abuse of prisoners, assaults, drug smuggling, and alleged cover ups." In this case, Wackenhut lost their contract to operate the facility and "a dozen former Wackenhut employees have been indicted on criminal sex charges" (2). In two New Mexico prisons run by Wackenhut, five prisoners died in the first year of operation. Some of the deaths were allegedly caused by excessive guard violence. At one of the prisons, a riot broke out, injuring 13 guards and 1 inmate. One Wackenhut employee was arrested and charged with beating shackled inmates. During a riot at the other New Mexico Wackenhut facility, a guard was fatally stabbed. New Mexico Department of Corrections staff, responding to news reports, inquired about the riot but were told by Wackenhut employees that conditions at the prison were uneventful. When state police officers were sent to the prison, they were held at the front gate for 30 minutes. Upon being allowed entrance, they discovered a riot in progress. This prison, too, was understaffed (3). In Louisiana, juveniles were removed from a Wackenhut prison where, according to Judge Mark Doherty, they were treated like animals (3).

A group of religious leaders who visited a Wackenhut prison in New York, a facility for non-criminals seeking political asylum in the United States, was shocked by what they saw. The prison, located in a warehouse district near JFK International Airport, was a 200-bed building without windows that held detainees, 22–23 hours each day, in dormitories and segregation cells. Detainees were forced to wear orange jump suits and to use toilets without doors. They were let out 60–90 minutes per day into small exercise areas. One religious leader said, "I was shocked by what I saw.... Imprisoned criminals have more freedom, access and opportunity." An archdeacon said,

"[W]hat I saw today was un-American.... In the name of God, let's open our arms and treat these people as human beings" (National Council of Churches 2001: 1–2).

Wackenhut's successor, Geo Group, has fared no better. Since its inception, Geo Group has attracted lawsuits, addressing issues like avoidable inmate deaths, failure to provide appropriate medical care and use of excessive force. For example, in 2013, inmates at a Mississippi prison sued the state for chronic conditions they described as "barbaric and horrific." This lawsuit involves, among other issues, cells that had non-working lights and toilets, rat overpopulation and lack of mental health services. This prison had been operated by the Geo Group and its predecessors from 1999 until 2012, when Management & Training Corporation took control. In 2009, a court awarded $40 million to the family of an inmate who had been beaten to death in a Geo Group (formerly Wackenhut) prison. There were allegations of a cover-up and of destruction of evidence. Geo Group resolved this lawsuit by paying the family of the inmate victim an undisclosed amount (Fischer 2013: 1–4).

In the mid-1990s, CCA and Wackenhut were the darlings of Wall Street: "Between 1996 and 1997, CCA's revenues increased by 58 percent, from $293 million to $462 million. Its net profit grew from $30.9 million to $53.9 million. WCC (Wackenhut) raised its revenues from $138 million in 1996 to $210 million in 1997" (Davis 1998: 3). One Wall Street firm labeled CCA "a theme stock for the nineties" (Parenti 1999: 3). However, media revelations about violence in and mismanagement of corporate prisons, resulted in an industry-wide downturn, but only for a while. For example, on January 1, 1998, CCA stock sold for $446.25 per share. On December 14, 2000, it hit a low of $1.88 per share. On October 10, 1997, Wackenhut Corrections Corporation stock sold for $36 per share. On December 21, 2000, it hit a low of $5.88 per share. Then, the comeback began. On August 2, 2002, CCA stock sold for $12.45 per share (Hoover's Online 2002a: 4). On August 2, 2002, Wackenhut Corrections Corporation stock sold for $12.73 per share (Hoover's Online 2002b: 4). Other corrections corporations also experienced the brief turndown in popularity. For example, Cornell Companies, Incorporated, the fourth largest corrections corporation in the U.S., in terms of market share, "runs 69 adult and juvenile 'slammers' with about 15,500 beds in 13 states and Washington, DC" (Hoover's Online 2002c: 1). On April 2, 1998, Cornell Companies, Inc., stock sold for $25.44 per share. On December 21, 2000, it hit a low of $3.31 per share. The upturn, however, had begun on August 2, 2002, when Cornell Companies, Inc., stock sold for $9.40 per share (4). Clearly, the first few years of the new century were hard on corrections corporation stockholders. However, in spite of numerous investigations, negative reports and lawsuits, the two major players in the "prisons-for-profit" game are alive and well.

In July 2015, CCA stock was trading at approximately $34 per share, and Geo Group stock was trading at around $37 per share.

Small prison corporations are also likely to experience operational problems. For example, a vivid incident of violence in a privatized prison occurred in 1997, at the Brazoria County, Texas Detention Center, then operated by Capital Correctional Resources. This incident was captured on video tape and was seen by viewers across the United States. The tape showed guards kicking inmates from Missouri while the inmates were lying face down on the floor. Guards used stun guns on the prone, incapacitated inmates and turned a vicious police dog loose on them. Missouri subsequently canceled their contract with Capital Correctional Resources and placed the inmates elsewhere (Schlosser 1998: 19).

In 1998, at the privately operated Huerfano County, Colorado Correctional Facility, a supervisor ordered the beating of an inmate who allegedly assaulted a guard. The inmate was taken to a room by five guards who "repeatedly beat and kicked him before slamming him face-first into a cement floor. The guards then allegedly made (the inmate) use his own shirt to clean the blood from the floor." Three of the guards involved pleaded guilty to the beating and served minimal sentences in federal prisons (Plasket 2001: B3). In 2015, a privately owned and operated Arizona prison erupted in violence for three days, leaving seven inmates and nine guards injured. Damage to the prison was extensive enough to require relocation of over a thousand inmates to other lock-ups. The prison, owned by the Management & Training Corporation, had a long history of problems with high guard turnover, rape, murder and escape (Townes 2015b: 1–2).

CCA has come up with a new tactic to use in its competition with Geo Group and other surviving prison corporations. CCA, after assembling a $250 million start-up fund, offered to purchase state-owned prisons. The basic deal is if your prison qualifies, CCA will purchase the prison. In return, the state department of corrections will enter into a 20-year or more agreement to supply enough inmates to keep the facility at a minimum of 90 percent occupancy. CCA, by contract, has the right to reject the least healthy and most dangerous inmates in a prison system. CCA is interested in buying only prisons in good physical condition (Rasor 2012: 1–2). The first such purchase occurred in 2012 with the CCA acquisition of a prison formerly owned and operated by the Ohio Department of Corrections (Pavlo 2012: 1–2).

Both CCA and the Geo Group have branched out considerably into a new profit-making sector of the prison industry called "extra-carceral services." For example, in 2013, CCA purchased, for about $36 million, California-based Correctional Alternatives Inc., a privately held community corrections company. This purchase allowed CCA to establish a foothold in the lucrative halfway house market (Takei 2014a: 1). In 2011, Geo

Group purchased BI Incorporated, the largest electronic monitoring firm located in the United States, for approximately $415 million (Stillman 2014: 3). BI Incorporated designs, manufactures and assembles electronic monitoring systems, colloquially called "ankle bracelets" on the street. BI Incorporated offers around-the-clock monitoring services and technical support.

In sum, with fewer than 20 percent of American inmates currently locked up in privatized prisons, there exists great potential for corporate growth in this industry. With the movement of immense wealth in the form of private equity firms into the American prison industry, there is, likewise, great potential for increased corporate takeover of work that public employees perform. On October 28, 2016, Corrections Corporation of America re-branded itself as CoreCivic, Inc. CoreCivic is divided into three branches: CoreCivic Safety to manage their prison and detention center empire, Core-Civic Community to manage and expand the corporation's urban residential re-entry facilities and CoreCivic Properties to manage and expand its real estate portfolio (Davis 2016: 2). With their movement into the prison industry, corporations, again, have mastered the art of profiting from the plight of the poor.

Arguments for, and against, privatized prisons

The number of arguments for, and against, privatized prisons is almost endless (Logan 1990). Here, we examine only the most important and compelling issues:

In favor:

- Privatized prisons can "be financed, sited, and constructed more quickly and cheaply than government prisons" (Logan 2000: 1).
- A for-profit corporation can reduce the levels of bureaucracy (red tape) involved in management decisions (2).
- Recidivism rates for inmates released from private prisons might be lower than recidivism rates for inmates released from government-run prisons (Corrections Corporation of America 2002: 2).
- Numerous independent cost comparison studies have illustrated that private prisons save an average of 5–15 percent on costs (Corrections Corporation of America 2015).

Against:

- It is morally wrong for corporations, their executives and their stockholders to extract massive profits from the imprisonment of human beings (The Economist 2010: 1–2).

- Recent, unbiased studies by the General Accounting Office, by the Institute on Taxation and Economic Policy, by the Arizona Department of Corrections and by a number of other organizations indicate that privatized prisons are not less costly to operate than government-run prisons. When the costs to public agencies of responding to escapes and riots, of monitoring corporate prisons, and of tax breaks and other incentives are factored in, privatized prisons very likely cost more to operate than state-run prisons (Krugman 2012: 1–2; Austin & Coventry 2001; Bates 1997; Mattera et al., 2001; Shichor 1995). In fact, recent research is indicating that corporate prisons may charge the state as much as $1,600 per year more per inmate for some types of inmates, than it would cost to house them in a state-run prison (Oppel, Jr., 2011: 1).
- Because they are paid for every day that an inmate is locked up, corrections corporations devise ways to keep inmates longer than would be the case in government-run prisons, resulting in higher costs to taxpayers (Bates 1997: 10).
- In order to maximize profits, administrators of privatized prisons cut corners in the areas of prison design and construction, staffing, health services and food provision (5–6).
- Privatized prisons can be more violent than government-run prisons due to bare-bones staffing policies, poor employee training programs and high rates of employee turnover (7).
- Government employees assigned to serve as monitors of privatized prisons can be easily co-opted by corporate administrators, potentially resulting in lax oversight of day-to-day operations within privatized prisons (Bates 1997: 4; Shichor 1995: 127; Friedmann 1999b).

Summary

Are hard times or good times ahead in the for-profit prison industry? It is difficult to say with certainty what is ahead for corporate prisons. On the negative side, a number of state legislatures are looking for ways to cut back on spending. Typically, the two easiest parts of a state budget to cut are funds for schooling and funds for prisons. State-level funds for education have been cut, and cut again. But prison budgets, the sacred cow of the "super-crime-fighter politician," have not gone untouched. For example, some American politicians sponsored successful legislation that eliminated, or minimized, imprisonment for first-time offenders and for minor drug violators.

Such legislation could result in a slowdown in the numbers of persons being sent into state prison systems. For example, in Mississippi, in 2001, the state found itself with 2,000 empty prison beds. This situation set in motion a competition, between the operators of privatized prisons, the managers of state-run prisons, and county sheriffs who rent jail bed space to the state for prison inmates, for legislative support in keeping their facilities full. CCA and Wackenhut, using corporate administrators, lobbyists and free meals, went into action securing the cooperation of key legislators. The result was a transfer of inmates from state-run prisons into privatized prisons (Gruley 2001: 1–5). A pecking order, and a precedent, were set, at least in Mississippi. Privatized prisons would receive state support, even in hard times when state-run prison beds sit empty.

Another potential negative force impinging on the profits to be made from prisons is dropping numbers of arrests by police officers in the United States. For example, in 2004, American police officers arrested just over 8.4 million persons. However, in 2013, the total number of arrests had dropped to just over 7.1 million persons (Federal Bureau of Investigation 2015:1). If American police willingness to arrest, or American police capacity to arrest, should continue this downward decline, there could be hard times ahead for at least some privatized prisons, in some states.

On the positive side, prison corporations will continue to benefit from the war on terrorism, and from the push of refugee families who are pushed up against the Southern U.S. border. These human events forced the U.S. government to put out offers of new contracts to build and operate facilities where thousands of refugee families, illegal aliens and alien criminal suspects will be incarcerated. The Geo Group, because it has experience setting up and operating immigrant camps on converted military bases in Australia, and CCA, because of its connections, are especially well-placed to benefit from this new boom (Tharp 2001: 1–4; American Civil Liberties Union 2011; Parker et al., 2014).

It is clear that the role of privatized prisons in the incarceration industry is in flux. As of late 2016, privatized prisons held 22,100 federal felons. As of late 2016, privatized prisons under contract with U.S. Immigration and Customs Enforcement kept 34,000 illegal aliens, scheduled to be deported, under lock and key (Associated Press 2016: 1).

Another positive is the movement of Big Money into the prison business, in the form of private equity firms. Big Money at play creates an imbalance when it comes to the interplay between corporate officials and prison administrators representing state and other governments in the United States. Executives of prison corporations, for the most part, are more wise and experienced in the ways of large-scale commerce for profit than are their counterparts in government. Corporate prison executives, representing Big Money, have at their disposal not just significant wealth but also access to legal and public relations resources that tilt the game of winning prison contracts in favor of the entity seeking profit. Corporate prison executives are armed with the funds to make things happen. Corporate prison executives are equipped with the right things to say in order to justify making money off of human misery.

There is, in prisons for profit, a simple economic process at play. This process guarantees higher costs. Corporate prison executives, when negotiating contracts, are obligated to make the most profit possible for their employer. Corporate prison executives will take advantage of any need, of any oversight, of any opportunity that presents, in order to maximize income and profits. Representatives of states and other governments in the United States will not be able to withstand the enticements offered by prison corporations. Crime-fighting politicians will facilitate, and will bring to fruition, negotiations in order to maintain a steady supply of new prisons – so that crime can be fought. We learned from German sociologist Max Weber that bureaucracies are, indeed, formidable structures, capable of performing monumental tasks. We might be learning from a modern form of bureaucracy the private prison corporation, that almost any human enterprise can be turned into a business if there is enough money to be made.

At the turn of the century, about 5 percent of all prison beds in the United States, including about 10 percent of all federal prison beds, were controlled by corporations. By 2015, private prisons were housing around 7 percent of state inmates and approximately 20 percent of federal prisoners. Imprisonment had become a $5 billion industry (Cannon 2015: 2). In 2013, there were approximately 133,000 inmates held in for-profit prisons throughout the United States (Carson 2014: 14). By 2024, it has been estimated that private prisons in the United States will hold over 350,000 inmates (Pelaez 2014: 1). However, in late 2016, the U.S. Inspector General's Office released an audit critical of safety and security levels in privatized prisons. Soon thereafter, the U.S. Attorney General's Office issued a memo ordering Federal Bureau of Prisons administrators to allow existing contracts with prison corporations to expire without renewal and to enter into no new contracts with prison corporations for the incarceration of citizen convicts. This policy had actually already begun to be implemented by the Federal Bureau of Prisons. By late 2016, the number of federal prisoners held in privatized prisons had shrunk to 12 percent of the total federal inmate population. This chain of events had no consequences for the rapidly expanding use of privatized prisons by the U.S. Immigration and Customs Enforcement, for the incarceration of immigrant families and other types of illegal aliens (Associated Press 2016: 1). In the face of this news, stock in Corrections Corporation of America and Geo Group fell by over 40 percent. It would appear that bad times are ahead for corporate prisons, since about one-half of their income derives from federal contracts. However, lawyers and lobbyists representing these large corporations will wage a powerful campaign in Congress to seek legislation that will eliminate, or dilute, the Attorney General's ability to exclude corporate prisons. Until these processes play out, we won't know whether corporate prisons will fade away, or will continue their intrusion into the incarceration industry.

Profiting from punishment

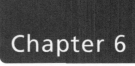

Chapter 6

The final solution – capital punishment

Contents

Introduction

Capital punishment, defined herein as killing authorized and undertaken by government authority in order to punish one or more persons for the commission of a criminal offense, is one of the oldest of all criminal sanctions, having been practiced for thousands of years. As late as the eighteenth century in England, torture followed by death was the punishment for hundreds of crimes, including theft. In the late eighteenth century, European nations began to reduce the number of capital crimes. Although capital punishment laws remain on the books in a handful of European nations, the last legal European executions took place in France in 1977 and in Turkey in 1984. The United Kingdom abolished capital punishment in 1969. Both the Council of Europe and the European Union make abolition of the death penalty a pre-condition of membership (Kleinsorge & Zatlokin 1999).

In 2002, records show that 3,248 persons were sentenced to death around the world. 1,526 inmates were executed in 31 countries. It is likely that many more were executed, but their deaths went unrecorded. Eighty-one percent of all known executions in 2002 were conducted in three countries — at least 1,060 in China, at least 113 in Iran and 71 in the United States. In 2010, about 2,024 new death sentences were imposed, and at least 527 executions (excluding China) occurred in 24 countries. Most executions were carried out in four countries: China (estimated in the 1000s), Iran (at least 252), Yemen (at least 53) and the United States (46) (Amnesty International 2011a). In 2014, just under 2,500 death sentences were handed out, and slightly over 600 executions were carried out, in 22 countries. These estimates exclude China, where records of death sentences and executions are kept secret and where, each year, experts estimate that thousands of death sentences are handed out and, at the very least, hundreds of executions occur. After China, in 2014, countries carrying out the largest numbers of executions were Iran, Egypt, Nigeria, Saudi Arabia, Iraq and the United States (Amnesty International 2015: 1–2). To date, 141 countries have abolished the death penalty, either by law or by practice. Abolitionist movements are afoot in many other countries. In late 2010, for the third time, the United Nations General Assembly adopted a resolution calling for a moratorium on the use of the death penalty. Each time this resolution has passed, more member nations have supported it. About 70 countries continue to authorize capital punishment. At the end of 2010, slightly less than 1,800 persons awaited execution around the world (Amnesty International 2011b).

Legally sanctioned executions were conducted in North America from the colonial period until 1966. In 1972, the U.S. Supreme Court temporarily declared capital punishment unconstitutional. In 1976, capital punishment was reinstated. In the colonial period, hundreds of crimes warranted execution. By the 1950s, only rape, murder and treason were capital crimes. Today, at the state level, only convictions for treason and murder can result in execution. At the federal level, however, capital crimes are more numerous. Murder of several types is a capital crime (examples: genocide, related to smuggling aliens, during a drug-related drive-by shooting, of a member of Congress, etc.). Many crimes that result in death are also capital offenses (examples: death resulting from aircraft hijacking, willful wrecking of a train resulting in death, civil rights conspiracy resulting in death, etc.). Espionage and treason are also federal capital offenses. In all, there are 41 federal capital crimes (ProCon.org 2012).

Early methods of execution

Capital punishment can be accomplished in a number of ways. What follows are descriptions of some of the most popular methods. *Death by stoning* was a popular ancient means of execution. It is still used today in a few Islamic nations. For example, in March 2002, a Nigerian peasant woman named Amina Lawal was sentenced to death by stoning for adultery as soon as her baby was weaned. She was to be buried up to her neck and stoned to death. Fortunately, in 2003, her sentence was overturned by a higher court. Later in 2003, another Nigerian court convicted a man of sodomy and sentenced him to death by stoning (Sengupta 2003). From the Middle Ages on through the colonial American period, *the wheel* was used to torture and kill criminals. Persons were tied to a wagon wheel and rolled over blunt or sharp objects or possibly down a steep slope, until death occurred. Others were tied to a wagon wheel, hit with a hammer breaking multiple bones and left to die a slow death. Yet others could be cooked, barbeque style, by turning the wheel over an open fire. *Burning at the stake* was a popular means of execution, used in the sixteenth and seventeenth centuries to eliminate "suspicious" women in Austria, England, Germany, Scotland, Spain, Switzerland and North America. This method of execution fell into disfavor throughout Europe in the early nineteenth century. *The axe or sword* were popular tools of execution in England and Germany in the sixteenth and seventeenth centuries. Executioners, wearing a hood, would decapitate criminals, often leaving their heads on display in a public place. The last legal beheading took place in England in 1747. However, legally sanctioned beheadings are still undertaken in some parts of the world (Amnesty International 2015: 2). For example, on May 18, 2001, seven men were beheaded in Saudi Arabia after having been convicted of alcohol use and of raping a man. That same day, two other Saudis were beheaded in Tabuk for drug dealing and murdering a police officer (Daily Times-Call, May 19, 2001). In late eighteenth-century France, a beheading machine named after Joseph Guillotin was invented. After testing on barn-yard animals and a few corpses, **the guillotine** was first officially used in an execution in 1792. It was last used to execute a French criminal in 1977.

American methods of execution

Between 1608 and 1987, approximately 14,634 executions were carried out in the colonies and, later, in the United States. Forty-nine percent of those executed were African American (Death Penalty Information Center 2004a). This number does not include the hundreds of thousands of Native Americans, African Americans and Mexican Americans who were put to death by legal authorities for resisting oppression and other forms of domination (Ginzburg 1962; Turner et al., 1984). Most such deaths went unrecorded.

In the late eighteenth and nineteenth centuries, death by firing squad and hanging became popular methods of execution in the United States. *Hanging* requires that a long rope be tossed over a large tree branch or some other strong object suspended several feet above ground. One end of the rope is tied off onto something solid, like a tree trunk. The other end of the rope is fashioned into a noose. The noose is placed around the neck of a person, who is on horseback or on a platform (preferably equipped with a hinged trap door) several feet above the ground. The person is then released from the horse's back, or from the platform, is dropped downward and is left to dangle, causing constriction of breathing, blockage of blood flow and possibly a broken neck. The bodies of hanged persons frequently lurch severely for several minutes. A somewhat less dramatic hanging can sometimes be achieved if the rope is soaked in a brine solution for a consid-erable period of time and then stretched while drying, in order to eliminate its tendency to stretch while under the stress of a suspended human body. Decapitation can usually be avoided by the use of an experienced hang person who can calculate an effective body weight/body structure/length of drop ratio (The Clark County Prosecuting Attorney 2002). It is notable that in 1933, Arizona installed a gas chamber after its gallows beheaded a condemned woman during a hanging (Solotaroff 2001). Because of the tendency of hanged persons to lurch, after having hung limp for several minutes, executed persons are best left at the end of the rope for at least one hour. Several Nazis convicted at the Nuremburg War Tribunal were exe-cuted by an experienced Army hangman. Somehow, the veteran U.S. Army executioner botched each hanging, leaving the condemned Nazis to suffer a bit longer than might have been necessary.

Death by shooting can be accomplished, Chinese-style, by a single exe-cutioner who places a pistol at the back of the head of a condemned person and pulls the trigger or by a *firing squad*. Firing squads range from three to six executioners, usually armed with rifles. The condemned person is tied to a chair or a stake in front of a solid backdrop, like a brick wall or a pile of sand bags. The firing squad faces the condemned person, standing several feet away and, when given the signal, shoot, aiming for the chest or head. Death is caused by destruction of the brain, ruptured heart and damage to major vessels, as well as by loss of blood and shock.

In 1977, Gary Gilmore and, in 1996, John Albert Taylor were executed by Utah firing squads, composed of five volunteer police officers. The 1996 execution attracted over 150 television news crews. As late as 2002, three states, Utah, Idaho and Oklahoma, authorized death by shooting as a back-up method of execution (The Clark County Prosecuting Attorney 2002). After the turn of the century, Utah was the only state that allowed condemned persons to choose between lethal injection or the firing squad. In 2003, two convicted Utah murderers requested that they be executed by firing squad. Over 40 men have been executed by Utah firing squads (Janofsky 2003). In early 2004, two Utah state legislators submitted a successful bill that eliminated firing squads and established lethal injection as the state's only method of execution (Denver Post 2004). However, in 2010, Utah condemned murderer, Ronnie Lee Gardner, exercised his right to select a firing squad instead of lethal injection. He was allowed to do so because he was sentenced to death before 2004. Gardner was executed on June 18, 2010, by a 5-person anonymous firing squad using .30-caliber Winchester rifles, standing 25 feet away from the man who was strapped to a chair. A small target had been placed over his heart. One rifle was loaded with blank ammunition, so that there would be some doubt about who actually delivered the lethal shot (Sanchez 2010). It appears that execution by firing squad is experiencing a renaissance in some parts of the United States. For example, in mid-2015, the Utah state legislature passed new legislation permitting some executions by firing squads (McCombs & Whitehurst 2015: 15A). Also in 2015, the Wyoming House of Representatives passed legislation authorizing the use of firing squads in some executions (Denver Post 2015b: 18A).

Execution by *electrocution* became popular in the United States in the late nineteenth and early twentieth centuries. In 1888, New York adopted electrocution as its main method of execution. Thomas Edison invented the first electric chair, at the request of New York corrections officials. Edison-sponsored tests of the electric chair involved common household pets, barnyard animals and an orangutan, all executed in laboratory settings in front of observers. Many observers reportedly became ill after watching. Perhaps Edison's crowning achievement was the electrification of Topsy, an adult elephant who allegedly killed three zoo workers, including one who tried to feed her a lighted cigarette. This electrocution occurred in 1903. Video of the pachyderm's execution by electrification can still be found on the Internet (ProCon.org 2012).

In 1890, William Kemmler was the first man executed in New York using Edison's machine. Kemmler killed his wife with an axe. Kemmler was strapped to a chair and was exposed to 1,000 volts of electricity for 5 seconds. But, he did not die. After four additional minutes of exposure to increasing amounts of electricity, the condemned man finally expired. During the ordeal, his body smoked, his head and arms caught on fire and blood ran from his body openings. A putrid stench, resulting from boiled body fats, filled the air. Many observers were sickened by the spectacle. Following Kemmler's execution, 25 states adopted electrocution as the preferred method of execution.

Pro-electrocution practitioners continued to work on the technology. In Florida, for example, executioners developed "Old Sparky," an electric chair that meted out 2,300 volts for 8 seconds, followed by 1,000 volts for 22 seconds, followed by 2,300 volts for 8 seconds (Committee on Criminal Justice – The Florida Senate 2002). Between 1930 and 1980, electrocution became the most common form of execution in the United States. Electrocution is hard on the condemned, as well as on observers. Persons executed via the electric chair tend to lurch violently against their restraints. Head banging is common. Skin color darkens considerably. Swelling occurs. The dying person can be set on fire, causing smoke to rise and stench to result from boiling body fluids. A South Carolina Attorney General who sent 11 men to death row once suggested that his state use "electric sofas" so that more condemned persons could be executed more quickly (Nelson & Foster 2001). As late as 2002, Alabama and Nebraska used electrocution as the only means of execution. Seven other states employed electrocution as a back-up method: "As of June 1, 2002, 147 of 780 executions (19%) performed (in the United States) since 1976 have been by electrocution" (The Clark County Prosecuting Attorney 2002: 7). On July 20, 2006, condemned murderer Brandon Hedrick was executed by Virginia corrections employees using an electric chair. Hedrick exercised his legal right, given in 1995 to condemned persons in Virginia, to select electrocution instead of lethal injection. A brine-soaked sea sponge, held in place by metal, was attached to his calf. Another brine-soaked sea sponge, held in place by metal, was attached to the top of his head. Power cables were attached to the metal. Lethal electrocution was then carried out (Clark County Prosecutor 2006). After that execution, states employing electricity dwindled to one. Finally, in 2008, the Nebraska Supreme Court ruled that execution by the electric chair was cruel and unusual punishment, thus ending its use in the last state to employ execution by electrification (Liptak 2008).

Lethal gas or *the gas chamber* is another modern method of execution. An airtight execution chamber is built, featuring windows for observation, a chair with restraints and a pan under the chair where cyanide pellets are placed. When sulfuric or hydrochloric acid is poured over the cyanide

pellets, deadly hydrocyanic gas fills the chamber. All of this is done by executioners stationed outside the chamber, using pipes, valves and remote
controls. Death of the condemned usually occurs 6 to 18 minutes after
exposure to the deadly gas. While dying of gas exposure, condemned persons are known to lurch violently against their restraints. Persons executed
in a gas chamber, like those who are hanged, sometimes "come back to
life," in the form of lurching after having gone limp for several minutes.
After death has been confirmed, executioners must pump the deadly gas
out of the chamber. Wearing gas masks and rubber gloves, they must scrub
the body with a bleach solution, pump all gas out of the body, strip it of
clothing, hose it down and redress it, before turning it over to a funeral
home or the family of the deceased. During the execution process, or practice executions, should the deadly gas escape from the chamber, or should
executioners be exposed to the gas while in the chamber, death of persons
not condemned can occur (Cabana 1996). In fact, while practicing, executioners at the gas chamber in Parchman, Mississippi, used to play jokes
on each other, feigning a mishap with the process and falling limp while in
the chamber, causing others on the execution team to run for their lives.
Gas chamber executions can also be botched. For example, in 1955, Mississippi's first execution in the gas chamber at Parchman State Penitentiary
did not go as planned. The condemned, Gerald Gallego, was restrained in
the gas chamber. An executioner dropped the lever allowing the cyanide pellets and sulfuric acid to combine. But nothing happened. While Gallego sat
restrained and cloaked in the chair, an executioner went into the chamber
to execute repairs. The lever was dropped again, but only a small amount
of deadly gas was generated, sickening, but not killing, Gallegos. Gas was
pumped from the chamber. Corrective measures were taken. A decision
was made to restart the execution. Eventually, Gallegos was successfully
gassed to death (Solotaroff 2001).

Nevada was the first state to adopt the gas chamber as a method of execution. In the United States, the first execution in a gas chamber occurred
in 1924. Between 1924 and 2000, 31 condemned persons were executed in
U.S. gas chambers. As late as 2002, Arizona, California, Missouri and Wyoming allowed the gas chamber to be used as a back-up method of execution.
In 1999, Arizona conducted the last execution by lethal gas: "As of June 1,
2002, eleven of seven hundred and eighty executions (1.4%) performed
since 1976 had been by the administration of lethal gas" (The Clark County
Prosecuting Attorney 2002: 8).

Lethal injection is today the execution method of choice in 31 states
that have authorized capital punishment. Lethal injection is also favored
by the federal government of the United States and its military branches.
In 1888, lethal injection had been proposed in New York. But instead,
electrocution was adopted. More recently, a University of Oklahoma

anesthesiologist, Dr Stanley Deutsch, was among the first to recommend injection as a method of execution, likening it to the medical use of a general anesthesia. In 1977, Oklahoma became the first state to adopt lethal injection as a method of execution. Texas, in 1982, executed the first inmate using lethal injection, a man named Charlie Brooks. By 2000, 97 percent of executions in the United States were carried out by lethal injection (Groner 2002). By 2010, all executions in the United States utilized lethal injection, although electrocution (9 states), lethal gas (3 states), hanging (3 states) and firing squad (2 states) were still kept as back-up solutions to be used, should lethal injection be prohibited by a federal court ruling (U.S. Department of Justice 2011a: 6).

The execution protocol for lethal injection is supposed to visually resemble what takes place in a hospital room during the early stages of surgery. For example, in California, the condemned is taken into an execution chamber equipped with windows for observation. S/he is strapped onto a gurney and fitted with a cardiac monitor. An IV is started in a functional vein in each arm, and a flow of saline solution is started. The IV in one arm will be used to perform the execution. The IV in the other arm is held in reserve, in case a malfunction occurs. After the warden signals to begin, 5 grams of sodium thiopental are injected, inducing sleep. The line is then flushed with saline solution. Fifty cc of pancuronium bromide (a muscle relaxer that causes paralysis) is administered. The line is then flushed with saline solution. Fifty cc of potassium chloride follows, inducing cardiac arrest. In the amounts injected, each chemical is lethal (The Clark County Prosecuting Attorney 2002). This form of execution is highly painful. But the condemned cannot show it, because s/he has been put to sleep and paralyzed. Thus, the image seen by observers is that of one simply going to sleep, a visual improvement over shooting, hanging, lethal gas and electrocution. Some argue that lethal injection is more humane (Associated Press 2006). However, many critics disagree: "Lethal injection is not humane nor 'painless' as death penalty advocates claim. Potassium is a metallic inert chemical.... In large doses, injected intravenously, it would burn and hurt horribly.... It makes all muscles lock up in extreme contraction that would hurt unbearably" (Death By Lethal Injection 2001: 1–2). Pancuronium bromide, marketed under the name Pavulon, paralyzes the skeletal muscles but does not deaden the brain or nerves. In Tennessee, a judge declared that Pavulon "has no legitimate purpose" in executions: "The subject gives all the appearances of a serene expiration when actually the subject is feeling and perceiving the excruciatingly painful ordeal of death by lethal injection" (Liptak 2003: 1).

Execution by lethal injection, however, has become more complicated, as shortages of some drugs commonly used occurred. In 2005, the European Union passed legislation intended to ban trade in "instruments of torture," including capital punishment equipment (European Union 2005). This legislation led to reduced manufacturing of some execution drugs. The sole American manufacturer of sodium thiopental reduced its production of the drug, creating shortages in the United States. As a result, in late 2010, it was necessary to acquire a supply of sodium thiopental from the UK, so that an execution in Arizona could be carried out (Amnesty International 2011c). Finally, in early 2011, the only U.S. manufacturer of sodium thiopental halted its production of the drug, leaving most capital punishment states facing shortages. Obtaining supplies from foreign manufacturers placed some state departments of correction at odds with the Food and Drug Administration, a federal agency charged with policing the importation of drugs into the United States (New York Times 2011). This shortage set in motion a movement to find other ways to accomplish execution by injection. By 2011, lethal injection practitioners in the United States were using four methods: execution by three drugs starting with sodium thiopental, execution by three drugs starting with pentobarbital, execution by one drug (thiopental) and execution by one drug (pentobarbital) (Death Penalty Information Center 2011). Such changes in the execution protocol set in motion a flood of legal challenges. Some advocates of capital punishment argue that moving to a one-drug execution protocol would lessen the pain inmates experience while dying. However, no execution method is perfect. An execution achieved by injection of a single barbiturate, for example, could result in a time lag of as much as 45 minutes before death is achieved (Grady 2006). This 45-minute wait could become quite uncomfortable for witnesses. In 2009, Ohio became the first state to execute a person using a one-drug lethal injection method. Lethal injection can be made macabre by the age and condition of the condemned party. For example, "California's first judicial killing of 2006 disposed of a man who had been on death row for 23 years. Seventy-six years old, legally blind from diabetes, suffering from heart disease, he made the journey to the death chamber in a wheelchair" (Hertzberg 2007).

A big problem for executioners involves finding functional veins in condemned inmates. This can be an especially difficult task when working with inmates who have injected prohibited drugs or who have suffered from diabetes. In such situations, a condemned person strapped to a gurney can experience close to 20 needle punctures, before a functioning vein is located. For example, in 1992, it took the execution team 45 minutes to find a functional vein in the arm of Arkansas murderer, Rickey Ray Rector. In order to accomplish his own execution, Rector, while strapped to the gurney, had to help with insertion of the IV. In 1996, a condemned man in Indiana lay strapped to the gurney for 1 hour and 20 minutes, while executioners looked for a functional vein, before they were able to inject him with the deadly chemicals. In 2001, Jose High, lay strapped to a gurney in

Georgia for 30 minutes while executioners probed his arm, hand, leg and foot, looking for a functional vein. In 2006, a Florida execution team had to lethally inject a condemned man a second time, when the first attempt left the man grimacing and mouthing words. In late 2009, an Ohio execution team, after trying for approximately 2 hours to find an open vein in the arms and legs of a condemned man, halted the execution attempt and returned the man to his cell on death row (New York Times 2009a).

Many lethal injection executions are botched in other ways. One such execution attempt resulted in a violent reaction to the drugs by the condemned man, causing one observer to faint. Another attempt featured the escape of a syringe from a condemned man's arm and the spewing of deadly chemicals towards observers. After 40 minutes, that inmate finally died. In 1997, a condemned man in Oklahoma experienced a violent reaction to the deadly drugs, inducing chest and stomach convulsions and the locking of his jaws: "After 26 convulsions, his body first turned a yellowish gray and then turned a deep purple. The death spasms lasted for more than twenty minutes" (Mears 2001: 3). In 2014, an Ohio inmate, instead of quietly passing away, "gasped for air for 11 minutes, and it took 25 minutes in all to end his life" (Denver Post 2014a: 15A). The Ohio condemned man, according to witnesses, eventually expired, but only after struggling with his bindings, clinching his fists and snorting and choking until the lethal drugs finally worked. The executioners had used a new three-drug combination. They had used up the last of one drug in a prior execution, and their foreign supplier had refused to resupply them, thus forcing the change to a new drug (Salter 2014: 11A).

Two other botched executions in 2014 illustrate just how wrong lethal injection can go. In late April 2014, Governor Mary Fallin announced that the Oklahoma Department of Corrections would hold their first double execution (two executions in a single day) in 80 years. Clayton Lockett was the first inmate to be executed on April 29, 2014. Another inmate, Charles Warner, was to be executed 2 hours later. Because their supply of one drug, the sedative that had been used in many Oklahoma executions, had run out, the Oklahoma executioners approached their work that day equipped with a new sedative, midazolam, in their three-drug combination.

Something went very wrong during Lockett's execution. The presiding doctor reportedly failed to properly place the needle through which the lethal drugs would travel into Lockett's femoral vein. The drugs, consequently, remained close to the point of injection, instead of traveling throughout the body and to the heart. At first, Mr Lockett seemed to fall asleep. But, then, he regained consciousness. For approximately 43 minutes, Mr Lockett lay on the gurney, writhing in pain, clenching his teeth and, from time-to-time, attempting to speak. The doctor, trying to end the execution, attempted to insert an intravenous line into a vein near the condemned man's groin. The doctor missed, hitting, instead, an artery. Blood spewed from Lockett's groin onto the doctor (Eckholm 2014: 23). Lockett's attorney, David Autry, who witnessed the botched execution, said, "[I]t was a horrible thing to witness. This was totally botched" (The Greeley Tribune 2014: A6). In a telephone interview with the first author, conducted on May 2, 2014, Attorney Autry had the following to say about the execution: "He was not unconscious. They conducted the execution like a junior high lab experiment." Mr Autry has witnessed numerous executions at the McAlester, Oklahoma, death chamber. Mr Lockett's was, by far, the most gruesome execution Attorney Autry has seen. Mr Warner's execution was delayed by an Oklahoma Court of Appeals for 6 months. In January 2015, the United States Supreme Court put three scheduled executions in Oklahoma on hold, until the Court could consider whether or not the sedative, midazolam, is sufficiently effective to prevent suffering at the "cruel and unusual" level (Denver Post 2015a: 13A). Florida executioners, having run out of their preferred sedative, had also switched to midazolam (Sherman 2015: 18A).

The second botched execution of 2014 occurred in Arizona in late July. Like their counterparts in Oklahoma, the Arizona executioners had run out of their preferred sedative. They decided to proceed with a two-drug combination: hydromorphone (an opioid pain medication) and midazolam (a sedative). Taken in sufficient quantities, hydromorphone can stop breathing. Instead of efficiently passing on, Joseph Randall Wood lay gasping for air for 90 minutes. In attempts to end Mr Wood's life, executioners injected him 15 times, each time using the same amount of the lethal drugs that they had originally intended to use for the execution (Galvan 2014: 18A). Mr Wood did die, two and a half hours after he received the first lethal injection. Executioners in some states, like Texas, set about locating a new supplier for pentobarbitol, their preferred sedative (Denver Post 2014b: 16A; Graczyk 2015: 14A). Colorado's execution protocol recently changed by replacing its preferred sedative, sodium pentothal, with the then available alternative, pentobarbital (Elliott 2013: 4B). Should Colorado executioners need to execute someone on their small death row, they will have to find a new source for pentobarbital, or they will have to come up with a new, effective sedative to add to their death cocktail. Executioners in most states will not reveal the drugs used in lethal injections (Welsh-Huggins & Salter 2014: 6A). In late June 2015, the United States Supreme Court, in a 5-to-4 decision, ruled that midazolam can be used in executions. In a dissenting statement, Justice Sotomayor suggested that her colleagues on the Court were sanctioning torture (Keim 2015: 3). It is likely that a few more executioners, in a few more states, will try midazolam as a component of their cocktails. Over time, through experimentation with living beings, we will know more about midazolam.

As we go to press, execution states are scrambling to find a drug, or a combination of drugs, that can be used to conduct an efficient, visually acceptable and timely way to extinguish a human life. To date, eight states have experimented with a single-drug style of execution (Texas, Arizona, Missouri, Georgia, Idaho, Ohio, South Dakota and Washington). Fourteen states have used pentobarbital as the sedative in their execution cocktails. Three states have used midazolam as the sedative in their death drug mix. A number of execution states have passed laws allowing for the use of back-up methods for executions, should lethal drugs become unavailable, or should the United States Supreme Court strike down the use of drugs in executions (Death Penalty Information Center 2015d: 1).

Another major concern with lethal injection is that it involves the participation of doctors and nurses who have pledged to "do no harm." Doctors are involved in writing prescriptions necessary to obtain drugs used in lethal injection executions (Groner 2002). Medical doctors provide other questionable services for the execution industry. For example, the U.S. Supreme Court ruled that inmates can be forced to take antipsychotic medication in order to make them sane enough to execute (Lewis 2003). This practice would, of course, require the participation of at least one medical doctor. The American Medical Association and other professional medical associations specify that doctors should not participate in executions. Most state departments of correction find it impossible to recruit doctors who will help with lethal injections. The rare doctor who will participate appears likely to be mistake-prone (Eckholm 2014: 23; New York Times 2007).

The foremost American producers of execution machinery are Fred Leuchter, of Massachusetts, and Jay Wiechert of Fort Smith, Arkansas. Leuchter, who designed and built a lethal injection system in the basement of his home, is the most notorious (Trombley 1992). In 1985, he sold that system to the state of New Jersey. He got $30,000 for his first execution machine. Leuchter also designs, manufactures and sells electric chairs ($35,000); gallows; ($85,000) and gas chambers ($200,000). Leuchter repairs and services everything that he sells. He provides training for executioners (Edwards 2015; Weber 1998). Weichert, who operates a custom machinery business in Fort Smith, Arkansas, is a designer of industrial machinery. He is also the foremost producer of electric chairs. He sold six for about $40,000 each (Bicknell 1997). Leuchter did not think much of Mr Weichert's machines. Leuchter reportedly wondered if Mr Weichert might like to torture condemned inmates (Sparrow 2009).

Capital punishment since 1977

Between 1976 and July 2015, 2,284 persons were executed in the United States. In the U.S. since 1977, 527 executions were carried out in Texas. Other leading capital punishment states are Oklahoma (112), Virginia (110), Florida (90), Missouri (85), Alabama (55) and Georgia (57) (Death Penalty Information Center 2015c). When executions are looked at as a percentage of all murder convictions in a state, Nevada leads the nation at 6 percent, followed by Oklahoma (5.1 percent), Texas (2 percent) and Virginia (1.3 percent) (Liptak 2004).

Between 1976 and 2013, 141 persons who received death sentences "volunteered" for execution, thus relinquishing all rights to appeal their convictions and/or sentences. Most inmates executed died by lethal injection, some by electrocution (Death Penalty Information Center 2013). Thirty-four of the 2,284 executions involved persons who were probably developmentally disabled. On June 20, 2002, the U.S. Supreme Court, in *Atkins v. Virginia*, ruled that execution of the mentally retarded constitutes cruel and unusual punishment. Twenty-two of the 2,284 persons executed were juveniles at the time they committed capital crimes. Thirteen of the twenty-two juveniles were executed in Texas. In January 2004, the U.S. Supreme Court agreed to review a 1993 murder conviction of Christopher Simmons, who was a juvenile at the time he committed the crime (Greenhouse 2004: 1). On March 1, 2005, the U.S. Supreme Court prohibited the execution of persons who were under the age of 18 when their capital crimes were committed (Canadian Coalition Against the Death Penalty 2010). At the mid-point of 2011, 63 American women were incarcerated on death row (Death Penalty Information Center 2012a).

Only 5–10 percent of all U.S. homicides are prosecuted as capital cases. Of each 50–60 murderers convicted in the United States each year, one is sentenced to death, and approximately one-third of those sentenced to death will have their sentences overturned on appeal. Of the 8,466 death sentences handed out in the United States between 1973 and 2013, only 1,359 executions have been carried out. In other words, approximately 16 percent of death sentences in the United States actually result in execution of the defendant (Baumgartner & Dietrich 2015: 1). Critics argue that capital punishment has an important symbolic component. By killing a few murderers, politicians and legal officials demonstrate that they have not surrendered in their fight against violent crime (Nelson & Foster 2001). In this sense, American legal officials execute criminals because they can. Capital punishment illustrates the power of the state.

Most capital murder prosecutions, and thus executions, occur in "death belt" states including Texas, Oklahoma, Missouri, Ohio and others extending eastward towards the Atlantic Coast (Solotaroff 2001; Death Penalty Information Center 2012a). "Death pockets," or "death counties," exist within the death belt and elsewhere in the United States. For example, at the turn of the twenty-first century, southern Georgia sent many murderers to death row. Northern Georgia did not. Memphis and East Knoxville sent many murderers to Tennessee's death row. Nashville did not. Of Texas' 254 counties, 42 send murderers to death row. One Texas county, Harris, supplied one-third of all Texas death row occupants. More than one-half of all murderers on Pennsylvania's death row came from a single city, Philadelphia, where over one-half of all murder trials were prosecuted as capital cases (Foster 2001; Nelson & Foster 2001). Between 1977 and September, 2011, 15 of the 3,148 counties in the United States accounted for 30 percent of the executions carried out in the United States. Nine of the fifteen death counties were located in Texas. Two death counties were located in Alabama. One death county could be found in each of the following states: Arizona (Pima County), Oklahoma (Oklahoma County), Missouri (St Louis County) and Ohio (Hamilton County) (Death Penalty Information Center 2012b).

Executioners

Early American executioners were a rare breed. They worked alone and were sometimes criminals themselves who escaped execution by agreeing to do the deed. Edwin F. Davis, who helped Edison design the first electric chair, executed William Kemmler and more than 250 others before retiring. Rich Owen, a guard at the Oklahoma State Prison in McAlester, built the facility's electric chair. In 1917, when the state executioner showed up too drunk to proceed, Owen stepped in and continued to execute condemned inmates until 1948, when illness ended his career. In the 1930s, 18-year-old George Philip Hanna watched as an Illinois sheriff botched a hanging. Hanna approached the sheriff, offered to help and proceeded to conduct a first-rate hanging. Word of Hanna's feat spread and led to a 40-year career as a traveling hangman. Grover Cleveland, when he was sheriff of Erie County, New York, conducted two hangings. John Hulbert pulled the switch, after over 140 inmates were hooded and strapped into the electric chairs at prisons in New York, New Jersey and Massachusetts. In Louisiana, Henry "The Hangman" Meyer and Gradys Jarrett, who operated the electric chair, became public figures. Florida and Texas, on the other hand, kept secret the identity of their executioners. From 1966 to 1977, during the unofficial moratorium on capital punishment, "all American executioners except one retired or died" (Solotaroff 2001: 4).

Modern American executions are conducted by a team, ranging from 3 members (Georgia) to 15 (Kentucky). Modern executions are broken down into small steps with a few steps assigned to each member of the team, thus diluting individual responsibility for the premeditated killing of a human being. Team members are volunteers selected from the pool of correctional officers who work at a prison where condemned persons are executed. Team members usually receive extra benefits, like release from normal duties so that they can practice executions, direct access to the warden and additional pay. Execution team members achieve a bit of notoriety, as news of their membership leaks out into the communities in which they live. Modern executioners undertake multiple, monotonous and realistic rehearsals. Eventually, as experience accumulates, some become "skilled death-work technicians" (Johnson 1990: 81).

Modern American executions are governed by massive written protocols, developed by legal officials and overseen by wardens inside the walls of prisons where executions occur. Protocols outline in fine detail "an execution etiquette" (Johnson 1990: 73). Stephen Trombley, a British writer and film maker, studied the execution protocol developed by the state of Missouri that was designed to choreograph lethal injection executions at the maximum-security Potosi Correctional Center, a prison exclusively housing inmates convicted of capital murder. Trombley's analysis features Fred Leuchter, who invented Potosi's lethal injection system, as well as executioners dispassionately explaining how rectal plugs and catheters help prevent soiling of the death chamber gurney. Warden Paul Delo likens executions at his prison to the early stages of surgery, when a patient is anaesthetized. The prison physician explains that he participates by pronouncing condemned inmates healthy enough to be executed, and then dead, after they are executed. He also signs death certificates. Executioners display no outward emotions as they describe their duties. As the video rolls, execution team members somberly go through the final practice for an execution just a few hours away, as if they were arena workers, setting up the seats and preparing the floor for an athletic event. Execution team members rationalize their participation in a methodical, premeditated killing by portraying themselves as instruments of the state and of the people. They are doing their jobs as directed (Trombley 1992; Trombley & Wood 1992).

The authors recently spent a day inside the walls of a maximum-security Midwestern prison with a member of its execution team. We visited the cellblock where condemned men are housed. We visited the execution chamber. Our host offered to let the first author sit or lie down on the gurney where lethal injections are administered. He declined, opting, instead, for a seat in the witness area. We asked our host how he handles the emotions that result from helping to kill another human being. He replied that, before each execution, he spent a good deal of time reviewing the details of the crime, or crimes, that had determined the condemned man's fate. This process, he explained, rid him of any guilt or ill feelings that might result from his part in the execution. He was, after all, just doing his job. Donald Cabana, a career prison official and former warden who had presided over executions at the Mississippi State Penitentiary, explained his philosophy of capital punishment in the following way:

My personal feelings were not germane to any part of the process. I had a job to do.... I tried to handle the situation as just another part of the job. I had often witnessed the cold, unfeeling violence of inmates, and over time my senses became numbed by it.

(1996: 17)

The federal death penalty

The federal government of the United States also punishes certain crimes with death sentences. Between 1790 and 1963, the U.S. federal government executed 340 persons, 336 men and 4 women. Persons condemned under federal law were executed by means of hanging, electrocution or the gas chamber. Criminals receiving the death penalty under federal law committed such crimes as murder, piracy, rape, rioting, kidnapping, spying and espionage. Between 1963 and 1988, when the federal death penalty was reinstated, no criminals were executed by the federal government. In 1993, President Bush instructed federal officials to use lethal injection as the preferred method of execution. On July 19, 1993, the United States Penitentiary at Terre Haute, Indiana, was designated as the site where federal executions would occur. On July 13, 2001, anticipating a need for a larger federal death row, an expanded Special Confinement Unit was opened at the United States Penitentiary in Terre Haute, Indiana. The Terre Haute Special Confinement Unit contains 50 single cells for inmates with federal death sentences (U.S. Bureau of Prisons 1999). Before the Terre Haute facility became operational, 34 federal executions, dating between 1927 and 1963, had been carried out at various sites throughout the country, utilizing three methods: hanging, electrocution and the gas chamber (U.S. Bureau of Prisons 2001). Between 2001 and 2003, the federal government executed three men at the U.S. Penitentiary in Terre Haute, Indiana. All three were lethally injected. Between 2003 and the end of 2011, there have been no subsequent federal executions (U.S. Bureau of Prisons 2004; Death Penalty Information Center 2012a). At the end of 2003, the U.S. government held 28 inmates on death row. Another seven death row inmates were held by the U.S. military. Attorney General John Ashcroft's order that federal prosecutors seek the death penalty in most murder cases suggested that death rows in federal prisons would soon house many more condemned persons (Glaberson 2003).

At the end of 2009, the federal government held 56 persons on death row, a 100 percent increase in a 10-year period (U.S. Department of Justice 2011a). Six other men were held in cells at the U.S. military death row. Since the federal death penalty was reinstated in 1988, 75 persons have been sentenced to death in federal courts. Only three condemned federal inmates have been executed. The last federal inmate to be executed, Louis Jones, Jr., died by lethal injection on March 18, 2003. At the mid-point of 2015, 59 condemned federal inmates sit on death row. Fifty-six of the condemned inmates are held at the Terre Haute, Indiana, execution unit. Three other condemned men were held at the infamous ADX prison in Colorado (Lavoie 2015: 10A).

A statistical look at capital punishment in the United States

Table 6.1 shows the number of death sentences in United States criminal courts for the years 1977, 1987, 1997, 2007 and 2014. We see in Table 6.1 that death sentences peaked in 1987 and dropped significantly since 1997. In 2014, only 72 death sentences were handed out by juries and judges in the United States, marking a significant downturn in the use of execution as a punishment for criminal activity.

Table 6.2 provides information about the number of persons on death row in United States prisons for the years 1977, 1987, 1997, 2007 and 2014. We see that the number of persons sitting on death row in the United States peaked in 1997 and has dropped, incrementally, since then. The reality that jumps out from Table 6.2 is the fact that the United States has created a significant backlog of persons waiting to be executed.

Table 6.3 shows the actual number of executions carried out in the U.S. for the years 1977, 1987, 1997, 2007 and 2014. We see that executions in the United States peaked in 1997, a year when approximately 1.4 persons were executed, each week. However by 2014, executions in the United States had

Table 6.1 U.S. death sentences, 1977, 1987, 1997, 2007 and 2014

Year	Sentences
1977	137
1987	289
1997	276
2007	126
2014	72

Source: Death Penalty Information Center 2004c; 2012a; 2015.

Table 6.2 Number of persons on death row in U.S. prisons, 1977, 1987, 1997, 2007 and 2014

Year	# of inmates
1977	423
1987	1,984
1997	3,335
2007	3,215
2014	3,054

Source: Death Penalty Information Center 2004d; 2012a; 2015b.

Table 6.3 Number of persons executed in the U.S., 1977, 1987, 1997, 2007 and 2014

Year	# of executions
1977	1
1987	25
1997	74
2007	42
2014	35

Source: Death Penalty Information Center 2004b; 2012a; 2015a.

dropped to only 35 for the entire year, for an average of approximately 0.7 of a person being executed each week.

Data presented in the Tables 6.1, 6.2 and 6.3 highlight an important set of dilemmas Americans confront about capital punishment. With over 3,000 condemned persons sitting in cells on United States death rows, and with the number of executions down to less than 40 per year, the death row backlog will remain large, as long as United States courts continue to issue death sentences to almost twice as many persons each year as are executed. In order to eliminate the death row backlog in the next 10 years, United States prison authorities would have to execute well over 300 condemned persons each year, far more than the system is now capable of eliminating and probably far more than citizens of the U.S. could likely tolerate. Were the U.S. to execute more than 1 person per day for 10 years, we Americans might be suspected of practicing barbarism on a large scale by many members of the United Nations and by our allies in Europe.

The costs of capital punishment

Capital punishment is costly. When trials and appeals are included, the costs of capital punishment become shocking. California, a state in deep financial trouble, spends $137 million each year on capital punishment. Florida, boasting one of the largest death row populations in the U.S., spends over $24 million per execution. Since 1972, Florida taxpayers have spent more than $1 billion on their death penalty system for 72 executions (Floridians for Alternatives to the Death Penalty 2004a; Death Penalty Information Center 2012c). In North Carolina, it costs over $2 million more to execute a murderer than to keep him or her in prison for life. Eliminating the North Carolina death penalty law would save taxpayers almost $11 million per year (Porter 1998; Death Penalty Information Center 2012c). In Indiana, the death penalty costs taxpayers 38 percent more for murderers than would life sentences without the possibility of parole. Texas death penalty cases cost approximately three times more than it would to keep a convicted murderer in a single cell for 40 years (Death Penalty Information

Center 2004e; 2012c). In Maryland, taxpayers shell out approximately $3 million for each capital murder case. California's capital punishment system costs taxpayers approximately $137 million each year. Eliminating capital punishment would allow Californians to spend less than $12 million per year for all murder cases (Amnesty International 2012: 5).

The costs of capital punishment cannot be measured solely by the amount of money spent. Watt Espy, a wise man and a leading historian of American executions, contended that "more than one person dies with each execution." The most obvious casualties are, of course, the victims of capital murder, whose lives have been extinguished by senseless, brutal acts of violence. Victims of capital murder are, forevermore, denied the opportunity to live among, to financially support and to love other members of their families. Family members and friends of the victims of capital murder suffer terribly. Some are consumed by hatred. Some suffer from debilitating unresolved grief. The financial burden of their loss can be overwhelming. The case of Richard Speck who, in Chicago, murdered seven nurses, illustrates this phenomenon well. Within a few years of the murders, most of the victims' parents had passed away. It should also be noted that families of condemned persons suffer greatly. The loss of their fathers and mothers, sons and daughters, brothers and sisters, nephews and nieces via execution has a lasting effect that can be described as a form of living hell.

Capital cases are also hard on attorneys. Capital murder cases require far more time and energy for preparation and litigation than do other murder cases. Most defendants in capital murder trials are indigents whose lawyers are public defenders. Public defenders typically have large caseloads. We have worked with public defenders who were given just a few days between trials to prepare for an upcoming capital murder case. Many public defenders lack the experience and funding needed in order to adequately prepare for a capital trial. Unfortunately, some "public defenders ... just don't care" (Nelson & Foster 2001: 115).

Even talented, experienced, dedicated attorneys in capital murder cases suffer. For example, Peter D. Greenspun and Jonathan Shapiro, gifted and dedicated defense attorneys representing John Allen Muhammad in the notorious sniper rifle trial, paid a great price for their beliefs and their efforts. They were severely criticized by the media for representing a man portrayed as a monster. Greenspun weathered threats against his family. The attorneys got to know Muhammad as a human being, who possessed many positive qualities. Greenspun described the trial as a "raw, gaping wound itself." After the verdict of guilt and the death sentence were handed down, Greenspun and Shapiro were left to confront the emotional aftermath and regrets about the trial that come naturally to a defense attorney who cares and who has lost (White 2004: C01). Since most, if not all, capital murderers are suicidal, and probably insane, defense attorneys who work with them suffer unimaginable frustration. For example, Greenspun and Shapiro, during the first day of the Muhammad murder trial, were fired by their client, thus critically compromising their ability to adequately defend him. In another murder trial, Attorney Shapiro was "sucker-punched" in court and knocked out by his client.

During the course of our capital murder trial work, we befriended a gifted, dedicated capital murder trial specialist who practices law in Oklahoma. We have learned about his continued visits with men on death row, long after their cases were lost; about money taken from his modest income to buy them small items – books, magazines, a television – in order to make their lives in prison slightly more tolerable; about his attending some executions, because he had been asked to by the condemned man. Such hidden suffering is the fate of a capital defense lawyer who cares.

Capital punishment takes its toll on executioners. In Robert Johnson's words, "a profound absence of feeling would seem to embody the bureaucratic ideal for the modern execution" (1990: 72). Executioners develop relationships with the condemned while they sit for years on death row. Executioners guard and care for condemned inmates during the "death watch," those several hours preceding the execution. Executioners conduct the execution, somehow controlling their own regret about, and ambivalence toward, helping to kill another human being. Through all of these experiences, executioners must suppress their own feelings by creating in themselves a state of emotional numbness. The cumulative aftermath for executioners can be debilitating. Some have morbid dreams about executions in which they participated. Some suffer from failing health. Some are compelled to change careers. Some commit suicide (Johnson 1990; Solotaroff 2001). In Donald Cabana's words, "there is a part of the warden that dies with his prisoner.... Both are victims, unwilling captives of a human tragedy" (1996: 16).

Randolph Loney, a literature professor turned minister who, in 1985, began visiting men on Georgia's death row, believes that all Americans are diminished by the existence of capital punishment. Loney writes about men who have murdered, who have rehabilitated themselves while awaiting execution, about "our brutality against the powerless" (2001: 7). Loney visits condemned men, again and again. Why? He answers, in Nietzsche's words, because, where condemned men live, "the absence of God fills the room." (33). Loney is speaking of the ability to forgive, and to love, even our worst enemies. Reverend Loney writes,

[T]he persistent carrying out of executions is an issue that touches us all. The condemned have died in our names.... As long as we speak these words of death ... there will be no genuine vitality in our national life.

(7)

Arguments in favor of capital punishment

The three most compelling arguments in favor of capital punishment focus on incapacitation, revenge and deterrence. *Incapacitation* is the most simple argument. By executing murderers, they are no longer around to commit future murders. *Revenge* springs from a popular biblical belief in "an eye for an eye." Many Americans believe that when a human takes the life of another s/he has relinquished his or her own right to live (Pojman 2004: 51). Prosecutors are often heard saying that they are seeking the death penalty on behalf of the victim and his or her family, that society demands vengeance. In support of this position, some religious scholars conclude that God commanded capital punishment in both the Noachian Covenant and the Mosaic Covenant and that "neither Jesus nor Paul abrogated capital punishment" (House 1997: 415). John Stuart Mill, arguing against the elimination of capital punishment for murderers, in his 1868 speech before the English Parliament, put this logic in secular utilitarian terms when he declared "that he who violates that right in another forfeits it for himself, and that while no other crime that he can commit deprives him of his right to live, this shall" (Pojman 2004: 4).

Finally, many Americans believe that capital punishment *deters* other would-be murderers. Simply put, the threat of execution, rather than some lesser penalty, keeps people who are contemplating murder from going through with it. Ernest Van Den Haag was the pre-eminent proponent of this position. Van Den Haag favored capital punishment for murderers "if probably deterrent, or even just possibly deterrent." He believed that the death penalty deters more than other possible punishments for murder "because people fear death more than anything else" (1997: 450). Van Den Haag acknowledged that innocent people are sometimes executed. But he saw that as acceptable, in order to achieve the deterrent effect. For decades, a majority of Americans have agreed with Van Den Haag. For decades, when asked by pollsters if they supported the death penalty, a majority responded in the affirmative. For example, in 1995, 77 percent of Americans favored the death penalty. In late 2000, 66 percent favored it (Solotaroff 2001). A Harris poll conducted in January 2004 that asked, "[A]re you in favor of the death penalty for a person convicted of murder?" reported 71 percent of respondents supported capital punishment (prodeathpenalty.com 2004). A November 2011 survey conducted by the Pew Research Center revealed that 62 percent of adults still favor the death penalty for murderers (Pew Research Center for the People and the Press 2012).

Arguments against capital punishment

Perhaps the most compelling argument against capital punishment, once again, has a religious basis: "The death penalty is the ultimate cruel, inhuman and degrading punishment. It violates the right to life" (Amnesty International 2004b: 1). The Ten Commandments, accepted by Judaism, Christianity and Islam as the most important rules of human behavior created by God, contain the prohibition "thou shalt not kill," affirming the human right to life. Some opponents of the death penalty note that it violates "the sanctity of the offender's life, which God has given and which God values despite the repulsiveness of what the offender has done" (Lutheran Church in America 1991: 4–5). In sum, Katya Lezin, in her book about six imprisoned capital murderers, explores the irony of killing murderers as punishment for killing: "An execution involves ending the life of an individual, often making us guilty of the very crime for which we are punishing someone. It also discounts any belief in redemption and forgiveness, reflecting a short-sighted and dismal view of humanity" (1999: xvii).

Another argument against capital punishment is that "it is irrevocable and can be inflicted on the innocent" (Amnesty International 2004b: 1). Between 1973 and January 23, 2012, 140 prisoners had been released from death row in the United States, after evidence emerged of their innocence (Amnesty International 2004a; Death Penalty Information Center 2012a; 2012d). Many condemned inmates released since 1973 sat on death row for several years, some barely escaping execution. They were the victims of misconduct by prosecutors and police officers, of statements made by unreliable witnesses, of botched or faked physical evidence, of forced confessions and of inadequate defense lawyers. For example, in Oklahoma, a police chemist, whose testimony helped convict 12 death row inmates, fell under a cloud of suspicion and is suspected of lying about, or faking, incriminating evidence (Hastings 2001; Yardley 2001). In Pennsylvania, a state court judge voided a man's death sentence after ruling that prosecutors had withheld critically important information from defense attorneys, in violation of Constitutional and ethical guidelines (Bonner, 2001a). In an Idaho case, a man sat on death row for 18 years after he was convicted of a murder on the basis of an FBI expert's testimony that his hair sample was similar to strands found on the victim and on the testimony of two jailhouse informers. He was released after a DNA test exonerated him of the murder (Bonner 2001b). No means exist to determine how many innocent persons have been executed in the United States. In Ohio, a man was held on death row for 20 years until, in 2012, he was released by a court ruling that the state had withheld key evidence from the defense. Condemned persons spend, on average, almost 10 years between receiving a death sentence and exoneration (Death Penalty Information Center 2012d).

In 1997, recognizing the of problems related to capital punishment, the American Bar Association House of Delegates passed a resolution calling for a halt to executions until U.S. courts could guarantee that capital trials were being impartially and fairly administered, and with a minimum risk of executing innocent persons. Bar associations in California, Colorado, Louisiana, New Jersey, New York, North Carolina and Pennsylvania have adopted death penalty moratorium resolutions. Bar associations in Illinois, Ohio and Washington passed resolutions calling for a review of their state's death penalty process (Texas Lawyers in Support of a Moratorium 2002).

The problem of executing innocent persons was revealed most extensively in Illinois where, since 1977, 13 death row inmates were exonerated and released from prison. In January 2000, Illinois Governor George Ryan, a pro-death penalty Republican, imposed a moratorium on capital punishment in his state. In January 2003, after extensive review of the death penalty process and of all death row inmates, Governor Ryan declared that the capital punishment system in Illinois was fundamentally flawed, as he pardoned four death row inmates and commuted the death sentences of 163 men and 4 women (Ryan 2004; Wilgoren 2003). Illinois is not the worst state in this regard. Florida leads the nation. Since 1973, 25 condemned persons have been exonerated and released from Florida's death row (Floridians for Alternatives to the Death Penalty 2004a).

In 2000, lawyers and criminologists at Colombia University released results from an exhaustive $1.25 million study of death penalty cases in the United States. Most notable was their finding that "of every three capital sentences reviewed, two were overturned on appeal. The researchers characterized capital punishment in the U.S. as "riddled with unfairness and incompetence ... as broken" (Herbert 2002: 1). The worst states, in terms of percentage of errors in death penalty cases were Kentucky, Maryland, Tennessee, Mississippi, California, Idaho, Montana, Georgia, Arizona and Alabama, with error rates ranging from 100 percent to 77 percent. According to Columbia Law School Professor, James Leibman, "they do too many too fast and prosecutors seek the death penalty too quickly" (Sowers 2002: 1–2).

Another argument against the death penalty is its disproportionate use African Americans. After reviewing this possibility, the U.S. General Accounting Office, based upon its examination of existing research, concluded that African Americans are disproportionately sentenced to death (1997). A study of the death penalty, conducted by the Texas Defender Service, affirmed this pattern. In Texas, when an African American kills a European American, the death penalty quickly comes into play. According to the Texas Defender Service, Texas has never executed a European American for the murder of an African American (Herbert 2003). Similarly, after analyzing almost 6,000 Maryland murder cases, researchers reported that prosecutors are far more likely to seek the death penalty in cases where African Americans are charged with killing European Americans (Paternoster & Brame 2003). In 2003, 8 of 12 men on Maryland's death row were African American. According to Jackson, Jackson, Jr. and Shapiro, "there is a special relationship between the death penalty and African Americans, a relationship going back to antebellum days, when the gallows was a principle means of punishing slaves, and through the worst years of Jim Crow" (2001: 72). In 2000, a study commissioned by Attorney General Reno reported that eight out of each ten death penalty charges referred to the Attorney General for approval involve African American or Hispanic defendants. Minority defendants had been charged in 72 percent of active federal death penalty cases approved by the Attorney General. European American defendants are twice as likely as African Americans and Hispanics to avoid federal capital charges via plea bargaining (73).

Another factor contributing to the argument against capital punishment is the absence of proof that executing murderers deters others from committing murder. The definitive data on this subject comes from a study commissioned by the United Nations, originally conducted in 1988 and updated in 2002. Its author, Roger Hood, concludes that "it is not prudent to accept the hypothesis that capital punishment deters murder to a marginally greater extent than does the threat and application of the supposedly lesser punishment of life imprisonment" (2002: 230). Hood further concludes "countries need not fear sudden and serious changes in the curve of crime if they reduce their reliance upon the death penalty" (214). Bailey and Peterson, after an exhaustive review of the research literature related to murder, capital punishment and deterrence conclude "the evidence on how different dimensions of capital punishment influence homicides is overwhelmingly contrary to deterrence theory" (1997: 153).

There is another unresolved issue related to capital punishment in the United States. Over 120 foreigners from 29 countries have been sentenced to death in the United States in violation of international law created in 1963 at the Vienna Convention (Simons & Weiner 2004). For example, in April 2004, the International Court of Justice ruled that the murder cases of 51 Mexican nationals held on death row in the United States should be reviewed because, when arrested, they were not given access to representatives of their government as prescribed by the Vienna Convention (New York Times, April 19, 2004). Germany and Paraguay have filed similar suits against the United States. Another unresolved issue involves over a hundred inmates held in American death rows who were sentenced by judges to be executed. In 2002, the U.S. Supreme Court ruled that juries, not judges, must determine the sentence in capital murder cases (Holland 2004). Since 1988, 28 foreign nationals have been executed in the United States (Amnesty International 2012: 1).

Summary

While we Americans continue our pursuit of kinder executions, most industrialized nations have turned away from this form of criminal punishment. For example, even when Anna Lindh, Sweden's foreign minister, was stabbed "repeatedly with a household utility knife as she shopped in a department store," her assailant and murderer was sentenced to life imprisonment rather than death (Cowell 2004). Giuliano Amato, Prime Minister of Italy, captured the essence of world opinion about capital punishment when he declared, "[T]he death penalty is disgusting, particularly if it condemns an innocent. But it remains an injustice even when it falls on someone who is guilty of a crime" (Amnesty International 2004c: 1–2).

Change is afoot in American society. Large pharmaceutical corporations are no longer willing to manufacture and market a critical drug commonly used in the lethal injection cocktail, although one boutique pharmacy seems to be filling the void. In 2009, New Mexico eliminated the death penalty. In 2011, Illinois repealed its death penalty. In 2015, the Nebraska state legislature repealed their death penalty law, overriding a veto by the governor. A number of other states, like Colorado, for example, have imposed a de facto moratorium on executions while their legislatures and courts examine the costs of execution as well as the legality of their execution protocols. Even super-crime-fighter legislators are beginning to realize that death penalty costs are too high. Consequently, at least until the American economy recovers a bit more, death sentences, and executions, will be on the wane. We do not, however, see the death penalty disappearing from American society. Instead, we see this fragment of the "war between the states" continuing on, well into the future.

Chapter 7

Less visible prison minorities – women, children and the elderly

Introduction

Throughout their history, American prisons have been dumping grounds for ethnic minority persons. This fact is well documented (Turner et al., 1984; Cahalan 1986; Shelden 2001). Receiving far less attention is the presence of other prison minorities, namely women, children and the elderly. These somewhat hidden prison minorities pose unique and challenging problems for politicians, prison administrators and workers, as well as for the rest of us who live in American society. We believe that the increasing flow of women, children and seniors into American prisons can be viewed as a hidden crisis.

Female inmates

Female inmates have always been treated differently in the United States. James V. Bennett, former Director of the Federal Bureau of Prisons, wrote, "[N]o one has really known what to do with the few women who are condemned to prison, least of all the federal government" (1970: 127). Others contend that female inmates "say they are being punished for breaking not only social laws but also unwritten moral laws. They often report that prior to incarceration, they were treated by judges, lawyers and others in the criminal justice system with contempt, as if they were 'tramps' or cheap women – basically 'anti-mothers'– for stepping out of place and threatening the status quo" (quoted in Watterson 1996: 34). Butler reports that the female inmate, "now a 'moron,' a 'whore,' a 'villainess' – no longer demanded public scrutiny. Society easily dismissed women sentenced to the penitentiary because they were 'real women' no longer" (1997: 27). Once in prison, because of their powerlessness and small numbers, women are often treated as afterthoughts, as nuisances and, all-too-often, as objects of sexual pleasure.

In 1820, America's 15 prisons held men, women and children, as well as persons with severe mental illness, sometimes all mixed together and sometimes somewhat separated from each other. For example, in 1825, at the Auburn State Prison in New York, women and men were held at the same facility. But female inmates at Auburn were kept in an attic room above the prison's kitchen and were not allowed to leave the attic to work or to exercise. In 1842, at an Illinois prison, women were worked in the kitchen by day and were crammed into a cellar below the warden's house by night. In the late 1800s, at another Illinois prison, women were incarcerated separately from the male inmates, on a top floor of an administration building, where they were put to work sewing for inmates and staff, manufacturing light objects and knitting. At this Illinois prison, women were allowed only one walk around the prison grounds each year. At other American prisons, like San Quentin, female inmates were put to work as barmaids and prostitutes serving the prison staff. Women, of course, were a prison minority, making up as little as 1 percent, and never more than 10 percent, of a prison's inmate population (Britton 2003).

In the late 1800s and early 1900s, state governments began building separate prisons for women. The Indiana Reformatory Institution for Women and Girls, opened in 1873, was the first American prison built exclusively for females. In the 1920s, sociologist Frank Tannenbaum wrote the following about a women's prison he visited in a Southern state:

> The dining room contains a sweatbox for women who are being punished by being locked up in a place with insufficient room to sit down and near enough to the table to smell the food. Over the table, there is a long iron bar, to which women are handcuffed when they are being whipped.
>
> (quoted in Bennett, 1970: 128)

Women's prisons were often built next to men's prisons. The first federal prison for women opened in 1945, at Alderson, West Virginia. Women's prisons were sometimes overseen by a "matron," the female equivalent of a warden. However, early women's prisons in the United States were, for the most part, under the control of a male-dominated prison hierarchy and were allocated fewer resources than prisons for men (Rafter 1990). As late as the 1970s, many women were still held on the grounds of what were predominantly men's prisons. For example, at the Utah State Prison, south of Salt Lake City, women were incarcerated in a single-story building, at the edge of the parking lot, next to the much larger men's prison. Female inmates had access to only a small fenced yard for exercise and to a small kitchen, where they could produce some baked items, like brownies, to share with each other. Women in the Utah facility, visited many times by the first author, appeared to be severely depressed and overweight. Women at the Utah prison were allowed out of their small building and exercise yard only once each week, when they were taken into the men's prison, where they could, for a short time, use the gymnasium, which was mostly a basketball court.

Table 7.1 shows a steady increase in female inmates held in U.S. state and federal prisons over the past hundred years. It is notable that, between 1970 and 1980, the number of women in U.S. prisons almost tripled. Between 1980 and 1990, the number of female prisoners in the U.S. almost tripled, again. More recently, between 1990 and the end of 2002, the number of U.S. women doing time more than doubled. Between 2000 and 2010, the number of women locked up in state and

Table 7.1 Number of women in U.S. state and federal correctional facilities, 1910–2013

Year	Number of women	Percent of total inmates female
1910	2,714	4%
1923	3,237	4%
1933	4,140	3%
1950	7,123	4%
1960	9,054	4%
1970	5,965	3%
1980	15,119	5%
1990	44,065	6%
2002	97,491	7%
2013	111,287*	7%

Sources: Cahalan 1986: 65; Butterfield 2003: 1; Harrison & Beck 2003: 1; Carson 2014: 3.
Note: *This figure is for December 31, 2013.

federal prisons grew by another 21 percent (Glaze & Kaeble 2014: 7). As Table 7.1 shows, by 2013, U.S. prisons held over 111,000 women.

In statistical terms, European American women are less likely to be sent to a U.S. prison than are women of color. Rhode Island holds the fewest women, per capita (15 out of each 100,000 women living in the state). Oklahoma prisons host the most women, per capita (121 out of each 100,000 women living in the state). Women are, for the most part, sent to prison for the commission of property and drug-related offenses. Over six out of each ten women held in a state prison have minor children from whom they have been separated. Almost three of each four women in a state prison report the presence of an ongoing mental health problem (Butterfield 2003: 4; The Sentencing Project 2012b: 1–3). At the turn of the century, approximately 43 percent of female prisoners in the U.S. were African American, about 42 percent of female prisoners were European American and about 12 percent of women in prison were Hispanic (The Sentencing Project 2003). It is notable that many violent American female inmates are incarcerated because they killed violent husbands or violent male friends (Butler 1997).

As late as the mid-1970s, only about one-half of the states in the U.S. maintained separate prisons for women. By the late 1990s, 40 state governments operated approximately 92 prisons for women and another 16 prisons that house both men and women (National Institute of Corrections 1998: 1). Female inmates in Federal Bureau of Prisons facilities are held in 6 women's prisons, 8 prison camps for women and 12 prisons where both men and women are kept (Federal Bureau of Prisons 2004: 1–29). Many states and the federal government contract with prison corporations to hold women in private facilities. No reliable estimates exist for the number of women's facilities in the United States operated by private corporations. The largest complex of women's prisons in the United States can be found in California. The infamous Central California Women's Facility (CCWF, located in Chowchilla, California) is the largest women's prison in the United States and, possibly, in the world. CCWF contains an inmate population approaching 4,000. California also operates the Valley State Prison for Women (also located in Chowchilla, California) and the California Institute for Women (located in Chino, California). The California Rehabilitation Center at Norco houses men and women. Together, the four California facilities hold about 10,000 women (Revolutionary Worker 1997; California Department of Corrections 2001f; Gottesdiener 2011: 1).

Female inmates and their children

Over 60 percent of the women in American prisons are mothers of young children. About 250,000 American children have mothers who are incarcerated. Over one-half of those children never get to visit their mothers in prison. Children of color are more likely than European American children to have a mother in prison (Mumola 2000; Glaze & Maruschak 2008). Nationally, most children of incarcerated mothers have lived with their grandparents, 17 percent with their fathers, while 6 percent have gone into foster homes (Johnson & Waldfogel 2003; The Sentencing Project 2012b). In California, on any given day in 2003, around 7,000 female inmates were locked up in a prison. Collectively, they were the mothers of about 18,000 children under the age of 18. Most children of incarcerated California women have been under the age of 10. Over 70 percent of the California convict mothers committed property or drug offenses. Historically, about 60 percent of the California children with inmate mothers lived with their grandmothers, 20 percent lived with their fathers and 10 percent to 15 percent resided in foster homes (Center for Children of Incarcerated Parents 2003).

One in four women in prison either have given birth within 1 year of their incarceration or have gone into prison pregnant. Some female inmates have become pregnant while in prison. It is estimated that 6 percent of the women coming into American prisons are pregnant. Less than one-half of American prisons have written policies directing employees in the handling of pregnant inmates. Less than one-half of American prisons provide prenatal care for pregnant women. Women prisoners who give birth almost always must be transported to a hospital, since few prisons have adequate facilities for safely delivering a child. While being transported to a hospital, and while at a hospital, most female prisoners are kept in restraints (shackles). According to Amnesty International, "shackling of all prisoners, including pregnant prisoners, is policy in federal prisons and the US Marshal Service and exists in almost all state prisons. Only 13 states have prohibited the shackling of female inmates during labor and delivery" (The Sentencing Project 2012b: 3). Unfortunately, where laws have been passed, they are often ignored. Hemorrhaging, decreased heart rate or brain damage to the baby may result from shackling during labor. In sum, most medical doctors view shackling during labor and delivery as a threat to the health of both mother and baby (Quinn 2014: 2). Within a few hours of birth, most babies are taken from female prisoners, with 10 percent going into foster homes; 45 percent going to parents, sisters, or other relatives of inmates; and 22 percent going to their fathers (Watterson 1996; The Sentencing Project 2012b). It costs taxpayers about $20,000 per year to keep a child in foster care. The National Institute of Corrections could find only three prisons, one in Nebraska and two in New York, with nursery programs that allowed inmate mothers to keep their babies near them while they are incarcerated (1998). Many children of inmate mothers who are placed in foster care will never live with their mothers again, because of the 1997 federal Adoption and Safe Families Act that requires states to take action severing parental custody after a child has spent 15 months out of any 22 month period in foster care (itvs 2004; Justice Works 2004).

Many men in prison are worried most about getting out. Many women in prison worry most about their children. Many female inmates believe that the most punitive aspect of their stay in prison is the separation from their children. Children with mothers in prison wet their beds more than other children. They underachieve at school. Some refuse to eat properly. Children with mothers in prison suffer financially. They live in shame, suffering from the stigma that has been attached to their mothers. They realistically fear for their mother's safety. The children of convicts are often treated poorly by school officials. They frequently become truants, dropouts and, consequently, join gangs. Children with mothers in prison more frequently become delinquent, experience early pregnancy and abuse drugs. Children often feel guilty and blame themselves because their mothers are in prison (Watterson 1996). Even children who are allowed to visit their mothers in prison suffer terribly. For example, one 8-year-old boy, not having seen his mother in years, after a 3-hour prison visit "clung to his mother, his arms and legs wrapped tightly about her. Weeping hysterically, the child had to be wrenched away. He was taken to another state to live with relatives" (quoted in Watterson 1996: 217). In short, life in a U.S. prison can be hell, for most inmate mothers and for their children.

Sexual abuse of female inmates

Throughout the early history of the American prison movement, female inmates were overseen by male guards and administrators. Consequently, the sexual abuse of female inmates started early and has continued (Butler 1997; Gottesdiener 2011). In fact, the sexual abuse of female inmates by male employees, when it occasionally became known to the American public, sparked the movement to build separate women's prisons. However, over 40 percent of all correctional officers working in women's prisons are male (Britton 2003; Piecora 2014: 1). It should be noted that many American women's prisons employ an even larger proportion of male correctional officers. For example, at the California Correctional Women's Facility, with a female inmate population of over 3,500, 70 percent of the approximately 360 correctional officers have been male (United Nations Commission on Human Rights 1999). Even though most sexual abuse of female inmates goes unreported, largely because of victims' fear of retaliation and/or prosecution, there exists considerable documentary evidence that American female inmates are raped and otherwise sexually assaulted, are sexually extorted, are groped during body searches and are watched by male prison employees while they undress, shower and use other bathroom facilities (Amnesty International 2004c). Female inmates are coerced by male corrections workers to perform sexual acts in exchange for goods, like cigarettes or sanitary supplies, and services, such as extra privileges or telephone calls to their families. Female inmates sometimes "consent" to sexual relations with male corrections workers, because of loneliness or because they need attention, love and affection.

Female inmates who refuse the advances of male corrections workers are subject to reprisal. For example, one woman who got in a fight at a women's prison was transferred to a segregation unit in a nearby men's prison. Her neighbors were male inmates. Her keepers were mostly male correctional officers. One night, she heard the lock of her cell door click open. A male inmate entered and attempted to sexually assault her. She fought back. She was injured and bleeding, but he fled, unsuccessful. A few nights later, she again heard the cell door lock click open. Another male inmate entered and attacked her. She fought him off, and he fled. She reported the incidents. She requested a transfer. But nothing happened. A few days later, at night, she heard the cell door open: "Then came the Sept. 22 attack. Throughout it the three men threatened her life, called her a 'snitch' and told her to 'keep her mouth shut'" (Siegal 1998: 4). Only correctional officers are supposed to possess the keys, and the freedom of movement at night, that allow for the opening of cell doors.

Women in prison are visited less frequently than their male counterparts. Women in prison are even less well-off financially than their male counterparts. Some believe that "stripped of their rights, money and contact with the outside world, they are powerless, helpless and easy to manipulate" (2). Researchers who studied sexual abuse of female prisoners in 11 state prisons located throughout the United States concluded that

> being a woman in U.S. state prisons can be a terrifying experience.
> If you are sexually abused, you cannot escape from your abuser.

Grievance or investigatory procedures, where they exist, are often ineffectual, and correctional employees continue to engage in abuse because they believe they will rarely be held accountable, administratively or criminally. Few people outside the prison walls know what is going on or care if they do know. Fewer still do anything to address the problem.

(Thomas et al., 1996: 5)

For example, a Special Rapporteur, sent by the United Nations Commission on Human Rights to investigate violence against women in California prisons, reported,

California appears to have inadequate administrative or penal protection against sexual misconduct in custody. This is compounded by the fact that the California Department of Corrections has no comprehensive procedures for reporting or investigating allegations of sexual abuse in its facilities. Sexual misconduct in custody was criminalized only in 1994 ... prison management ... still used the term 'overfamiliarity' to refer to acts of sexual abuse ... the use of this euphemism obscures the serious nature of the acts concerned.

(1999: 3)

This situation has improved somewhat, largely due to the 2003 federal Rape Elimination Act. However, according to a California female inmate, "guards have sex and women are harassed by the guards.... Women get pregnant. Babies are born. These things happen here and the guards are responsible" (quoted in Gottesdiener 2011: 3).

Correctional officers in many states have access to female inmates' files and can therefore monitor any complaints that are lodged against them by inmates. Correctional officers in many states can fabricate rules violations, can have inmates placed in "the hole" and can influence whether or not inmates are allowed visitors. These and other tactics are used by male correctional officers to intimidate female inmates who have filed, or who might file, formal complaints against them. In some states, female inmates who have sexual contact with male prison employees can be held criminally liable for their behavior. In some states, consent on the part of a female inmate is viewed by legal officials as a mitigating factor when a male correctional officer is caught having sexual contact with one of the women he is employed to oversee.

In a survey that covered all 50 states, Washington, D.C., and the federal prison system, Amnesty International researchers concluded the following: as late as 2002, 14 states had no law in place prohibiting sexual contact between inmates and prison employees. As of 2004, six states still had no such law on the books. No states have laws in place that meet the six recommendations made by Amnesty International that, if effectively enforced, would provide adequate protection for all inmates against sexual abuse. At least 45 states allowed pat-down searches of female prisoners by male correctional officers. Six states routinely allowed cross-gender pat down searches. Only Florida, Michigan and the federal prison system prohibited pat-down searches of female prisoners by male correctional officers. Given the fact that sexual abuse of female inmates by male correctional officers continues, even where written law prohibits it, Amnesty International recommends that women in prison should be handled solely by female correctional officers (2003).

Available data suggest sexual abuse of American female inmates, at least in some prisons, reached epidemic proportions. For example, in 1977, the U.S. Department of Justice joined a class action lawsuit, originally filed by 31 female inmates, alleging that women incarcerated at the Crane and Scott prisons had been subjected to sexual abuse and misconduct and illegal invasions of privacy. The Michigan Department of Corrections and the Department of Justice settled the lawsuit out of court. However, representatives of Human Rights Watch protested that the settlement left female prisoners in Michigan "vulnerable to sexual harassment and abuse by corrections staff" (1999: 1). In 1999, at least 22 state departments of correction were confronted with lawsuits involving charges of sexual misconduct perpetrated by prison employees (LIS, Inc., 2000).

Women prisoner advocates protested a change in policy at the California Valley State Prison for Women in Chowchilla authorizing pat down searches "involving the touching of the breasts and fondling of the pubic area of female prisoners by male guards," claiming that this practice "constitutes heightened sexual harassment in that prison" (Greenspan 2003: 1). In 2003, an inmate at the Indiana Women's prison filed suit against three guards and the Indiana Department of Correction alleging that, in 2002, she was raped in the prison chapel by one guard. She told police she consented to sexual activity between herself and the other two guards. Two other female inmates at the prison have accused the same guards of sexual misconduct. The guards were fired in August 2002 (Ryckaert 2003:1). In 2003, after deliberating 30 minutes, a federal jury awarded a female Texas inmate $4 million, concluding that she had been raped by a correctional officer. According to her testimony, she was raped in a supply room. The inmate, no longer in prison, reported continued suffering from panic attacks, depression and nightmares (Heinzl 2003).

We should note that sexual abuse in prison is not limited to female inmates. In 2002, female corrections officers, who work as nurses in Florida prisons, filed a class action lawsuit against the Department of Corrections, alleging that "the Department had engaged in system-wide policy and pattern and practice ... of subjecting the Plaintiffs and the class to unwelcome, severe and pervasive sexual harassment by male inmates." The nurses, who are required to provide healthcare services to inmates in their cells, contend that male corrections officers take no action to stop male inmates from masturbating, pointing and shooting at the nurses, a practice called "gunning" (Angelfire 2004: 2). The nurses further claimed "that the prevailing attitude among security officials in the Department to the harassment has been indifference, condonation and hostility" (5). In 2003, two veteran female correctional officers filed another suit against the Florida Department of Corrections, alleging that they "were repeatedly harassed and pressured to perform sex acts while on the job." They reported that such abuses occurred for many years and that other Florida female corrections officers were sexually harassed and abused as well (Tardy 2003: 1).

Children as inmates

In the 1820s, most facilities in the United States that confined law-violating children on a long-term basis were called "prisons" or "houses of refuge." In the 1850s, the name for many long-term children's lock-ups was changed to "reformatories." Regardless of what they were called, early American long-term lock-ups for children were usually located in rural areas and were operated as punitive, work-oriented prisons. Many nineteenth-century American child convicts were encircled by thick concrete walls, were housed in cellblocks behind locked doors and were subject to constant violence, rigid rules of conduct and harsh discipline. Corporal punishment and inmate violence extinguished all but the most determined efforts at rehabilitation of young inmates. In the 1850s, a few progressive juvenile lock-ups moved children out of cellblocks and put them into sets of cottages dispersed throughout a prison grounds. In the early 1900s, as probation and parole became more common, more and more juvenile prisons moved to the cottage system and introduced elements of rehabilitation into their programs. This system has endured. Most long-term children's prisons in the United States currently house children in cottages. In recognition of a recent move toward some efforts at rehabilitation, many prisons for juveniles are called "industrial schools" or "training schools." In the 1940s, camps, farms and ranches began to receive some law-violating children on a long-term basis. Such facilities are usually located in forested or agricultural areas, where children are put to work under minimum-security conditions. Today, almost all long-term children's prisons in the United States combine some elements of punishment with rehabilitative goals. In other words, incarceration, isolation, denial of privileges and corporal punishment operate alongside counseling, medical care, educational programs, vocational offerings and recreational activities in children's prisons (Musick 2001).

Growth in long-term U.S. children's lock-ups

As data presented in Table 7.2 indicate, in the 1880s only 53 children's lock-ups existed in the United States. Even as late as 1923, there were still relatively few places in American society where law-violating children could be locked up. However, by 1966, well over 600 such facilities had been constructed in the United States. Locking children up was on its way to becoming an American industry. Most juvenile facilities were operated by local, state or federal legal agencies. By 1982, we see that tremendous growth has occurred in the number of U.S. children's lock-ups. By the 1980s, about two-thirds of the almost 3,000 children's incarceratories were under the control of for-profit and non-profit private organizations, and 2,277 of the facilities were long-term children's prisons. This growth trend continued into the late 1980s. By 1987, 3,299 children's lock-ups had been built in the United States, over 2,500 of those were long-term facilities. The pattern of growth dropped slightly in the 1990s. In 1991, there were 3,130 children's lock-ups in the United States. By 2000, the number of children's lock-ups had shrunk slightly to 3,061. In 2010, we see a notable downturn in the reported number of juvenile residential facilities located in the United States. This reduction, however, was accomplished by researchers at the U.S. Department of Justice, not by an actual reduction in U.S. children's lock-ups. The government researchers implemented a narrowed definition of the term "residential facility."

Table 7.3 provides historical information about the number of children locked up in the United States. These data are only approximate because, in some jurisdictions, juvenile authorities hold persons over the age of 18 in children's prisons. For example, the California Youth Authority, the

Table 7.2 Number of U.S. juvenile residential facilities in the United States, 1880–2010

	1880	1923	1966	1982	1991	2000	2010*
Total number	53	145	656	2,900	3,130	3,061	2,111
– Public control	–	123	507	1,023	1,098	1,203	1,074
– Private control	–	22	149	1,877	2,032	1,848	1,037

Source: Cahalan & Parsons 1986: 138; U.S. Department of Justice 1990: 565; U.S. Department of Justice 1993a: 579; Sickmund 2002: 2; Hockenberry et al., 2013: 2.
Note: *Definitions of "residential facility" were narrowed for the research that yielded 2010 data, thus creating the appearance of a sharp downturn in the total number of U.S. facilities.

Table 7.3 Children held in U.S. juvenile correctional facilities, 1880–2010

	1880	1923	1960	1980	2000	2010
Number present	11,468	27,238	57,883	59,414	110,284	66,632

Source: Cahalan & Parsons 1986: 130; U.S. Department of Justice 1993b: 580; Sickmund 2002: 2; Hockenberry et al., 2013: 2.

largest children's prison system in the world, holds some persons in their early- to mid-20s in their juvenile prisons. In 1880, 11,468 young persons were incarcerated in American prisons. By 1923, that number had more than doubled. By 1960, the number had more than doubled again. Almost 60,000 children were held in U.S. juvenile facilities. From 1960 to 1980, the number of children in prison stayed relatively constant. However, by 2000, children's prisons were hosting over 110,000 young souls (Sickmund 2002: 2).

Two somewhat divergent movements would soon cut into the number of children being held in U.S. juvenile correctional facilities. First, in some states, legislators successfully passed revisions in juvenile and criminal law diverting many criminal-law violating children into adult criminal court and, eventually, into adult prisons. Second, in a number of states, legislators successfully passed revisions of juvenile and criminal law that diverted a number of law-violating children away from juvenile courts and long-term lock-ups and, instead, into community-based alternatives. California experienced some of the largest reductions. In 2004, California juvenile prisons held over 3,900 male inmates. Due to changes in California law dating from 2007 through 2012, the 2015 estimated male juvenile in-facility population shrank to 685 inmates. It is noteworthy, however, that the total California juvenile prison population is projected to begin increasing again in 2016 (California Department of Corrections and Rehabilitation 2016: 26). By 2010, we see the effects of changes in law, as they show up in juvenile incarceration statistics. Table 7.3 shows that, in 2010, America's more than 2,000 children's lock-ups held approximately 66,632 inmates, a reduction of about 40 percent from the juvenile prison population 10 years earlier.

At the turn of the century, almost 1 in 4 incarcerated American children were 14 years old or younger (U.S. Department of Justice 2002). Sixty percent of all U.S. children's lock-ups were operated by private organizations. Locking children up had become a profitable industry. For example, by the late 1990s, Youth Services International was operating 20 juvenile lock-ups in 12 states with a total bed capacity of 4,000. Corrections Corporation of America and Wackenhut were each running seven juvenile lock-ups. Corrections Services Corporation had opened six. Many other corporations were either already in the business of locking up children or were getting into this lucrative business (Friedmann 1998). At least 40 percent of American juvenile lock-ups held more children than they were equipped to house. In other words, "facility crowding affects a substantial proportion of youth in custody ... facilities reporting fewer standard beds than residents were significantly more likely than other facilities to say they transported youth to (hospital) emergency rooms because of injuries resulting from interpersonal conflict" (Sickmund 2002: 3). Congressional investigators reported that, in 2003, 15,000 American children who suffered from psychiatric disorders were incarcerated "because no mental health services were available" (Pear 2004: 1).

The character of children's prisons

Many training and industrial schools appear identical to older adult prisons, especially if they have been in use for a while. Many recently constructed training and industrial schools tend to, from the outside, resemble private boarding schools. Cottage-style housing is common in both settings. Newer maximum-security children's prisons look a lot like maximum-security adult prisons. It is difficult to tell from exterior architectural styles whether punishment or rehabilitation is emphasized within the confines of a children's prison. However, some aspects of punishment prevail almost everywhere in juvenile corrections. For example, children are locked up in all medium- and maximum-security facilities. Violence is commonplace in all long-term prisons. Corporal punishment of children is legal in most states. Almost all long-term juvenile prisons employ an arbitrary and inclusive style of discipline. Arbitrary and inclusive discipline gives prison workers control over almost all inmate activities and can result in abuses of authority (Rothman 1979; Mendel 2011).

Problems abound in children's prisons. In 1994, Rebound, Inc., lost a $150 million contract to operate a Maryland juvenile prison because too many children had escaped. In 1995, a Rebound, Inc., children's prison in Colorado was closed because investigators found "a consistent and disturbing pattern of violence, sexual abuse, clinical malpractice and administrative incompetence at every level of the program" (Friedmann 1998: 2). In 1997, Rebound, Inc., lost another contract to operate a Florida children's prison "due to inadequate performance" (2). In 1994, a child escaped from a Maryland prison operated by Youth Services International. That same year, at the same prison, a female employee was raped by an inmate. One year later, at the same prison, seven prisoners overpowered four employees, stole a bus and escaped, injuring several other children when the bus crashed. In 1997, Corrections Corporation of America lost a contract to operate a South Carolina juvenile prison after investigators from the governor's office concluded that guards had used excessive force with children. The guards were accused of hog-tying juveniles as well as denying them food, medical care and access to toilet facilities. In 1996, six children escaped from the prison. In 1997, another eight disappeared from the facility (2). In 2002, the head of an Arizona children's boot camp was arrested and charged with second-degree murder, related to an incident where a child in custody at the camp died from exposure. The head of the boot camp was also charged with eight counts of child abuse and aggravated assault. He was accused of holding a knife against the throat of another teenage inmate at the camp (Sterngold 2002).

The Swanson Correctional Center for Youth, called "Tallulah Prison" because it is located near Tallulah, Louisiana, is perhaps the most dangerous and cruelly operated children's lock-up in the United States. Just six weeks after it opened, in 1994, a federal judge declared a state of emergency at the prison "due to riots and an inability of staff to control or protect youth (Bervera 2004: 2). In 1995, Human Rights Watch asserted that Tallulah prison staff misused the facility's tiny, bare isolation cells and failed to provide adequate education and other programming for children held there. According to the U.S. Department of Justice, in the month of August 1996, 28 children held at Tallulah Prison were sent to hospitals suffering from serious injuries. In 1998, Louisiana became the first state to be sued by the federal government in an attempt to force improvements at Tallulah and other children's lock-ups. According to one parent whose child was held at Tallulah, "you can't imagine the things they do to children at Tallulah.... These children are abused by guards.... Guards beat on the children, sell them drugs and have sex with them ... the children are afraid to say anything about it" (2). In 1999, the state of Louisiana seized control of Tallulah from its private operators. In 2003, due to a grassroots political movement, legislation was passed in Louisiana that will force the eventual closing of the children's prison at Tallulah.

Severe problems are also found in children's prisons operated by government agencies. For example, in 1998, a 15-year-old girl hanged herself to death at the aging juvenile prison in Middletown, Connecticut. Escapes also regularly occurred at the prison. In reaction to the hanging, state authorities set about building a new children's prison, on a 34-acre campus about 2 miles from the old prison. The new prison opened in 2001 and was supposed to hold 240 boys and girls. Through May 2004, only boys had been confined at the new prison, leaving girl inmates without permanent quarters. Connecticut taxpayers eventually spent $57 million for the facility and another $130 million to operate it between August 2001 and June 30, 2004. The new facility ended up costing Connecticut taxpayers $774 per child per night to operate, around $282,000 per child per year. The exorbitant costs of the prison are likely the result of cronyism during the design and construction process. Taxpayers got little for their money. The prison has been described as "forbidding." Many of its cells lack windows and children, therefore, cannot be held in them. Other 7-by-10-foot cells have only tiny "slit" windows. State officials uncovered a pattern of overuse of mechanical restraints and seclusion at the new prison. They noted that "children are not always properly monitored," due to staffing shortages (Cowan 2004: 5). In 2002, a top administrator of the Maryland Department of Juvenile Justice resigned after it was discovered that he had twice understated the number of incidents involving guards assaulting youthful inmates in the state's lock-ups (Richissin 2002).

As we moved further into the new century, largely due to dwindling tax revenues, state legislatures moved to reduce the number of American children held in juvenile lock-ups. This resulted in a 47 percent decrease in the number of children held in residential placement facilities between 2000 and 2010 (Hockenberry et al., 2013: 8) However, in terms of the treatment of incarcerated children, little has changed. For example, facility overcrowding is still a fact of life for a substantial number of children held in long-term juvenile lock-ups (6–7). In any given year, at least 10 percent of young persons held in U.S. juvenile prisons report that they were the victim of one or more incidents of sexual abuse. Staff members and other juvenile inmates are the most frequent perpetrators (Mendel 2011:6). According to the Government Accountability Office (GAO), "youth maltreatment and death occurred in government and private residential facilities across the nation ... however, data limitations hinder efforts to quantify the full extent" (Brown 2008: 3). An independent study of police and state monitoring records of 100 juvenile residential treatment centers, conducted by the *Chicago Tribune* and Northwestern University's Medill Watchdog program, uncovered "hundreds of reports of rape, sexual abuse and physical assault" (D. Jackson et al., 2014).

Children held in adult lock-ups

Throughout the United States' history as a sovereign nation, children have been found "doing time" inside adult jails and prisons (Musick 1995: 267). Policy about this process ebbs and flows. Early in American history there were few, if any, restraints on jailing and imprisoning criminal-law violating children in the same facilities with adult inmates. In the 1830s, Illinois began restricting the numbers of children who could be sent to an adult prison. In 1855, Chicago opened a prison for juveniles, called a "reform school." In 1867, the Illinois State Reform School was opened. In 1876, the Women's Centennial Association opened a reform school for girls. With this change in policy, and with the building of three prisons for children, Chicago and Illinois created a new model for the legal incarceration of most children living in the United States. By the early 1900s, the "reform school movement," along with passage of new juvenile codes restricting the numbers of children who could be incarcerated with adults, spread throughout the United States.

In the late 1970s, the legal wall that had been built to keep criminal-law violating children away from adult offenders began to crumble. In 1977, Washington's children's code was changed, making it easier to transfer some children charged with criminal offenses to adult criminal court for trial and sentencing. In 1981, Colorado changed its law, making provisions for the routine transfer of repeat, and serious, child offenders to adult criminal courts for trial and disposition. Most state legislatures followed suit, revising their children's laws making it easier to routinely transfer children to adult criminal court jurisdiction (Musick 1995: 213–215). This movement gained momentum in the 1990s. Consequently, since 1992, 45 states passed new laws or revised old laws making it easier to transfer juvenile criminal law violators into adult courts for trial. However, in the late 1990s, children's law and policy, driven by a large-scale disappearance of tax revenue, leaned back towards keeping children out of U.S. adult prisons. Today, all 50 states have laws in place that allow juveniles to be routinely tried as adults. In 14 states, children of any age could be transferred to adult criminal court for trial. In some other states, children can be as young as 10, 12 or 13 and still be transferred to adult criminal court for trial (Equal Justice Initiative 2014: 1). However, most states have recently been less willing to pay for the incarceration of children alongside adult inmates.

Table 7.4 provides information about the number of children under age 18 held in adult state prisons, at the mid-year point, for four recent years. We see that, in 1985, 3,400 children were serving time in America's adult prisons. This number grew considerably by 1995. However, by 2000, the number of children held in adult prisons had shrunk and had shrunk even further by 2012.

Some states, like Maine, Kentucky and West Virginia hold very few, or no, persons under age 18 in their adult prisons. On the other hand, as Table 7.5 indicates, adult prisons in ten other states have held over two-thirds of all American children below 18 years of age who were incarcerated in U.S. adult prisons. Florida led the nation with almost 400 children incarcerated in adult lock-ups. Adult prisons in Connecticut held over 300 children.

What kind of child ends up in adult prisons? Nathaniel Brazill became a poster boy for those who advocate locking children up in adult prisons. On May 26, 2000, on the campus of his Florida middle school, the then 13-year-old boy, on the last day of the school year, in a fit of rage, shot and killed his favorite teacher. The child was feeling the emotional turmoil of an adolescent love-life that had gone sour. The child had just returned to school, after a suspension for throwing water balloons. The murdered teacher had prohibited Nathaniel from talking to two girls during class. In 2001, at

Table 7.4 Number of children under age 18 held in adult prisons, 1985–2012

	1985	1995	2000	2012
Number present	3,400	5,309	3,896	2,700

Source: Austin et al., 2000; Harrison & Karberg 2004: 5; Campaign for Youth Justice 2012: 4.

Table 7.5 States with largest numbers of children under age 18 held in adult prisons, midyear, 2009

State	Number of children in adult prison
Florida	393
Connecticut	332
North Carolina	215
New York	190
Arizona	157
Texas	156
Michigan	132
Alabama	118
Nevada	118
Illinois	106

Source: Griffin et al. 2011: 25.

the discretion of a prosecuting attorney, Nathaniel was tried as an adult. He was found guilty of second-degree murder and was sentenced to a 28-year prison term, without the possibility of parole or time off for good behavior. At his trial, the young defendant testified that he had only intended to scare the victim, that the gun had fired accidentally (Riddle 2001). Nathaniel will be 42 when he is released from prison.

Lionel Tate is another poster boy for those who advocate putting children in adult prisons. When he was 12, the Florida child killed a 6-year-old girl. Lionel, at the discretion of a prosecuting attorney, was charged as an adult with murder. At the age of 14, he was tried, convicted and sentenced to life inside a Florida prison. In December 2003, Lionel Tate's murder conviction was overturned by an appellate court, because the trial court judge had failed to order a psychiatric examination of Lionel, in order to determine whether or not he was competent enough to be tried. In 2004, Lionel Tate was released from prison (Waters 2004).

Adult prisons are dangerous and debilitating places for children to do time. When compared to juvenile prisons, according to Physicians for Human Rights, children in adult lock-ups are "five times more likely to be sexually assaulted … twice as likely to be beaten by staff … 50 percent more likely to be attacked with a weapon … eight times as likely to commit suicide" (Physicians for Human Rights 2004a: 1; see also Schiraldi & Zeidenberg 1997 and Tesfaye 2015). There is no evidence indicating that incarcerating children in adult prison deters crime. Quite the opposite, children held in adult prisons are likely to commit additional crimes after their release.

Children and the American death penalty

The United States was a world leader in executing persons who were juveniles when they committed capital crimes. In fact, according to Physicians for Human Rights, "in the past 10 years, the United States has executed more juveniles than the rest of the world combined" (2004b: 1). This practice started in 1642 when Thomas Graunger, a child found guilty in Plymouth Colony, Massachusetts, of bestiality, was executed. Between 1642 and 1973, 344 Americans who were juveniles when they committed capital crimes were executed. Between 1973 and 2003, 22 juveniles were executed in the United States. Almost two-thirds of those executions were carried out in Texas (Streib 2004; Coordinating Council on Juvenile Justice and Delinquency Prevention 2000). At the beginning of the twenty-first century, 19 states still permitted the execution of persons who were under age 18 when they committed a capital crime. In 2004, 81 Americans were sitting on prison death rows in 13 states, awaiting execution for crimes they committed when they were juveniles (Physicians for Human Rights 2004b; see also Streib 2004). In 2005, in *Roper v. Simmons*, the U.S. Supreme Court ended the practice of executing persons for crimes they committed when they were children.

Almost all countries have ratified the United Nations Convention, Article 37a, stating that "neither capital punishment nor life imprisonment without possibility of release shall be imposed for offenses committed by persons below eighteen years of age" (quoted in American Academy of Child & Adolescent Psychiatry 2000: 1). Iran and the Congo are the only remaining countries still executing persons who committed capital crimes when they were under age 18 (Physicians for Human Rights 2004b). Proponents of executing persons for crimes they committed when they were juveniles argue that the practice deters crime and that murderers, regardless of their age at the time of the offense, deserve to lose their lives. Psychiatrists who oppose this practice maintain that "adolescents are cognitively and emotionally less mature than adults. They are less able than adults to consider the consequences of their behavior, they are easily swayed by peers, and they may show poor judgement" (1). Lawyers who oppose this practice argue that children are less able than adults to help their defense lawyers during the murder trial and therefore are more likely than adult defendants to be convicted of a capital offense. Evidence shows that many persons who have been executed, or who are sitting on death row awaiting execution for crimes they committed when they were children, suffer from head injuries, from neuropsychological and/or psychotic disorders. Many condemned children have IQs below 90 and cannot read. Most have been sexually and psychologically abused during their childhoods. Others were sodomized (Coordinating Council on Juvenile Justice and Delinquency Prevention 2000: 5).

Elderly inmates

America's prison population is growing old, quickly (Aday 2003; Rudolph 2012). According to Jonathan Turley, founder of an early advocacy group for older inmates and professor of law at Washington University, "there is a crisis in the making. The national prison population is graying at an unprecedented rate, and the prison system is simply not prepared to deal with gerontological disease and geriatric care" (quoted in Schreiber 1999: 2). We have reached a point in this crisis where in excess of $16 billion is spent, on an annual basis, to incarcerate elderly inmates in U.S. state and federal prisons (Rudolph 2012: 1). A number of factors contribute to the aging of inmates in the United States, such as "three-strikes laws," longer mandatory sentences meted out by criminal courts, increases in sex offenses and murders committed by older Americans and an influx of "baby boomers" into prisons.

Prison inmates, because age-related health problems occur earlier in life for them, are considered "old" when they reach 50 or 55 (Chettiar et al., 2012: i; Aday 2003; Morton 1992; Schreiber 1999; Maker 2001). Inmates over the age of 50 suffer from the same assortment of cumulative and catastrophic illnesses that plague all Americans, including cancers, blocked blood vessels, heart disease, Alzheimer's disease, lung ailments and arthritis. Americans over 50 use more prescription drugs than younger persons. The elderly spend twice as much time in medical facilities and incur three times the healthcare costs that younger Americans do (Morton 1992). The cost of clearing a blocked blood vessel is around $4,500 per vessel, per attempt. The cost of heart bypass surgery can easily exceed $150,000 (Associated Press 2004; Morton 1992). State departments of corrections currently spent between $20,000 and $30,000 per year to house reasonably healthy, younger inmates. The costs of caring for an inmate over 60 years of age can average $70,000 annually. A seriously ill older inmate can cost taxpayers as much as $200,000 per year to keep in custody (Aday 2003; Prison Talk 2002). These costs will increase considerably in future years.

Growth in the elderly inmate population

In 1974, there were about 11,500 inmates over the age of 50 in U.S. state and federal prisons, representing 5 percent of the total inmate population (U.S. Department of Justice 1977). In 1992, the number of American inmates over the age of 50 had increased to around 60,000. By 2002, the prison system housed over 120,000 state and federal inmates over 50 years of age, representing almost 9 percent of the total inmate population (Associated Press 2004; Harrison & Beck 2003). By 2012, inmates over 55 years of age made up approximately 17 percent of the state and federal prison population. If current practices continue, by 2030, one in three inmates (about 400,000) in the United States will likely be more than 55 years old (Chettiar et al., 2012: i; Maker 2001).

California's 33 prisons host around 6,000 inmates over 55 years of age, three times the number held in 1990. The rapid increase in elderly California prisoners is largely a result of the state's frequent use of its "three strikes and you're out" law, passed in 1994, a law supported by the governor. Between 1994 and mid-2001, California criminal courts sentenced 6,721 persons to lifetime prison terms without parole by invoking the "three-strikes" law, and another 43,800 persons to long prison terms by invoking the state's "two-strikes" provision (King & Mauer 2001). Unless legal changes occur, in 20 years, California prisons will host as many as 50,000 elderly inmates. This situation, described as "a ticking time bomb," if allowed to happen, will cost California taxpayers $4 billion per year, approximately what the entire state prison system costs to operate as we entered the twenty-first century (Thompson 2004a).

According to the California Legislative Analyst's Office, it costs tax-payers two to three times more to care for elderly inmates than it does to care for younger ones (McMahon 2003). In 2001, California spent almost $700 million for prisoner medical services, although California Department of Corrections officials do not know how much of the total was spent on elderly inmates. According to a 2002 report, one geriatric inmate in California received medical care for four separate cancers and a stroke and, furthermore, consumed medication costing $1,800 per month. Elderly California inmates are dispersed throughout the state's 33 prisons and are mixed into the general prison population. A proposed 1999 law that would have provided for the release of some inmates over the age of 60 into nursing homes and home detention arrangements was defeated in the Assembly, even though research indicates that men over the age of 55, when paroled, are highly unlikely to return to prison (Associated Press 2002a). In 2010, there were about 13,600 inmates over the age of 55 in California prisons. The number of elderly California inmates has been doubling every 10 years. This situation, if allowed to happen, will cost California taxpayers $4 billion per year, approximately what the entire state prison system costs to operate as we entered the twenty-first century (Legislative Analyst's Office, 2010: 1–2).

In Florida, as of mid-2001, the oldest inmate was 89 years old. In 1997, Florida prisons held 4,176 inmates over the age of 50. By 2001, the number of elderly inmates held in Florida prisons had grown to 6,172. In 2001, Florida prisons held 7,636 elderly inmates, 3,194 age 50 to 54; 1,526 age 55 to 59; 771 age 60 to 64; 403 age 65 to 69; and 278 age 70 and over, an increase of 12 percent over the number of elderly inmates held in 2000 (Florida Department of Corrections 2004; McMahon 2003). The Florida Department of Corrections, in cooperation with the Florida Department of Elder Affairs, operates two facilities for elderly male inmates and one facility for elderly female inmates, staffed by younger inmates, that provide special services and special diets (Morton 1992). In 2000, Florida opened a work camp, adjacent to the State Hospital in Chattahoochee, with 378 beds, mostly occupied by "able-bodied" inmates over age 50.

Almost 10 percent of inmates confined to prisons operated by the Tennessee Department of Correction are age 50 and over. The oldest inmate in the Tennessee prison system is 83. About 50 percent of the elderly Tennessee inmates are housed at the Deberry Special Needs Facility or a boot camp in Wayne County for "able-bodied" seniors. The other 50 percent of elderly Tennessee inmates are dispersed among the inmate populations at 13 other prisons (Tennessee Department of Correction 2002). Elderly Tennessee inmates suffering from disabilities, disease and illness, like many elderly inmates throughout the prison system, get special help with grooming; require security-approved aids like canes, walkers, wheelchairs, oxygen tanks, toilet safety rails, pull-up bars for beds and diapers; must receive medical treatment and medication; and need help dying. Elderly Tennessee inmates, like elderly inmates everywhere, suffer from a wide range of illnesses, disease and disabilities, including heart attacks and strokes, hypertension, high cholesterol, amputation, Parkinson's disease, Alzheimer's disease, prostate cancer, lung cancer, menopause, dementia, infectious hepatitis and AIDS. Tennessee taxpayers and Department of Correction officials are facing a real "senior inmate care crisis" in the years ahead.

It is noteworthy that the U.S. federal prison system has identified elderly inmates as the fastest growing segment of their population. Elderly federal inmates increased from 24,857 in 2009 to 30,962 in 2013, an increase of 25 percent. It is estimated that the Federal Bureau of Prisons spent approximately $881 million to incarcerate elderly inmates in 2013, comprising 19 percent of its total budget (Office of the Inspector General, U.S. Department of Justice 2015: i).

Problems faced by elderly inmates and their keepers

Elderly inmates, when mixed into the general population of a prison, often fear for their safety, feeling vulnerable to attack by younger convicts (Bowers 1996; Corwin 2001). Senior citizen inmates run the risk of being exploited by younger prisoners. The first author, early in his career, worked at the maximum-security Washington State Prison, in Walla Walla, a violent and highly dangerous place. One of his lasting memories of Walla Walla is seeing small groupings of old men, often with canes, walking together in small groups around the massive exercise yard where violent, inmate-against-inmate attacks regularly occurred. The old men looked so frail, so vulnerable against the backdrop of one of America's most violent prison yards. Implements seniors often need in order to function – canes, bed rails, prosthetics, hand bars and wheelchairs, for example – are usually seen by prison personnel as posing security risks. Elderly inmates left in a general prison population often need help with brushing their teeth, shaving and pushing their wheelchairs to the cafeteria

(Chettiar et al., 2012; Aday 2003). Such help is all too often not available (Fletcher 2000).

It is possible that in the near future, every prison system in the United States will operate at least one nursing home or assisted living facility for elderly prisoners (Aday 2003). A 1991 survey of state prison systems and the federal prison system revealed that 14 prison systems operated special units for elderly men and 4 systems operated special units for elderly women. Twenty-two prison systems reported having some form of specialized programs for elderly inmates (Morton 1992). A 2000 survey of 46 prison systems identified 16 that operate separate facilities for elderly inmates. Many prison systems report having specialized programs for older inmates that are operated within the confines of its regular prisons. Oklahoma, for example, in order to prevent the exploitation of elderly inmates, assigns them to single-person cells (McMahon 2003). Twelve prison systems, including the Federal Bureau of Prisons, operate formal hospice programs for dying inmates. Other prison systems are developing formal hospice programs (Aday 2003; LIS, Inc., 1998).

Sex offender, 74-year-old Rudy Suazo died of a stomach cancer that ate away at his shrinking body in a Colorado prison hospice. The Colorado facility, located inside the Territorial Correctional Facility in Canon City, was the first state-certified prison hospice in the United States. Inmates are allowed to move into the Colorado prison hospice if they are expected to die within 6 months and if they are willing to sign a "do not resuscitate" agreement. Between 1995 and 2002, 95 inmates died there. Prison hospice care inmates received more pain-killing medication than would be allowed for an inmate in the general prison population. They got to watch television, and some were frequently visited by relatives (Sanchez 2002).

Elderly female inmates

Because they are a small minority of the totality of prisoners, representing about 6 percent of all state and federal elderly inmates, elderly female inmates are largely ignored. However, their numbers are growing (Aday & Krabill 2011). The presence of elderly inmates in women's prison systems is beginning to cause significant problems for prison officials and taxpayers. In California, for example, in 2010, there were 532 women age 55 or older locked up in three prisons, the California Institution for Women, Valley State Prison for Women and Central California Women's Prison. In 2030, assuming that women age 50 and older will represent about 10 percent of California's total elderly inmate population, there will be approximately 3,300 elderly women doing time in California prisons (Sundaram 2009: 2). Eighty-eight-year-old Helen Loheac, at the time the oldest woman in the

California prison system, serves as an example of just how costly incarcerating the elderly can get. Unable to clearly see and hear, besieged by kidney failure and Alzheimer's disease, Helen passed away in early 2009 in a hospital near her prison. She was shackled at the waist and ankles. To the end, she was guarded by two uniformed correctional officers. In all, before her passing, Helen was costing the California prison system about $250,000 per year to maintain. It is notable that, just a few months before her death, Helen, serving a prison term for "conspiring to murder," had been deemed by a parole board as too dangerous to release via "compassionate parole" (1–2). Prison officials and social scientists have only recently begun to examine the needs of, and special problems posed by, growing numbers of elderly female inmates (Caldwell et al., 2001).

In terms of problems, risks and fears, almost all that has already been written about elderly inmates applies to women as well as men. Similarly, when considering the healthcare needs of elderly female inmates, they will suffer from the same array of chronic and catastrophic illnesses and diseases that have already been enumerated in this chapter. For example, in New York, at the Bedford Hills Correctional Facility, 74-old Martha Weatherspoon hobbles and sits behind bars and razor wire, serving out a 20-year-to-life sentence for drug dealing. Weatherspoon, imprisoned at the age of 60, has had knee replacement surgery and suffers from a chronic foot condition. She is the type of inmate who can cost taxpayers huge sums of money in medical care. And her incarceration has done nothing to reduce the flow of illicit drugs in and around her former Syracuse apartment complex (Purdy 2002). However, female elderly inmates will also require somewhat different medical services as they experience extreme weight gain; severe depression; menopause; osteoporosis; breast, cervical and uterine cancer; and as they undergo hysterectomies (Caldwell et al., 2001; Morton 1993; Genders & Player 1990).

What should be done?

If for no other reason than cost containment, special prisons for elderly inmates will be built in increasing numbers. For the same reason, special programs within regular prisons will be developed everywhere in American society where seniors are locked up. Therefore, as American inmates gray, the cost of operating a massive national prison system will increase at unprecedented rates. However, the debate is growing about what to do with elderly inmates. On the one side, many argue that the best thing to do in order to head off the looming financial crisis incarcerated elders will precipitate is to release all nonviolent older inmates who pose no ongoing threat to society. This argument is supported by ample evidence that paroled seniors rarely recidivate (Chettiar et al., 2012: 12; Sundaram 2009: 2).

On the same side, others argue that seriously ill older inmates, especially those in the process of dying, should be released into the custody of their families, where that is possible, or into nursing homes and hospices outside of the prison system. On the other side, some victim's advocates and "tough-on-crime" politicians declare that inmates, regardless of their age or physical condition, were put into prison for punishment and that they should stay there for the longest amount of time possible. So far, for the most part, the pro-punishment side has prevailed.

Summary

Somewhat hidden behind the looming image of a typical prison in the United States – a big house, a warehouse, full of violent, drug-dealing men – we find growing numbers of women, children and seniors doing time. In fact, female, child and graying inmates are among the fastest-growing segments of modern American imprisonment. If treated humanely, if given a fair chance at rehabilitation, women, children and senior inmates require specialized treatment that cannot be provided in a warehouse prison.

It is inhumane to separate women from their children while mom is doing time. Yet it would be inhumane, and expensive, to put children in women's prisons so that families could continue living together. Far too many women who give birth while incarcerated in a U.S. prison, are treated harshly, if not brutally. Women who work in U.S. prisons as well as female inmates, deserve respectful treatment and effective protection from sexual harassment and violation. We Americans are now facing the dilemma of massing refugee families along our Southern border. Many of the refugees who make it over the border have their spouses and children with them. As prisons have been quickly built to accommodate refugees who are apprehended, thousands of Latin families find themselves serving time in a new type of American prison. Uncounted numbers of families have been broken up as this mass arrest and incarceration takes place. Uncounted numbers of refugee women and their children are being held by private contractors while U.S. officials decide what to do with them. These are the same private contractors the U.S. Inspector General and the U.S. Attorney General recently deemed unworthy to house citizen convicts who are under the jurisdiction of a U.S. federal court.

Over the past 15 years or so, there has been a strong push to get most children out of U.S. prisons. This push has met with some recent success. However, the numerical decline, which appears in statistical tables, appears to have been done with the use of smoke and mirrors. A significant number of child law violators who might have been sentenced to a juvenile prison, are now under new sentencing reforms, sent to an adult prison, thus shrinking the numbers of children counted as incarcerated in juvenile prisons. A change in the way federal research agencies define a children's lock-up made about 30 percent of the children's "residential facilities" in the United States go away, only for the purpose of record-keeping. By far, the most important risk we take by incarcerating masses of children is in how those children will think about themselves, and their captors, later in life. Children who find themselves imprisoned are being taught that they are powerless and worthless. Locked-up children are barraged by hurtful messages about their misdeeds and about faults in their make-up. Negative labels are attached to incarcerated children. Some children will resist the messages and labels. All-too-many imprisoned children will accept or absorb the negative labels. Such children become entrenched in the ways of crime and disrespect. In increasing numbers, such children form the core of American gang culture.

Senior inmates are at great risk, especially if mixed into the general population of a typical American warehouse prison. Old folks are "easy pickins" for predatory inmates. Their property will be stolen. They will be bullied. The senior author, when much younger, worked in a dangerous warehouse prison, located in the western part of the United States. He remembers a bunch of "old guys" who used to huddle together, as they walked around the huge, dangerous exercise yard used by all inmates. In numbers, the old inmates gained a bit of temporary strength in an otherwise hostile and dangerous exercise yard. One can only imagine what forms of oppression awaited those old men as they broke up and headed back to their cellblocks, back to their cells, often shared with younger inmates, back to the cellblock showers, shared by all inmates, in groups. Simply put, as inmates get older, their ailments and medical bills pile up. The graying of the U.S. inmate population is already taxing the finances of corrections systems throughout the country. For the next 20 to 25 years, problems related to locking up seniors are likely to grow more serious and costly.

Prison by-products – violence and disease

Introduction

Prisons are dangerous, forboding places where humans are locked up and are forced to behave in ways they would not if they were free. Prison by-products, namely rape, other forms of prison violence and disease, help to accomplish the societal goal of punishing criminals by making the convict's life a living hell. However, prison by-products also make another societal goal, that of rehabilitating offenders, almost impossible for many, if not most inmates. Prison by-products make the work of honest, humane corrections officers far more difficult. Prison by-products help twist and corrupt less savory corrections workers. Endemic rape, gratuitous violence and dreaded disease make American prisons breeding grounds, places where mental and physical illness spread and, eventually, flow back into American communities as inmates are released and come home.

Prison rape

Even though it is a basic human function and need, sexual activity in prison is prohibited for most inmates. Policymakers, prison officials, corrections officers and criminologists, for the most part, act as if sex in prison does not exist. Except for the few who are allowed conjugal visits, prison inmates are prohibited from having sexual relationships. Even though conjugal visitation programs promote family stability and tend to reduce violence among inmates, they are rare in American prisons. And, in recent years, a number of prison systems have eliminated their conjugal visitation programs (Hensley 2002a; see also Smith 2006). Some inmates get around this dilemma by having sexual affairs with corrections workers. For example, Rierden writes about Katie, an inmate inside a women's prison, who "started up a love affair with the electronics instructor at the prison school. Word got out ... and the instructor was fired" (1997: 28). Susan Smith, who is serving a life sentence in a South Carolina prison for drowning her two sons, reportedly had sex four times with a 50-year-old guard. The guard was suspended (Daily Camera 2000: 13A).

For the vast majority of inmates who either choose not to have illicit sexual contact with corrections workers or who have no opportunity to do so, the options are limited. They can abstain. Or they can masturbate. In fact, masturbation is a common practice in both men's and women's prisons. However, masturbation is stigmatized in American society. Consequently, many inmates choosing masturbation are left with guilt feelings and with the need to conceal their behavior from other inmates as well as from correctional officers (McGaughey & Tewksbury 2002).

Inmates can have consensual homosexual relations, usually with other inmates. This option is relatively easy to achieve. While formally prohibited, many corrections workers tolerate prison homosexuality (Koscheski et al., 2002). However, in prisons, especially men's prisons, homosexual contact is generally stigmatized and, thus, comes only with significant costs. Heterosexual inmates, who choose to practice consensual, situational homosexuality while in prison, must deal with the identity conflict that can arise. They must conceal their situational homosexual behavior from most other inmates and from corrections workers. Once released from prison, they must pretend that it never happened. For this, and for many other reasons, most inmates and ex-convicts refuse to talk about sex in prison. The conventional wisdom among social scientists is that female inmates adapt somewhat better than male inmates to consensual, situational homosexual behavior (Rierden 1997; Hensley 2002b).

Prison rape

Another sexual option for aggressively violent inmates is coerced homosexual contact, in its most extreme form commonly called "prison rape." Rape is that point in prison life where sex and violence meet. Largely because there is no standard definition of rape, it is one of the most difficult aspects of prison life to study and to write about. We define prison rape herein as "sexual intercourse with a human against his or her will." The more benign concept, namely "forced sexual contact," in prison ranges from "genital fondling and failed attempts at intercourse" to "completed rapes ... defined ... as forced oral, anal, or vaginal intercourse" (Struckman-Johnson & Struckman-Johnson 2000: 379).

The existence of widespread prison rape has been either denied or downplayed by most American prison officials (Mariner 2003; Hensley & Tewksbury 2005). Correctional officers and inmates are far more likely than prison officials to acknowledge that rape is a common fact of prison life (Dumond & Dumond 2002; Mariner 2003). Many prison wardens, apparently, aren't around when sex occurs in their prisons. A study using data gathered from anonymous surveys of 226 male and female prison wardens shows that "wardens generally believe sexual activities, consensual and coercive, are relatively rare in their institutions" (Hensley & Tewksbury 2005: 186). Ironically, according to recent U.S. case law, the less wardens know about their prisons, and about what goes on inside them, the less risk they take of legal liability if laws are broken. Prison rape occurs in men's prisons as well as women's prisons, although research suggests that it is more common among men (Beck & Johnson 2012: 21; Kunselman et al., 2002). It is estimated that "more than 200,000 men are raped behind bars each year" (Harris 2013; Reese 2012).

Until recently, there was no existing body of data that reveals the extent of rape in America's prisons. In one study of seven U.S. men's prisons, using anonymous, written surveys of inmates and security staff, researchers found "that 21% of the inmates had experienced at least one episode of pressured or forced sexual contact since incarceration.... 16% reported that an incident had occurred in their current facility. At least 7% of the sample had been raped in their current facility" (Struckman-Johnson & Struckman-Johnson 2000: 379). It is possible that more than 140,000 male inmates have been anally raped (Mariner 2001). According to the United States Congress, "experts have conservatively estimated that at least 13 percent of the inmates in the United States have been sexually assaulted in prison. Many inmates have suffered repeated assaults. Under this estimate, nearly 200,000 inmates now incarcerated have been or will be the victims of prison rape. The total number of inmates who have been sexually assaulted in the past 20 years likely exceeds 1,000,000" (quoted in Carnell 2003: 2).

Like elsewhere in society, much, possibly most, prison rape goes unreported: "Only a small minority of victims of rape or other sexual abuse in prison ever report it to the authorities. Indeed, many victims – cowed into silence by shame, embarrassment and fear – do not even tell their family or friends of the experience" (quoted in Carnell 2003: 130–131). Male rape is a taboo subject. Male inmates fail to report having been raped because they fear that their sense of masculinity will be taken from them by other males. They fear that other male inmates will perceive them as weak, defenseless and, therefore, easy prey for sexual aggression. Rapes go unreported because victims fear reprisal from other inmates if they are caught snitching. Rapes go unreported because victims fear revenge rapes and beatings if perpetrators catch them snitching. Rapes go unreported because victims sense that correctional officers and administrators are indifferent towards such offenses and, thus, they will receive no support and protection (Mariner 2001; Dumond & Dumond 2002). According to the United States Congress, "prison rape often goes unreported, and inmate victims often receive inadequate treatment for the severe physical and psychological effects of sexual assault – if they receive treatment at all.... Most prison staff are not adequately trained or prepared to prevent, report, or treat inmate sexual assaults" (quoted in Carnell 2003: 3).

The senior author is reminded of two prison rape victims he worked with. The first victim, though slight in physical stature, had survived his long prison term by using his wits and social skills to manipulate others, but in likable ways. This man proved to be a valuable asset, as I went about re-investigating an 11-year-old murder that had occurred in his prison. In the midst of one of our many interviews, while talking in general terms about prison rape, he shared with me that he had been raped. I was stunned, since inmates almost never want to talk about prison sex, let alone prison rape. I was also overwhelmed with compassion for this man who, as a young inmate, experienced intense, embarrassing trauma and who, as a man in his 40s still carried the pain of such violation in his soul. The second victim was a young man still in his 20s. He had been out of prison for about 2 weeks when I met him. This young man was neither large nor muscular. This young man went into prison carrying with him mental health problems. In prison, his mental health issues were treated with prescription drugs that rendered him "unable to raise my arms." In this condition, the young man found himself confined to a prison mental health unit that also hosted a violent sexual predator. When an opportunity arose, the young man was raped by the predator. When I met the young man, though released from prison, his rectum was still bleeding.

Prison rape can be used by corrections officers as a disciplinary tactic. For example, four California Department of Corrections officers indicted by a Kings County Grand Jury were charged with conspiracy to carry out a sodomy and with preparing false reports. These indictments were based upon evidence provided by the state attorney general's office alleging planned rapes and cover-ups at the Corcoran State Prison. Charges against the guards were made possible when a former corrections officer stepped forward, breaking Corcoran's code of silence, and described to a Los Angeles Times reporter how guards ordered the transfer of a troublesome young inmate into a cell occupied by a much larger inmate, nicknamed the "Booty Bandit," knowing that the "Bandit" would probably rape his prey. During investigation of this crime, evidence emerged suggesting that at least one other troublesome inmate had been placed by guards in the "Booty Bandit's" cell as an unofficial punishment for misbehavior (Arax & Gladstone 2004: 1; see also CBS News 2001; Dickey 2002). The four guards were eventually acquitted. In Texas, the American Civil Liberties Union filed suit in federal court on behalf of a gay inmate, alleging that "he was raped hundreds of times and forced to become a 'sex slave' for vicious prison gangs" while "correction officials winked and nodded as violent prisoners preyed on him over an 18-month period" (Dowdy 2002: 1). In Colorado, an inmate was paid a $70,000 settlement when the Department of Corrections failed to protect him from a known prison rapist. The inmate victim was subsequently transferred to a prison "where 76 percent of the population are sex offenders" (Mitchell 2009: 1B). In another Colorado case, ten female inmates filed a lawsuit in federal court alleging "repeated acts of sex abuse by male corrections officers" at two prisons (Ingold 2011: 11A) Some believe that many corrections officers and administrators allow gang-related rape as a "trade-off," in exchange for gang members abiding by other important prison rules.

Groth, Burgess and Holmstrom report that prison rapists use three main techniques in preying on victims: entrapment, intimidation and force (1977; see also Mariner 2001). *Entrapment* involves a complicated scheme whereby a rapist has accomplices stage aggression towards a victim. The rapist steps in and defends the victim, initiating a friendship. This might occur several times. The victim comes to rely on the rapist for protection and, in return, begins to do favors for the rapist. Gradually, the rapist begins to make sexual demands, and the victim reluctantly and helplessly agrees. Once the victim is entrapped in this manner, the rapist owns him. The victim will be required to perform sexual and other chores for the rapist. The rapist can rent, lease or sell the victim, if he wishes to do so. At this point, the victim has become a "prison slave" (Dumond & Dumond 2002). Entrapment can come in the form of favors done by the rapist for the victim, or gifts given to the victim by the rapist. The victim will be given cigarettes, drugs, liquor or canteen items. After a period of gift giving or favor doing, the rapist will inform the victim that he must repay his debts by performing sexual acts. *Intimidation* is a far more straightforward technique. A rapist might simply approach a victim and tell him "fight, run or fuck," leaving the victim with a set of difficult choices to make. Or, a rapist might approach a victim and tell him "either you suck my cock, or my boys over there will stab you," pointing towards a group of mean-looking nearby inmates. Rape by *force* could begin with a knife being placed next to a victim's throat while he lay in his cell bunk, or being jumped by a gang of men while taking a shower. Gang rape is particularly violent and frequently has an ethnic conflict dimension (Kunselman et al., 2002). Unfortunately, cries for help in a prison often go unheeded (Mariner 2001).

Prison rape is disastrous. For the victim, it leaves life-long emotional and physical damage. Victims of prison rape can suffer from

> vaginal or rectal bleeding, soreness and bruising (and much worse in the case of violent attacks), insomnia, nausea, shock, disbelief, withdrawal, anger, shame, guilt, and humiliation. Long term consequences may include post traumatic stress disorder, rape trauma syndrome, ongoing fear, nightmares, flashbacks, self-hatred, substance abuse, anxiety, depression, and suicide.
>
> (Stop Prisoner Rape 2004a: 1)

Prisoner rape spreads disease, both inside the prison and back into American communities, as infected inmates return and share their afflictions with others (Stop Prisoner Rape 2004b). According to the United States Congress, "prison rape endangers the public safety by making brutalized inmates more likely to commit crimes when they are released – as 600,000 inmates are each year" (quoted in Carnell 2003: 3). For the perpetrator, rape becomes the most perverse of all forms of prison sex, twisting the personality and rendering him or her unable to engage in healthy sexual relationships once released from prison.

Rapists are frequently older than their victims but younger than the general prison population. Rapists usually go to prison at a young age and are quite familiar with their surroundings (Chonco 1989). Rapists sometimes have a menacing look and belong to violent gangs. Prison rape victims come in many forms. For example, the authors recently worked on a capital murder case involving a big, tough member of a white supremacist gang. He was known in prison as a particularly violent inmate who always had access to weapons and the support of his fellow gang members. He was known in prison as a quick-tempered murderer. We knew him during our work on his murder trial as a highly dangerous man diagnosed with paranoid schizophrenia. In spite of his formidable physical appearance, in spite of his penchant for violence, in spite of his connections, he was raped by three other inmates, after returning to his cell from a shower. However, the most likely prison rape victims usually possess some combination of the following characteristics: they are young, frail, slim or small. Victims often have "feminine" qualities like long hair, a high voice or perhaps a sway to their walk. They may be homosexual. They may be unable, or unwilling, to fight. They may be first-time offenders, possibly convicted of sexually violating a child or of a property or drug crime. In short, potential victims are seen by rapists as weak and unable to defend themselves (Mariner 2001). According to the United States Congress, "young first-time offenders are at increased risk of sexual victimization. Juveniles are 5 times more likely to be sexually assaulted in adult rather than juvenile facilities – often within the first 48 hours of incarceration" (quoted in Carnell 2003: 3).

Sykes and Messinger (1960) developed a typology of inmates that focuses on the sexual statuses they occupy. *Wolves* are predators who rape and who provide protection for weak inmates in exchange for sexual and other services. *Punks* are heterosexual inmates who are raped, usually by wolves and must, therefore, function as passive homosexual objects. If "owned" by a wolf, a punk must do the bidding of his master. A punk can be rented, leased or loaned out as a sexual object. A punk can be lost to another in a card game. *Fags* are homosexual inmates who engage in voluntary homosexual activity within the walls of the prison, sometimes functioning as prostitutes. Although the labels will change from prison to prison, this typology was created some time ago by inmates and is still used.

In a women's prison, the typology is somewhat different. Some *homosexual couples* form. Homosexual couples are in love with each other and form lasting relationships. Most female inmates are *situational homosexuals* who engage in sex with other women while behind bars but who revert to heterosexual relationships when released. Some female inmates are *studs*, promiscuous and aggressive, sometimes forcing others to engage in sex against their will (Rierden 1997). *Stud, bitch* or *pimp* are labels used to denote "masculine" female inmates. *Fox, femme* or *broad* are labels attached to more "feminine" females. Female prostitutes are called *tricks* or *chippies* (Giallambardo 1966). In broader American society, ideas and practices related to gender and sexuality are changing. Rigid gender stereotypes, like male/female and heterosexual/homosexual, are being replaced with more "gender fluid" nuances. However, ironically, American prisons are bastions of traditionalism. It will be some time before ideas and practices based upon "gender fluidity" filter into U.S. prisons, especially prisons housing men.

Words of inmates tell the prison rape story far better than the writings of academics, who might occasionally work in prisons, but who get to go home at night and to shower alone. For example, S.M., at the age of 18, entered prison. The sexual harassment started immediately, but he held out for 3 years. Finally, "two of them held me down while the other raped me.... I stayed in my cell all day, skipped lunch. I didn't say anything to my cellmate about it. I was so embarrassed I had it happen to myself" (quoted in Mariner 2001: 19). That event opened the flood gates. S.M. was forced to pay for protection. S.M. was raped again, this time by a violent cellmate. He reported the assaults to correctional officers but received little help. He began violating prison rules in order to be placed in isolation, thereby avoiding his assailants. But S.M. was eventually placed, in spite of his pleas, back into living quarters with rapists. S.M. eventually ended up in a psychiatric unit after attempting suicide.

C.R. went into a Texas prison when he was 19. He was beaten and raped by six Texas Syndicate gang members. Two years later, he was repeatedly beaten by members of the Mexican Mafia. The Mexican Mafia enslaved C.R. and sold him to African American inmates for use as a sexual object. He was again beaten and raped. Later, a cellmate beat C.R. for refusing to engage in sex with him. After a move to another section of the prison, C.R. was again raped and forced to pay for protection. C.R. received no effective help from his custodians, but he did contract HIV (23).

Abating prison rape

In the landmark *Farmer v. Brennan* case, the United States Supreme Court declared that prison employees who allow prison rape are violating the Eighth Amendment to the U.S. Constitution that prohibits "cruel and unusual punishment" (1994). In *Farmer v. Brennan*, the Supreme Court affirmed that "prison officials have a duty under the Eighth Amendment to provide humane conditions of confinement. They must ensure that inmates have adequate food, clothing, shelter, and medical care, and must protect inmates from violence at the hands of other prisoners." Unfortunately, this strong declaration was rendered almost useless, in terms of protecting inmate victims, when the Supreme Court added the following: "a constitutional violation occurs only where the deprivation alleged is, objectively, 'sufficiently serious,' ... and the official has acted with 'deliberate indifference' to inmate health or safety." In other words, as long as prison employees and officials do not act with "deliberate indifference," prison rape can continue. This part of the court ruling can be interpreted to mean that the less prison officials know, or admit that they know, about prison rape, the less likely that they can be held accountable for its aftermath. In essence, the 1994 *Farmer v. Brennan* decision creates a dynamic whereby prison employees and officials gain insulation from legal culpability by knowing as little as possible about prison rape, a regrettable dynamic if the primary goal is protecting inmates from "cruel and unusual punishment."

Largely in response to growing media coverage of prison rape issues and cases, the U.S. House of Representatives and the U.S. Senate unanimously passed the Prison Rape Elimination Act of 2003 (PREA). The Act creates, within the Department of Justice, a Review Panel on Prison Rape. PREA's purpose was "to provide for the analysis of the incidence and effects of prison rape in federal, state, and local institutions and to provide information, resources, recommendations and funding to protect individuals from prison rape" (National PREA Resource Center 2013). The National Prison Rape Elimination Commission was created. A by-product of the Commission's efforts is the Second Chance Act, passed by Congress in 2008: "The Act provides grant money to programs that assist in helping released inmates readjust to society and find a way to be productive, healthy members of their communities.... Congress has decreased the allocations to this program increasingly since 2010" (Reese 2012: 3). The commission also developed a set of prevention recommendations. Those recommendations were submitted to the U.S. Attorney General in June 2009.

PREA required the U.S. Department of Justice, Bureau of Justice Statistics to "develop new national data collections on the incidence and prevalence of sexual violence within correctional facilities" (U.S. Department of Justice, Bureau of Justice Statistics 2006: 1). The first PREA research product was a first-ever 2004 national survey of administrative records on sexual violence in adult and juvenile correctional facilities. In 2005, the national survey was repeated and expanded. The 2004 survey located 284 allegations of sexual violence in federal prisons and 3,172 allegations of sexual violence in state prisons. The 2005 survey located 268 allegations of sexual violence in federal prisons and 4,341 allegations of sexual violence in state prisons. Approaching the study of prison sexual violence in this way, the Bureau of Justice Statistics uncovered a relatively small problem. The Bureau reported "that there were an estimated 0.40 substantiated incidents of sexual violence per 1,000 inmates in 2005, down from the 0.55 recorded in 2004" (1).

In 2007, the Bureau of Justice Statistics surveyed a national sample of prison inmates about their experiences with sexual violence. These findings were extrapolated so that nation-wide estimates of prison violence could be generated. The Bureau estimated that 60,500 incidents of sexual violence were reported by inmates in 2007. Staff sexual misconduct was somewhat more common than inmate-on-inmate sexual violence. The Bureau concluded that sexual violence impacted about 4.5 percent of all inmates in the United States (Beck & Harrison, 2007:1). Based upon their 2008–2009 survey, the Bureau of Justice Statistics estimated that 64,500 inmates reported sexual victimization. Staff sexual misconduct, again, was somewhat more commonly reported than inmate-on-inmate sexual violence (U.S. Department of Justice, Bureau of Justice Statistics, August, 2010: 7). A 2008 U.S. Department of Justice study estimated that about 10 percent of state prison inmates are sexually abused while serving their sentences (Frieden 2012: 10).

We will see what comes of PREA. Powerful forces work against prison rape reform. For example, prison administrators achieve the highest level of insulation from legal culpability by knowing as little as is possible about prison rape. Many inmates and corrections workers reap benefits from prison rape. It is possible that *Farmer v. Brennan* and the Prison Rape Elimination Act of 2003 will produce significant reform. It is also possible that *Farmer v. Brennan* and the Prison Rape Elimination Act of 2003 will turn out to be mostly "smoke and mirrors," tactics used by politicians and legal officials to create the appearance of action, when inaction is their real goal. We fear that "the wall of silence" about prison rape is far stronger than a court ruling without "teeth" and a federal law. Silence about prison rape is underpinned by many factors, including "the shame of the convicts that they could not defend themselves, prisoners' fear of possible reprisals ... the general public's radical lack of concern for prison conditions" and "homophobia" (Paczensky 2001: 135).

In 2011, the U.S. Department of Justice began finalizing rape-prevention policies that will eventually become mandatory for the federal prison system and for state prison systems receiving federal money. These policies are based upon rape-prevention recommendations the Attorney General received from the National Prison Rape Elimination Commission in 2009. On February 3, 2011, the Department of Justice published in the *Federal Register* a document titled "National Standards to Prevent, Detect, and Respond to Prison Rape" (U.S. Department of Justice 2011b). This 54-page document is a "notice of proposed rule-making." This most recent attempt at prison rape reduction will unfold in the next decade or so.

Effective abatement of prison rape could be achieved, if corrections officials and officers acted swiftly, locking down perpetrators in isolation cells, protecting victims from the "snitch" label and transferring victims to other prisons where their safety can be ensured. Such simple, straightforward solutions are not likely as long as corrections officials and officers, as well as large segments of the American citizenry, believe that rape of inmates is justified by the fact that they have committed crimes and, thus, deserve whatever punishment comes their way while in prison (Dickey 2002). The levity with which non-inmates react to prison rape is well-illustrated by a soft drink commercial aired in 2002 on a number of television networks. The commercial depicts a spokesman for their product, in prison, among inmates. When the spokesman drops a can of the product, he refuses to bend over in order to pick it up. The commercial ends with a view of the spokesman, sitting in a prison cell with the arm of a hulking inmate draped over his shoulder. A representative of the soft drink corporation responded to inquiries about the commercial by saying, "[T]he commercial was very well received by consumer audiences" (Mother Jones 2002: 2). A popular movie, released in 2015, titled *Get Hard*, keeps alive and exploits the imagery of looming, almost certain prison rape as the background for comedic performances. Against this persistent cultural background of humorous indifference, far too few Americans hear the cries for help coming from prison rape victims. Prison rape is one of the many reasons why male prison inmates have a suicide rate six times higher than the suicide rate for men in the general population (World Health Organization 2007: 3). Between 2001 and 2013, 2,577 suicides were reported as having occurred in America's state prisons (Noonan et al., 2015: 20).

After conducting a survey of sexual violence in U.S. adult correctional facilities, covering a recent 3-year period, the U.S. Department of Justice released data indicating that as many as one-half of all prison sexual assaults may be committed by guards. Prosecution of such offenses is rare, and only about 1 percent of correctional officers accused are convicted (Rantala et al., 2014: 1–12; see also Sapien 2014: 1–2). If, in fact, correctional officers are a major part of the rape problem in prison, it is difficult to see how PREA will be of much help to inmate victims.

Other forms of prison violence

The United States boasts a strong heritage as a racist and violent society. American soil was taken from its indigenous peoples through the use of wide-spread violence. Large-scale agriculture in this country was established, and expanded, on the backs of enslaved Africans and from the sweat of exploited Hispanics. Today, we Americans are still largely segregated, by wealth disparity and by ethnic preference, in terms of residence, education, occupation and patterns of association. As a nation state, we are prone to solving our problems with other countries through the use of large-scale violence. We Americans love violent sports. American media saturate our senses, and our brains, with depictions of violence. In interpersonal conflict, we are all too often quick-tempered and violent. Many of our children are disciplined in violent ways. Such qualities of the national character are found almost everywhere in American society, certainly in our prisons (Bernard & McCleary 1996). In these ways, prison life reflects life elsewhere in America, where "man's will to hurt" and "the male capacity and willingness to inflict pain on others" is endemic (Sabo et al., 2001: 12). In prisons, the American culture of violence is often found in one of its most extreme forms. The dynamics of violence are exaggerated inside a prison, largely because of the stress, tension and danger posed by living within the walls of a lock-up (Zoukis 2013: 1).

Herein, we define violence as

> any incident in which a person is abused, threatened, or assaulted. This includes an explicit or implicit challenge to their safety, well-being or health. The resulting harm may be physical, emotional, or psychological ... violence is not just about physical assault, but anything that induces fear.
>
> (HM Prison Service 2005: 2–3)

Prisons are places where violent criminals are locked up for long periods of time with persons who have committed property offenses as well as with drug law violators. Added to this potent mix of humanity are 200,000 to 300,000 American prison inmates suffering from "serious mental illness, including schizophrenia, bipolar disorders and major depression. Tens of thousands of these men and women experience active psychosis on any given day" (Abramsky & Fellner 2004: 1).

Gangs and prison violence

"Gang" is a word commonly used to identify an association of criminals or a group of individuals who have adopted a common name and who gather together on a regular basis in order to commit crimes. Gang members tend to acquire unique tattoos, to wear distinctive clothing and jewelry and to use hand signs that signify membership. In prison, officials frequently refer to gangs as Security Threat Groups (STGs). A Security Threat Group is defined as "a gang or inmate organization that is acting in concert posing a threat to the safety of staff, to the secure and orderly operation of a correctional institution, or to inmates" (Massachusetts Department of Corrections 2005). One feature that compounds the damage done by gangs is their tendency to be led by the most violent, exploitive and uncaring members. As one inmate put it, prison gangs are led by "the hog with the biggest balls." Gangs are important because "affiliation increases the probability of violence and other misconduct" in prison settings (Gaes et al., 2001: 23). For example, of the 36 homicides in California prisons in 1972, 30 were committed by members of a gang called the Mexican Mafia. Of the 25 murders in Texas prisons in 1984, 20 were committed by gang members (2). The deadly riot at a Lucasville, Ohio, prison, during which one correctional officer and nine inmates were murdered, was organized by members of three gangs (Huff & Meyer 1997). Between 2006 and 2009, California prison officials experienced 19 formally recognized riots in their vast prison system. At least six of those riots were gang-related (Associated Press 2009: 2). In 2015, another notable gang-related riot broke out, at a California state prison, located near Sacramento. This riot was precipitated by the stabbing of an infamous inmate one day after he had been released from decades in solitary confinement. As Hugo Pinelli, a notorious member of the "San Quentin 6," was stabbed by a number of inmates, a larger riot broke out around him involving members of a number of rival gangs. Eleven inmates received medical treatment, outside the prison, for stab wounds (Graham & De Graaf 2015: 1–3).

There are two general types of gangs, street gangs and prison gangs. *Street gangs* originated outside of prison. However, many members of street gangs are, today, in prison where they maintain their ties to, and affiliation with, a street gang. Prison gangs originated inside of prison. However, many members of prison gangs are, today, outside of prison, back in the communities and cities from which they came and are actively maintaining their ties to, and affiliation with, a prison gang.

Since the 1700s, American cities have been the birthplace of hundreds of street gangs. For example, in New York, the Latin Kings boast thousands of members. There are as many as 30 separate Mexican gangs in New York. New York hosts several Crip factions. New York Bloods, Latino Bloods and White Bloods operate around Staten Island. DDP (Dominicans Don't Play) prey on victims in Washington Heights and the Bronx. Yugoslavians, Albanians and Pakistanis belong to a gang called YAPS. Salvadoran gangs, known as MS-13 and SWP (Salvadorans with Pride), are found in the Bronx and on Long Island. New York City Police Department's 300 Gang Division officers infiltrated and sent to prison hundreds of gang members, including many leaders, producing a temporary downturn in gang activity (Donaldson 2002). Unfortunately, as street gang members go to prison, they set up shop there, targeting other inmates and correctional officers as their victims.

Chicago is notorious for its street gangs. In the early 1900s, Frederic Thrasher identified over 1,300 gangs in the Second City (1927). Today, gangs populate the streets of Chicago with names like:

- Ambrose
- Bishops
- Black Disciples
- Black Gangsters
- Black P. Stones
- Black Souls
- Familia Stones
- Folk Nation
- Four Corner Hustlers
- Gangster Disciples
- Gangster Stones
- Gangster Two Six
- Gaylords
- Harrison Gents
- Imperial Gangsters
- Insane Ashland Vikings
- Insane C-Notes
- Insane Deuces
- Insane Dragons
- Insane Orquesta Albanies
- Insane Popes (North Side)
- Insane Popes (South Side)
- Insane Spanish Cobras
- Insane Two Two Boys
- Insane Unknowns
- La Raza
- Latin Brothers
- Latin Counts
- Latin Dragons
- Latin Eagles
- Latin Jivers
- Latin Kings
- Latin Lovers
- Latin Pachucos
- Latin Souls
- Maniac Latin Disciples
- Mickey Cobras
- Milwaukee Kings
- Party Players
- Party People
- People Nation
- Saints
- Satin Disciples

- Simon City Royals
- Spanish Gangster Disciples
- Spanish Lords
- Stoned Freaks
- Twelfth Street Players
- Vice Lords

Since the 1970s, most of the large Chicago gangs have been run from inside prisons (Chicago Gang History Project 2005).

Los Angeles is the national capital of street gangs. Los Angeles gangs boast around 45,000 members. In Los Angeles, 209 Latino gangs, 152 African American gangs, 31 Asian gangs, 16 "stoner" gangs and 8 white gangs compete for turf, for victims and for other scarce resources. Gang wars in Los Angeles, for decades, have been led by the Crips and Bloods. There are 109 Crip gangs and 43 Blood gangs in Los Angeles. The Rollin 60s is the largest African American gang in Los Angeles. Latino gangs, like 18th Street, and a Salvadoran gang called Mara Salva Trucha, have thousands of members. Many Los Angeles street gang members come into, and go out of, prison. A founder of the Crips, Stanley "Tookie" Williams, is held on death row at San Quentin (Barrett & Kandel 2004). Los Angeles gang members have moved all over the country, opening up new chapters as they settle. Los Angeles gang members operate in many prisons throughout the United States.

Florida legal officials list 197 gangs operating in every city, "from Pensacola to the Florida Keys," throughout the state (Florida Department of Corrections 2005: 13). Most notable among Florida street gangs are

- 2nd Street Fellows
- 35th Street Players
- American Nazi Party
- Aryan Nations
- Black Gangster Disciples
- Bloods
- Crips
- Folk Nation
- Gangster Disciples
- Gaylords
- Imperial Gangsters
- Insane Gangster Disciples
- International Posse
- Ku Klux Klan
- La Familia
- Latin Counts

- Latin Disciples
- Latin Eagles
- Latin Force
- Latin Gangster Disciples
- Latin Kings
- Maniac Latin Disciples
- N.S.W.W.P.
- Northside Nation
- People Nation
- Simon City Royals
- Skinhead
- Solidos
- Spanish Gangsters
- Spanish Lords
- Vice Lords
- West Side Crips
- White Aryan Resistance
- Worldwide Folk

Members of all 197 gangs move into Florida prisons and eventually move back out into Florida cities and communities. Particularly problematic in Florida is the large number of gang members who hold white supremacy or neo-Nazi beliefs.

Six major *prison gangs* dominate correctional populations throughout the United States. *Aryan Brotherhood* (other names: Brand, AB, Tip, Alice, Alice Baker) first appeared in San Quentin State Prison in 1967. In the 1950s, founding members of the Aryan Brotherhood belonged to gangs called the Bluebirds, the Diamond Tooth Gang and the Nazi Gang. Members of the Aryan Brotherhood espouse a white supremacist, neo-Nazi philosophy. Their hatred towards African American individuals is legendary. Enemies of the Aryan brotherhood include African American gangs including the Black Guerilla Family, Crips, Bloods and El Rukns, as well as La Nuestra Familia. Allies include the Mexican Mafia, the Dirty White Boys, the Silent Brotherhood, many motorcycle gangs and La Cosa Nostra. Recently, the Aryan Brotherhood has shifted away from an emphasis on racism, towards the acquisition of power in prison, as well as in American cities. The gang admits some non-European American members and, according to a federal indictment, formed a partnership with Asian gangs to import heroin from Thailand (Hughes 2002: 27). Like most major prison gangs, the Aryan Brotherhood is a "blood-in-blood-out" organization. In other words, as a rite of passage, people who aspire to join must murder a person designated by the gang. Membership is for life. The only way to exit the Aryan Brotherhood is by death. Although a relatively small gang, the Aryan

Brotherhood dominates many American prisons and is also active in many cities. While not having "made their bones" as full-fledged members, thousands of inmates affiliate with the Aryan Brotherhood and obey the orders of its leaders. When released from prison, AB members are expected to do whatever they can to support those who are still incarcerated.

The Aryan Brotherhood, along with their allies, smuggle illicit drugs into prison, sell drugs to inmates, loan shark, rape, practice extortion and sell protection. AB members do whatever they can to disrupt prison discipline, including fomenting ethnic conflict and riots among other segments of inmate populations. AB members have been known to successfully bribe prison guards (Hughes 2002: 27A). Aryan Brotherhood members are particularly murderous. For example, "from 1975 to 1985, members committed 40 homicides in California prisons and jails, as well as 13 homicides in the community. From 1978 to 1992, AB members, suspects and associates in the federal system were involved in 26 homicides, 3 of which involved staff victims" (Florida Department of Corrections 2005: 5). AB members murdered correctional officers at the federal prison in Marion, Illinois, and at a prison in Oxford, Wisconsin (Hughes 2002: 27A). Barry Byron Mills and Tyler Davis Bingham, leaders of AB's Federal Commission, ran the gang from inside the walls of the Federal Bureau of Prison's super-maximum-security prison at Florence, Colorado (Hughes 2002: 1A). In 2002, 40 members of the Aryan Brotherhood were charged in a federal indictment with stabbing and murdering rival gang members, snitches, correctional officers, inmates who stole their drugs, inmates who owed them money, prisoners who were gay, African Americans and persons convicted of child molestation. One Aryan Brotherhood leader bragged that "the guards controlled the perimeter of the prison and we controlled what happened inside it" (Grann 2004: 161). It was alleged that "the gang's one-hundred or so members ... had gradually taken control of large parts of the nation's maximum-security prisons, ruling over thousands of inmates and transforming themselves into a powerful criminal organization" (158).

While the Aryan Brotherhood is, by far, the most notorious white supremacist prison gang, many others exist. Other white racist prison gangs include Aryan Nation, Aryan Warriors, Aryan Society, White Aryan Resistance, 211 Crew, Ku Klux Klan, Neo-Nazis, biker gangs like the Prison Motorcycle Brotherhood, Nazi Low Riders and Outlaws, Peckerwoods, Brothers of the White Struggle (B.O.W.S.), Northsiders (in Illinois), Simon City Royals (in the Midwest), Texas Mafia, White Gangster Disciples, White Supremacists, Young and Wasted and Church of the New Song (CONS) (Knox 1999). All of these gangs are dangerous and highly criminal. For example, 24 members of a racist Colorado prison gang, called the 211 Crew, were indicted by a state grand jury, charging them with murder (in prison), racketeering, witness tampering, selling guns and drug dealing, among other crimes (Montero 2005: 4A). Five members of the gang were charged with the murder of a Colorado prison inmate, so that one could "earn his stripes" as a full-fledged 211 Crew member. The gang boasts about 300 members. 211 Crew leaders in prison communicated with gang members outside of prison via coded telephone messages and letters. 211 Crew members outside of prison sell drugs and guns, smuggling some of the profits back into prison so that incarcerated members can live more comfortably. Those outside of prison also "settled scores" with members who refused to take orders (Pankratz & Mitchell 2005: 23A).

Another important prison gang is the *Black Guerilla Family* (BGF). BGF originated in 1966 in California's San Quentin State Prison. Its originator was George L. Jackson who preached a compelling mixture of Marxist, Maoist and Leninist philosophy that advocated eliminating racism, maintaining individual dignity while in prison and overthrowing the United States' political structure. Their mortal enemies are Aryan Brotherhood, Texas Syndicate, Aryan Brotherhood of Texas and Mexican Mafia members. Allies of the Black Guerilla Family include Black Liberation Army, Symbionese Liberation Army, Weather Underground and La Nuestra Familia members. BGF maintains cordial working relationships with numerous African American street gangs and heavily recruits their members when they are sent to prison. Their anti-government and anti-official philosophy makes corrections officers and officials targets for BGF-sponsored acts of violence. BGF members participate in acts of individual, ethnic-oriented violence, including rape, as well as in riots fueled by racism.

La Nuestra Familia (other names: LNF, NF, ENE, F and Nancy Flores) is one of two potent Hispanic prison gangs. LNF was formed in the mid-1960s at Soledad State Prison in California. LNF originated in order to provide protection for young Mexican American inmates who had lived in the rural parts of California and who were victimized by Mexican American inmates who had lived in California's large cities, especially Los Angeles. Their primary rival is the Mexican Mafia. Other enemies include the Texas Syndicate, Mexikanemi, F-14s and the Aryan Brotherhood. Allies include the Northern Structure and, sometimes, the Black Guerilla Family. The Northern Structure may be a subsidiary of the LNF. LNF members perpetrate a good deal of prison violence directed toward other inmates as well as toward correctional officers. They are active in the prison drug trade. They sell contraband food, rape, loan shark, gamble, extort and sell protection to weak inmates. Before they were transferred to a federal prison in 2001, Nuestra Familia leaders ran a large criminal syndicate, spread across a number of Northern California cities, by smuggling orders out of super-maximum-security Pelican Bay State Prison, written on small pieces of paper inserted into body cavities of visitors and parolees. The smuggled messages included orders to commit armed robberies and deposit the cash into specified bank accounts, directives to kill misbehaving gang members and prosecuting attorneys, instructions for collecting "taxes" from drug dealers and orders to perpetrate violence toward enemy gangs (Geniella 2001). Once released from prison, members of La Nuestra Familia are expected to assist those who are still incarcerated.

Another potent Hispanic prison gang is the *Mexican Mafia* (other names: EME, Emily, Emeros). The Mexican Mafia emphasizes ethnic solidarity and drug dealing. It was formed in the late 1950s at the Duel Vocational Center, a California prison for youthful offenders. EME was the outgrowth of a Los Angeles street gang. Most members of the Mexican Mafia are Mexican Americans who have come from big cities, especially Los Angeles. Its enemies are La Nuestra Familia, Northern Structure, Black Guerilla Family and members of African American street gangs. The Mexican Mafia has a strong working relationship with the Aryan Brotherhood and La Cosa Nostra. Other allies include Arizona's Old Mexican Mafia, Mexikanemi, the New Mexico Syndicate and a number of Latino big city street gangs. Wives, girlfriends and relatives of Mexican Mafia members are held in high esteem because of their willing participation in "drug transactions, financial activities, and mail-forwarding activities" (Florida Department of Corrections 2005: 8). EME members are known best for premeditated, gruesome prison murders, especially of Nuestra Familia members. The brutal nature of their murders is intended to instill fear, and to intimidate, other inmates and correctional officers. EME members also sell drugs, extort, rape, loan shark and sell protection to weak inmates. Additionally, the Mexican Mafia provides protection for La Cosa Nostra members. The Mexican Mafia is particularly active in the federal prison system.

Neta (other name: Asociacion Neta) was formed in 1979 in a Puerto Rican prison called Rio Piedras, in order to protect weak inmates from a gang called G'27. Neta members view themselves as people oppressed by the United States. They espouse independence from the United States for Puerto Rico (Segag.org 2011). They have strong ties to a Puerto Rican revolutionary organization called the Los Macheteros, as well as to a number of Puerto Rican street gangs. Their enemies are members of Los Solidos, Latin Kings and 20 Luv. Members of Neta are particularly active in Puerto Rican prisons, prisons throughout the Northeastern United States and Florida. Neta performs contract murders of inmates. Neta members extort, rape and deal drugs. Neta engages in acts of violence aimed at correctional officers and other prison employees.

Neta is one of the largest imported gangs to infest American prisons. An estimated 70,000 to 100,000 Neta members roam the streets and communities of Mexico and other Central American countries, especially in Honduras and El Salvador (G. Thompson 2004). Many gang members from Mexico and Central America find their way into the United States. For example, Mara Salvatrucha and the Mara 18 are two of the fastest-growing street gangs in Los Angeles, catering to illegal alien Central Americans. As a consequence, non-citizen inmate populations in U.S. prisons are growing (U.S. Department of Justice 2002: 499, 511). In 1998, a little over 77,000 non–U.S. citizens were held in U.S. prisons, almost 28,000 in federal prisons and a little over 49,000 in state prisons. By 2011, about 103,000 non–U.S. citizens were held in U.S. prisons, almost 31,000 in federal facilities and over 72,000 in state prisons (U.S. Department of Justice 2011a: 1). By 2013, over 26 percent of inmates in U.S. federal prisons were not citizens of the United States (U.S. Department of Justice 2011b: 1). Given these facts, we anticipate that the influence of foreign gangs on U.S. prisons will increase dramatically in the near future.

Another Mexican American/Hispanic prison gang, the *Texas Syndicate* (other names: Syndicato Tejano, TS, ESE TE, Teresa Sanchez), originated in the early 1970s at California's Folsom State Prison. It was formed by Texans at Folsom who were being victimized by gangs like the Aryan Brotherhood and the Mexican Mafia. TS now accepts members from Latin American countries, especially Columbia, Cuba and Mexico. TS is strongest in California and Texas prisons, but its members can be found in distant Florida prisons. Texas Syndicate allies are Texas Mafia and Dirty White Boys members. Its enemies include members of the Aryan Brotherhood, La Nuestra Familia, Mexican Mafia, Mexikanemi and the Mandingo Warriors. Texas Syndicate members perpetrate violence against other inmates and correctional officers. TS members deal drugs, extort, rape, loan shark and sell protection to weak inmates. Its membership is on the rise, largely due to the aggressive recruiting of non–U.S. citizen members.

Just how serious is the gang problem in American prisons? In 1993, the American Correctional Association (ACA), funded by the National Institute of Justice, undertook a national study of gangs in U.S. prisons. American Correctional Association researchers utilized a methodology whereby a single, state-level prison administrator was identified and was asked questions about gang activity in all prisons within his/her state. Using this strategy, ACA researchers concluded that only about 6 percent of all adult state prison inmates were gang members (American Correctional Association 1993). This finding became the benchmark for estimates of gang density in U.S. prisons. In 1999, researchers for the National Gang Crime Research Center (NGCRC) contacted 133 wardens of state prisons, located in 47 states, and asked them a series of questions about prison gang activity. Using a strategy that collects information from persons closer to the situation, in this case wardens, NGCRC reported that approximately 25 percent of the adult male inmates in state prisons and 8 percent of adult female inmates are gang members. Almost 33 percent of adult male inmates and 9 percent of adult female inmates in state maximum-security prisons are gang members (Knox 1999: 5). Wardens surveyed identified Crips, Black Gangster Disciples, Bloods/Piru factions, Vice Lord factions, the Aryan Brotherhood and Latin Kings as the largest gangs operating in their prisons (11). NGCRC researchers report that prison gangs are operating in all 50 states and in the District of Columbia and that "the vast majority of wardens in adult state correctional institutions do in fact believe that in the next few years the gang problem will dramatically increase behind bars" (48). Ironically, some argue that major prison gangs have grown so powerful that their leaders control much of what happens on a day-to-day basis within the walls of America's long-term lock-ups (Lessing 2016).

As cellular telephones spread throughout American society, they also spread throughout state and federal prison systems. A functioning cellular telephone can be sold for $200–$500 in most American prisons. A broken cellular telephone can be sold for as much as $100 in many American prisons. Cellular telephones often arrive in prisons via prison employees, as well as via persons visiting inmates. The best place to hide a cellular telephone is in the rectum. A shaped bar of soap can be used to train the rectum to better function as a cellular telephone repository. In 2013, California corrections officers seized over 12,000 cellular telephones from inmates (Wood 2014: 5). In 2013, officers in Florida prisons seized 4,200 cellular telephones from prison inmates (Roose & Harshaw 2015: 1). By extrapolating from these important pieces of information, we believe it is likely that a majority of American prison inmates now have access to cellular telephone use. It is certain that imprisoned gang leaders, through the use of cellular telephones, can maintain a good deal of control over gang activities in the communities and cities from which they came. Inadvertently, a robust cellular telephone black market has been a boon to inmate economies, as well as to some prison employee incomes. Technologies exist that can be used to block cellular telephone use on the grounds of a prison. The senior author has visited a few such prisons. However, most American prisons, to date, do not use cellular telephone blocking technologies. Why? Costs of installation and maintenance of such technologies begin at about $500,000 per prison and can quickly escalate to well over $1,000,000 per prison. Cellular telephone calls made by prison employees and administrators must be "washed" through the blocking system, before they can be connected to a party outside the prison. Finally, cellular telephone blocking technologies must be continuously calibrated so that they do not extend beyond the boundaries of a prison (Jackson 2013: 1–3).

Inmate-on-inmate violence

We have already examined the specter of rape that hangs like a dark cloud over American prisons. In his classic study of Stateville Prison, James

Jacobs observed that the "most distinctive manifestation of prison violence is homosexual rape" (1976: 79). However, the bulk of prison violence takes the form of non-sexual inmate-on-inmate confrontations. Social science research suggests that prisoner-on-prisoner "assault," or "attack" rates range from 3 per 100 inmates per year to as many as 20 per 100 inmates per year, depending upon the prison under examination and the examiner (Bowker 1980; Crouch & Marquart 1989; Silberman 1995; Federal Bureau of Prisons 2015a and 2015b). The actual rate is likely much higher, since most inmate-on-inmate violence goes unreported. By the turn of the century, experts estimated that every year, approximately 25,000 inmates are assaulted by other inmates (Clear & Cole 2000: 258). More recent research indicates that about 20 percent of American inmates are assaulted by another inmate, each year (Wolff et al., 2013: 2).

Inmate-on-inmate attacks usually involve the use of prison-made knives (called "shanks"), meat cleavers stolen from prison kitchens and clubs fashioned from chair legs, mop handles or pieces of pipe. The senior author, while working at the maximum-security Washington State Prison in Walla Walla, rarely walked inside the walls without seeing at least one homemade weapon laying on the ground. Very little fist-fighting occurs in contemporary American prisons. Instead, prison weapons are used in order to speed up the confrontation and to intensify the damage that can be done.

Inmate-on-inmate violence can occur for an infinite number of reasons. For example, a few years ago, the authors worked on a capital murder case involving a senior member of the Aryan Brotherhood (AB). One day, while he was walking down a cellblock stairway, a rival gang member lunged at him from behind, striking his head with a piece of pipe. The AB member fought off his assailant and then staggered to the prison medical clinic, where he told clinic personnel that he had fallen down a metal stairway, hitting his head. For several years after this incident, the AB member was plagued by "screaming headaches," which he self-medicated with marijuana. Later, while doing time at San Quentin, the same AB member, feeling threatened and at-risk by his cell assignment, acquired a 4-foot-long steel rod, took it to his cell and sharpened one end, using the concrete floor. He waited, sitting on his bunk, with the rod between his legs, until corrections officers escorted a rival gang member towards the front of his cell. As they moved in front of his cell, the AB member lunged forward, stabbing his rival three times in the chest, before an officer, using his baton, could knock the rod away. Why did the stabbing occur? The AB member had requested a cellblock change and was denied. He decided the best way to get his transfer was by stabbing someone. His strategy worked. At another American prison, fights, featuring shanks, break out over preferred seating in the cafeteria, in the television area and in the yard. In the yard, fights were over who owned a pile of dirt (Zoukis 2014: 1–4).

American prison wardens estimate that approximately 30 percent of all violence among inmates in their facilities is caused by gangs or gang members (Knox 1999: 31). Others who study this issue suspect that a far larger percentage of prison violence is attributable to gangs (Wood 2014). Violent acts in prison serve as ways to demonstrate, and test, manhood. Fighting is likely necessary if an inmate is jostled during an athletic event or while walking, if an inmate stares directly at another inmate, if an inmate is sitting in another inmate's accustomed place, if an inmate makes unwelcome sexual overtures or if just about anything else "pisses" an inmate off.

In federal prisons, inmate violence is categorized in the following way (Harer & Langan 2001: 517):

- Code 100: killing or attempting to kill any person
- Code 101: assaulting any person (serious)
- Code 104: possessing a weapon
- Code 201: fighting
- Code 203: threatening bodily harm
- Code 224: assaulting any person (less serious)

Harer and Langan report that female inmates rarely commit 100-level acts of violence. In general, "women commit less violence and less serious violence than men" (513).

Inmate-on-inmate violence takes on an even more sinister quality when it is facilitated by correctional officers. Perhaps the most infamous example of inmate-on-inmate violence precipitated by guards allegedly occurred at California's Corcoran State Prison, in the Secure Housing Units. According to a federal indictment, four correctional officers

> purposely released an African-American inmate into the prison yard with two Southern Mexican inmates from a rival faction.... The defendants then watched the fight without acting to prevent it.... Afterwards, they falsified a written report to cover up the fact that they had intentionally staged the fight.
>
> (U.S. Department of Justice 1998: 2)

On another occasion, four correctional officers allegedly let "two African-American inmates into the yard with members of the Southern Mexican faction, even though guards were aware that there were 'problems' likely to occur between inmates ... the two members of the Southern Mexican faction violently attacked the other inmates" An officer

> then allegedly fired two shots at the inmates ... which hit an inmate ... in the head and killed him. Following the shooting, the four officers involved

allegedly prepared false and misleading written reports designed to cover up the fact that they had encouraged the inmates to fight, knew the fight would occur, and intentionally failed to act to protect the inmates from one another.

(2)

Ultimately, federal prosecutors were unable to penetrate the correctional officer "Code of Silence" that dominates California prisons. In 2000, the eight guards were acquitted.

How do inmates respond to prison violence? Unfortunately, many state-raised inmates thrive on it. They have been exposed to violence since child-hood, long before coming to prison. State-raised inmates use violence to gain a "leg up" in prison and to demonstrate their superiority in a hostile environment. Mentally ill inmates often engage in violence, because they lack self-control and because they are not receiving effective counseling and medication. Peaceful inmates, inmates who are fearful, older inmates and socially isolated inmates often use avoidance techniques to decrease their risk of being violated in prison. They keep to themselves. They avoid areas of prisons where the risk of violence is high. They stay in their cells as much as possible. Some ask to be placed in protective custody. Many young inmates, especially those who have been victimized and those who have already served long prison terms, employ aggression as a means of deter-ring violent attacks. They are likely to "get tough" with another prisoner, as a way to show that they will fight back if provoked. They lift weights to dem-onstrate their power. They keep handy a "shank," or some other weapon, in case it is needed (Correctional Service of Canada 2004). Everett Hodges, founder of the California-based Violence Research Foundation, believes that excessive manganese in prisoner diets leads to increased violence. He recommends feeding inmates food rich in iron and calcium in order to counterbalance the manganese. In a 6-month trial, this recommendation was tested using 133 U.S. inmates as experimental subjects. "Violence fell by 38 percent" (ABCNews 2001: 1). This strategy has also been tested in some Mexican prisons.

Inmate-on-correctional officer violence

While at work, correctional officers are almost always outnumbered by inmates. Correctional officers work in places throughout prisons where, if attacked, back-up help must come through several locked "grills" (doors and gates) that take precious minutes to open. Correctional officers do not carry firearms in most American prisons. They must protect themselves with their wits, maybe a can of pepper spray, some martial arts training and, pos-sibly, an alarm carried on a belt or shoulder harness. Correctional officers represent "authority" to inmates and must enforce harsh rules. Correctional officers work among mentally ill and pathologically violent inmates. Correctional officers must break up fights. As a consequence, it is not surprising that correctional officers are frequently hurt at work. For example, in 1995, over 14,000 prison workers were injured by inmates (Clear & Cole 2000: 261). In 1998, another approximately 14,000 correctional officers were seriously assaulted. That same year, seven correctional officers died in the line of duty (Metz 1999). Between 1999 and 2008, 47,500 experienced nonfatal injuries that resulted from assaults and other violent acts. During that same 10-year-period, 28 correctional officers died as a result of prison homicides. Another 17 correctional officers committed suicide while at work, via "self-inflicted gunshot wounds" (Konda et al., 2012: 2–3).

A few examples will serve to illustrate the extreme danger inherent in the working life of correctional officers. In 2002, at a prison in Limon, Colorado, an inmate serving a lengthy sentence for killing a baby fatally stabbed a food service supervisor so that he would be separated from the general inmate population (Associated Press 2002b: 18A). In 2003, a veteran Florida correctional officer accompanied by two trainees was conducting a routine dormitory search. He confiscated a contraband piece of wire from an inmate's boot. The correctional officer informed the inmate that a disciplinary report would be written about the incident. The inmate reacted by stabbing the officer in the neck and jaw, using a "shank." Seriously injured, the officer fought the inmate off for several minutes, protecting the trainees from harm, until back-up officers arrived (Florida Department of Corrections 2003a). In 2003, another Florida correctional officer was struck in the head from behind by an inmate using a baseball bat. A fight ensued with other correctional officers and inmates joining in. Inmates were swinging horseshoes and the baseball bat. With the help of chemical agents, the inmates were eventually subdued. Five officers were transported to hospitals suffering from serious injuries (Florida Department of Corrections 2003b). In 2004, a prisoner serving 92 years to life for robbery and murder at Attica State Prison in New York, wielding a sharpened steel rod, attacked and stabbed three correctional officers. It took several other officers to subdue the inmate. The three officers were hospitalized and treated for multiple stab wounds (WIVB TV4 2004). In 2012, during a large-scale riot at a Mississippi Corrections Corporation of America prison for illegal immigrants, a 24-year-old guard was beaten to death by inmates while 16 other employees were injured (WAPT News 2012: 1). In 2016, four correctional officers working at an Iowa women's prison received multiple injuries while attempting to break up a fight in the cafeteria (Oldach 2016: 1–3). Later in 2016, a veteran correctional officer was seriously injured after an inmate punched him in the face. The blow knocked the officer head-first to the floor. The officer lost consciousness. Other officers coming to his aid were injured in the melee that ensued. This incident occurred at a New Jersey prison for youthful offenders. (Merriman 2016: 1).

In sum, life in prison for correctional officers consists of monotonous routines that are, nevertheless, charged with tension and frayed nerves. Their hours are spent watching inmates, while the inmates watch back. This routine is punctuated by sporadic episodes of extreme violence, carrying with it the risk of serious injury or death. This is not an easy way to make a modest living.

Correctional officer-on-inmate violence

Correctional officers, under certain circumstances and in some situations, are authorized to use reasonable force against inmates. For example, when attacked by one or more inmates, when inmates are trying to escape, when enforcing prison rules, when inmates resist discipline or orders and during riots where violence erupts, correctional officers are empowered to use reasonable levels of force. Legitimate, authorized use of force occurs frequently in American prisons.

Unauthorized use of violence by correctional officers is not systematically tracked by any American legal authority and, therefore, is impossible to enumerate or describe with accuracy. However, a number of corrections officials, inmates and human rights advocates assert that frequent "physical and sexual abuse of prisoners ... takes place in American prisons with little public knowledge or concern" (Butterfield 2004: 1). According to Chase Riveland, who served as Secretary of Corrections in Colorado and Washington state, "in some jurisdictions in the United States there is a prison culture that tolerates violence, and it's been there a long time" (quoted in Butterfield 2004: 2). Many correctional officers believe that the use of violence is a right they were given when hired to oversee a nation's criminals. Wardens and supervisors of correctional officers often "look the other way," in order to support line workers they must depend upon to control inmates. Higher level prison administrators are frequently skeptical of reports by inmates that they have been abused by guards. When charged with crimes of violence against inmates, correctional officers are almost always acquitted, due in large part to the reluctance of brother and sister guards to break the "correctional officer code of silence" that dictates acceptable behavior in their occupation. Below, we list examples of alleged unauthorized correctional officer-on-inmate violence.

"A prisoner at the federal penitentiary in Atlanta was held for five days in what is called a 'four-point restraint.' He was chained by his wrists and ankles, on his back, in a spread-eagle position. He was forced to urinate and defecate on himself. For five days" (Lewis 2001: 1). The inmate eventually sued, and the Federal Bureau of Prisons settled the case out of court, paying him $99,000. Use of such restraints is not uncommon in the federal prison system. For example, in 1996–1997, approximately 100 federal inmates were held in "four-point restraints." One inmate was held in four-point restraints for about 2 months (2).

In 1999, a Florida inmate was forced to wear a "stun belt" that delivered a 50,000-volt shock when activated by remote control while he appeared in court at his murder trial. On the second day of the trial, the soft-spoken inmate suddenly started screaming and cussing. A deputy had accidently triggered the "stun belt's" remote control. Shock devices are used by approximately 19 prison systems in the United States. A common "stun belt" model attaches to the waist with the shock device placed next to a kidney. Each shock lasts 8 seconds, causing intense pain and possible loss of bladder and bowel control. "Stun belts" can be fatal if used on inmates with heart problems (Wilkinson 2000).

A group of prison guards, nicknamed the Cowboys, who worked at the U.S. Penitentiary near Florence, Colorado, was accused by a former Federal Bureau of Prisons correctional officer of routinely beating African American inmates. In exchange for his cooperation, the former officer was given a shorter sentence as punishment for his own crimes. According to the former federal officer, the Cowboys ruled the prison by intimidating inmates and other officers. In fact, "with the approval of their superiors ... inmates and other officers were threatened with physical retribution if they told of the Cowboys' activities" (Plasket 2000: A1). As the investigation unfolded, a second former Federal Bureau of Prisons correctional officer stepped forward and, in exchange for a plea agreement regarding her own participation in the beatings, offered to testify against the Cowboys. She was allowed to plead guilty to a misdemeanor (Associated Press 2000: 17A). In November, 2000, seven of the Cowboys were indicted by a Denver grand jury on nine counts of depriving inmates of their civil rights while acting in an official capacity. The indictment listed 52 incidents including slamming inmates' heads into walls, dropping handcuffed inmates on their faces, kneeing inmates in their kidneys, choking inmates, squeezing inmates' testicles, mixing feces and urine in inmates' food, spraying inmates with a fire extinguisher and filing false reports. Recently, two officers employed at the federal Coleman Correctional facility, in Coleman, Florida, pleaded guilty to striking an inmate in the head, again and again, and to filing false reports about the incident (U.S. Department of Justice 2016: 1–2).

In 1997, a correctional officer was fatally stabbed by an inmate in a New York state prison. According to a lawsuit filed by 600 inmates, correctional officers at the prison waged a war of reprisal against them that featured beatings and other forms of abuse. Surveillance videotapes showed correctional officers dragging an inmate down a steel set of stairs. Tapes showed another inmate being dragged along a floor, while begging to be allowed to walk. Audio tape captured a supervisor's voice saying, "[D]on't pick him up, drag him.... I want him drug along the floor, just like that, like a pig." Inmates alleged that they had suffered broken bones, lost teeth and experienced internal bleeding. New York State Department of Corrections and FBI investigators were not able to corroborate the inmates' allegations. Then, in 2003, a retired correctional officer, a 16-year veteran of corrections work in New York, told the *New York Times* what she saw during that period. One day at work, after the correctional officer had been fatally stabbed, she observed several guards rushing past her. They attacked and severely beat an inmate who was carrying garbage from the prison cafeteria. As he lay on the ground, weathering a beating by several officers, the inmate howled and screamed like an animal. He pleaded, again and again, "I haven't done anything. I haven't done anything." She reported, "[T]hey were going to beat him anyway. They were going to get someone" (Sullivan 2003: 1).

On July 17, 1999, a Florida prison captain approached the death row cell of inmate Frank Valdes and ordered him to submit to handcuffing. When Valdes refused, the captain used pepper spray on Valdes and called in the prison's cell extraction team. During the struggle that ensued, Valdes died. Frank Valdes was not a nice person. Valdes had been imprisoned, and was awaiting execution, for murdering a correctional officer. Officials said, the day before his death, Valdes had threatened to kill another correctional officer (Associated Press 1999). Eventually, seven correctional officers were charged with second-degree murder for killing Frank Valdes. They were arrested and, after pleading not guilty, were immediately released on their own recognizance (Schneider 2001). One guard charged with second-degree murder defied the "code of silence" and offered to testify against the others, although his testimony was never heard by a jury. In 2002, the first murder trial, involving three correctional officers, was held in their home community, where approximately one out of every 11 residents work for the Florida Department of Corrections (Long 2001). As the trial approached, a large sign hung outside a local church read "Correctional Officers, look up. God loves you" (Lee 2002: 1). A number of inmates who witnessed the cell extraction testified for the prosecution. They asserted that Valdes had been beaten and stomped by the guards. The guards testified that Valdes had inflicted his own fatal injuries by throwing himself off his bunk onto the concrete floor. There was testimony that Valdes' body was covered with boot marks. In the end, the jury returned a verdict of "not guilty" on the second-degree murder charges. In 2001, another guard had been acquitted by a jury of criminal charges that he had beaten Valdes the day before he died (2).

Perhaps the most notorious examples of alleged Correctional officer-on-inmate violence can be found in the nation's largest prison system, in California, where approximately 128,000 adults are locked up. In February

2004, an adult inmate at Corcoran State Prison bled to death after pulling a dialysis shunt from his arm. It was reported that the inmate's cries for help were ignored by guards watching the Super Bowl. State-funded experts accused juvenile prison authorities of overusing "mace, drugs, physical restraints and wire mesh cages on misbehaving youths while ignoring or delaying mental or physical health treatment" (D. Thompson 2004a: 1).

In 1998, eight correctional officers who worked at California's maximum-security Corcoran State Prison were indicted in a federal court on charges they had conspired "to deprive inmates of their civil rights under color of law" (U.S. Department of Justice 1998: 1). The indictment alleged that Corcoran guards had staged numerous "gladiator fights" in small Secure Housing Unit exercise yards between inmates belonging to rival gangs. The officers would watch the fights for a while, then they would fire dum-dum or wooden bullets from high-powered rifles at one or more of the combatants. Since 1988, when Corcoran opened, "more than 30 inmates had been shot – eight of them killed – during these fights" (CBS News 2001: 1). A former Corcoran guard told federal prosecutors that the defendants "knew when the fights were going to happen and did nothing to stop them, then used the fights as an excuse to use their weapons" (LaMotte 2000: 2). Defense attorneys argued that the 84 fights, in less than a 6-month period, were spontaneous occurrences and that the guards had in no way staged them. After 31 days of litigation, all 8 guards were acquitted of all charges. Six of the defendants were reassigned to other California prisons. Two of the defendants retired.

At the maximum- and medium-security High Desert State Prison in Susanville, California, where almost 3,500 inmates are incarcerated in a facility designed to hold 2,324, according to a report released by the Office of Inspector General, a longstanding "entrenched culture" of racism and violence practiced by guards was found. Guards allegedly allowed gang members to control much of the prison, in exchange for their help and cooperation. Guards allegedly rewarded some inmates who assaulted other targeted inmates by giving them items that had been seized from the inmate population. It was alleged that, twice, guards had not interceded for some time while inmates were being stabbed by other inmates. The Inspector General found that inmates likely to be sexually assaulted were housed with inmates who were likely to assault them. High Desert State Prison has gone through seven wardens in less than a decade (St John 2015: 1–4).

In Florida, eight former correctional officers were charged with abuse of inmates at the Henry Correctional Institution. Alleged abuse included forcing some inmates to eat food off of floors if they refused to accept sexual aggression. Other inmates were allegedly forced to clean toilets with their tongues. Another inmate was reportedly beaten and choked by guards.

In all, 13 employees were fired at the prison. The warden and assistant warden resigned (Associated Press 2007a: 1). A new inmate transferring into Florida's Santa Rosa Correctional Institution had begged guards for protection from his new cellmate, a man known to be violent. After less than 2 days at Santa Rosa, the new inmate was found dead in his cell. His skull had been crushed, and his underpants had been pulled down by his violent cellmate, Shawn "Jiggaman" Rogers (Townes 2015b: 1–2). In Florida, 32 guards were fired after alleged criminal misconduct that resulted in inmate killings at four state prisons. A notable death occurred after guards placed an inmate, naked, under scalding water from a shower, for almost 2 hours. The inmate screamed for some time. Eventually, as his skin broke down, the inmate died. This mentally ill man had relieved himself in his cell and had not been able to clean the mess up by himself. Officers at the Florida Department of Law Enforcement are investigating 85 recent inmate deaths that occurred for reasons other than natural causes (Henry 2014: 1–4).

During a recent 5-year period in New York, state corrections officials attempted to fire 30 prison guards who were accused of abusing inmates. After the cases were filtered through an arbitration process dictated by union contract, only eight officers were fired. Eighty other cases of alleged correctional officer abuse were settled through a union-dictated negotiation process that results in brief suspensions of offending officers, instead of termination (Robbins 2015: 1–8).

Prison riots

Riot is defined herein as a group of persons acting in concert in order to cause disorder, to engage in acts of violence and to destroy property. Prison riots are common and have been occurring for a long time. While the senior author participated in a week-long workshop for prison administrators, offered by the National Institute of Corrections, that focused on "Advanced Management Strategies in Prison Disturbances," he learned that prison riots occur with great frequency in American prisons and that the media and the general public rarely learn about them. In this section, we review a cross section of prison riots, dating from 1774 to the present. Please be mindful that what follows is just a sampling of the riots that have occurred in America's prisons.

One of the first recorded American prison riots was in 1774 at Newgate Prison in Simsbury, Connecticut. Little is known about how it came about or how it was suppressed. We know somewhat more about the California Folsom Prison riot of 1927. Sometime in the morning of November 29th, Warden Court Smith notified Governor Clement Calhoun Young that 1,400 inmates were rioting. Young called out the National Guard, sending 450 Guardsmen to the prison. An unknown number of local police officers and deputy sheriffs joined in as well. Armed with machine guns, rifles and gas bombs, Guardsmen, police officers and deputy sheriffs entered the prison, throwing the gas bombs through windows into buildings where the rioters had clustered. Inmates fired back, using weapons they had seized. A retreat ensued and lasted through the night. By morning, realizing they were outnumbered, and outgunned, the inmates surrendered and went peacefully back into their cells (Wilson 1927).

In 1945, six inmates escaped from their cellblock at the old Sugarhouse Prison in Utah. They released 30 other prisoners and began destroying the cellblock. Officers from the Utah Highway Patrol and from a number of local police departments responded. After 9 hours, the inmates agreed to return to their cells. In 1951, four guards were taken hostage at the old Point of the Mountain Utah State Prison, located south of Salt Lake City. Shortly thereafter, 260 rioting inmates seized control of the prison's security building and proceeded to rip their cellblock and the security building apart. A call was made from the prison, asking for help. Soon, 60 Highway Patrol officers and almost a hundred officers from neighboring police departments began to arrive. Armed with handguns, shotguns, sub-machine guns and tear gas, officers surrounded the prison. Four hours later, all rioting inmates surrendered, released the hostages and peacefully returned to their cells. On February 6, 1957, a correctional officer was stabbed by five Utah State Prison inmates. One day later, the prison erupted in a 14-hour riot, resulting in heavy property damage. Once again, Highway Patrol and local police officers moved in, eventually extinguishing the riot (Utah Highway Patrol 2005).

On September 9, 1971, inmates began to fight next to a large, old gate that separated critical sections of Attica Prison, located 30 miles east of Buffalo, New York. Fights were common at Attica where the prison operated at 140 percent of capacity, where inmates were allowed to shower once a week and where each inmate had to make a single roll of toilet paper last for a month. Prisoners assembled to watch the fight and pressed against the gate, eventually breaking one of its rusted hinges. Watching the gate swing free, inmates realized that they could pass through it and seize the prison's control room. They did so, and one of the nation's bloodiest prison riots was under way. Dozens of hostages, including many guards, were captured. One was beaten to death with a club. Several other guards were beaten by inmates wielding baseball bats, sections of chain and pieces of pipe. Several buildings were set on fire. Inmates spread throughout the prison and gained control. Governor Nelson Rockefeller was notified, and soon thereafter, hundreds of police officers began to mass around the prison's walls. Five days of negotiating followed, with prisoners making speeches and issuing demands for better treatment. Prison officials negotiated and stalled, negotiated and stalled.

Finally, on September 13, Governor Rockefeller issued the order that the prison would be forcibly seized. Around 10 a.m., a state police helicopter began dropping tear gas throughout the prison, and officers, armed with handguns, shot guns, rifles and clubs, stormed the prison. In 6 minutes, an estimated 2,200 bullets and shotgun shells were discharged. Attica prison was seized, and 39 people, 10 hostages and 29 inmates lay dead. State officials claimed that all deaths were perpetrated by inmates who had slit the throats of their captives. Autopsies revealed that all 39 victims had been killed by the gunfire of law officers. In the aftermath of the takeover, Attica prisoners were stripped naked and were beaten with batons while being forced to crawl into the prison yard. In 1974, hundreds of Attica inmates filed a class action lawsuit against state and prison officials. In August 2000, the state of New York settled the lawsuit by paying the inmates' lawyers $4 million, and 500 surviving inmates, $8 million. In 2002, surviving Attica hostages, and close relatives of hostages who were killed by law enforcement gunfire, petitioned the state of New York for $30 million in reparations and an apology (Haberman 2002; PBS 2005).

We have read scores of books and articles about the Attica riot. We have watched documentary films about the Attica riot. It is our opinion that Tom Wicker's powerful book, *A Time to Die* (1975) is the most authoritative and sensible source of information about this testament to human stupidity and cruelty. After the riot had begun, inmate leaders, correctly fearing that New York state authorities might simply overrun the prison and perpetrate mass violence, invited a group of observers to come, hoping that their presence would serve a useful purpose. Wicker, a distinguished journalist and writer, was one of the observers who actually came to Attica. Wicker and the other observers shuttled back and forth, into and out of Attica, negotiating with inmate leaders and corrections officials. Finally, a few hours before the bloody takeover was begun, Wicker and the other observers were barred from entering Attica and were pushed aside. What happened next stands as an infamous chapter in American prison history. Wicker was appalled and outraged by what he viewed as the needless killing of 39 human beings. Wicker believed that, had corrections officials and Governor Rockefeller negotiated in good faith with inmate leaders, a peaceful resolution could have been found. His angst soon turned into a classic book.

In the early 1970s, the Oklahoma State Prison at McAlester was boiling over with violence. Operating at 200 percent of capacity, between 1970 and July 1973, 19 inmates died violently, 40 others were stabbed and another 44 suffered serious beatings. Then, on July 27, 1973, McAlester Prison erupted into mass violence. The event had started peacefully with a three-day hunger strike. But, on July 27, suddenly two guards were stabbed in the mess hall. Other prisoners, armed with "shanks," began taking hostages. Within 15 minutes, the riot was in full bloom. Many inmates brought out their supplies of prison brew, sometimes called "pruno," and proceeded to get drunk. Other inmates raided the prison infirmary, seizing narcotics, and proceeded to get high. At the prison paint shop, prisoners found glue and paint thinner to inhale. Inmates armed themselves with the usual prison weapons – "shanks," clubs, screwdrivers and hammers. Twenty-four persons were taken hostage, including twenty-one correctional officers. Inmates and hostages were beaten. The mess hall turned into a bloody mess, described by one observer as a "butcher shop." Twenty-four buildings were set on fire.

Governor David Hall was notified, and soon, 250 Oklahoma Highway Patrol officers and National Guardsmen arrived. Negotiations ensued. Governor Hall arrived and offered to negotiate with the inmates. Hostages were released, and peaceful inmates were allowed to safely exit the prison. More negotiations occurred. Promises were made by Governor Hall and additional hostages were released. Eventually, Highway Patrolmen and National Guardsmen entered the prison and regained control. In the end, most of the Oklahoma State Prison at McAlester was destroyed or badly damaged by fire, costing taxpayers $20 million. Three prisoners were fatally stabbed. One died of heart failure, and three others escaped (Oklahoma Department of Corrections 2005).

In the early morning of February 2, 1980, 15 correctional officers were guarding 1,000 inmates at the Penitentiary of New Mexico, located near Santa Fe. Like most American prisons, the Penitentiary of New Mexico was overcrowded, and illicit drugs were freely available. But here, guards exploited "snitches" as a main control mechanism, causing a violent and dangerous rift between a group of inmates who, for favors, would "rat" on others and the remainder of the inmate population. The prison at Santa Fe was a dangerous place. Doors and gates were left unlocked and open by irresponsible guards. Four guards were taken hostage. Inmates exploded through the unlocked doors and gates, smashed glass windows in the prison control room and gained access to most keys that secured locks within the prison. Eight more guards were taken hostage, bringing the total to twelve. Buildings were torn apart and set on fire. The infirmary was seized. Drugs and "pruno" flowed. Many inmates were stabbed and beaten. Some guards were stabbed and beaten. Some prisoners gained entrance into the cellblock where "snitches" were housed. "Snitches" were hanged, decapitated and otherwise brutalized. One died after having a blow torch held to the side of his head. Governor King was alerted and soon the National Guard arrived. Negotiations ensued, but produced no progress. Inmates sensed that a violent takeover loomed. Some inmates surrendered. Hostages were released. Dead and wounded persons were carried to the front gates and were taken away in ambulances. After 36 hours of revolt, the remaining inmates surrendered. Thirty-three inmates had been killed. One hundred other inmates were taken to a hospital, suffering from brutal wounds and drug overdoses.

Fire had destroyed most of the prison. A large-scale investigation of the riot followed. Many problems were identified. Twenty years later, as the century ended, little progress had been made in correcting problems that plague the Penitentiary of New Mexico (Gallagher 1999).

In 1986, 700 inmates rioted at South Carolina's Kirkland Correctional Institution. In 1987, Cuban detainees seized Atlanta's federal penitentiary, taking 100 hostages and holding the facility for eleven days. In 1988, two-thirds of Oklahoma's Mack Alford Correctional Center was seized by rioting inmates. Eight hostages were taken. In 1988, a riot occurred in the Special Housing Unit (SHU) of New York's Coxsackie Correctional Facility. One correctional officer was stabbed and several others were taken hostage. In 1988, drunk on "pruno," rioting inmates at Idaho's State Correctional Institution broke into a control center and seized the prison's close-custody housing unit. In 1989, two riots occurred on the same day at Pennsylvania's State Correctional Institution at Camp Hill. In all, 13 hostages were taken. In 1991, Cuban detainees rioted at Alabama's Talladega Federal Correctional Institution. Hostages were seized and held for ten days (Useem et al., 1995).

In 2000, a prison at Lamesa, Texas, erupted in violence, leaving 1 inmate dead and 31 others injured (Ivins 2000). In 2000, 200 inmates rioted at California's infamous Pelican Bay State Prison. Dozens of prisoners were seriously injured, and one was shot to death (Associated Press 2003a). In 2001, a California Mojave Desert prison riot left five inmates in critical condition, suffering from "deep puncture wounds," while 12 others received medical treatment for cuts (Ananova 2001: 1). In 2002, at California's Folsom State Prison, approximately 80 members of rival Hispanic gangs were released by correctional officers into the same exercise yard. A brutal riot ensued. Several current and former employees at Folsom alleged that the riot was staged by correctional officers and then covered up. In 2004, the United States Attorney, based in the Eastern District of California, issued a press release stating that his office had begun a review of the 2002 Folsom Prison riot (U.S. Department of Justice 2004b, February 6). In 2002, at California's New Folsom State Prison, 16 inmates fought with correctional officers. Several officers and inmates were injured. Officers fired rubber bullets at the inmates and live rounds of ammunition overhead (Walsh 2002). In 2003, 75 inmates again rioted at Pelican Bay State Prison in California (Associated Press 2003a). In 2003, more than 100 inmates rioted at a prison in Baker, California, operated by private vendor, Cornell Companies. Nineteen inmates were stabbed, and a fire was set (Associated Press 2003b). In 2004, between 150 and 300 prisoners rioted at Colorado's Crowley County Correctional Facility, a prison operated by Corrections Corporation of America. Thirteen inmates required medical treatment. One suffered from severe stab wounds. Equipment was smashed and fires were set. Four housing units were damaged (Gonzales et al., 2004: 1A; Sanko & Woullard 2004: 6A). Finally, in 2004, inmates rioted at Kentucky's Lee Adjustment Center, a prison owned by Corrections Corporation of America. A housing unit was severely damaged, and the prison's administration building was set on fire (Pitsch 2004).

In 2007, at an Indiana prison operated by the for-profit Geo Group, inmates, angered over their transfer from Arizona, "rioted" by taking off their shirts in the prison yard, in defiance of direct orders from correctional officers to remain fully clothed. In the melee that followed, two prison employees were injured. Fires were set in a prison yard. County, city and state police, wearing riot gear, assembled at the prison. Ample quantities of tear gas were used during the police take-over of the prison. Five inmates were sent to hospitals for treatment related to tear gas exposure (Associated Press 2007b: 1–2).

On April 20, 2008, at the U.S. Penitentiary in Florence, Colorado, a number of white supremacist inmates were celebrating Hitler's birthday in the exercise yard. Fueled by prison brew, armed with shanks, clubs and rocks, the white supremacists began yelling in a mean-spirited manner, toward a group of African American inmates. The ensuing riot involved about 200 inmates. In response, guards used 200 rounds of ammunition fired from M-16 rifles. They fired hundreds of pepper balls from a device inmates often mistake for a shotgun. Tear gas canisters and sting grenades were thrown. After peace was restored, two inmates lay dead, shot by guards positioned on towers above the riot. Thirty inmates and one correctional officer received treatment for injuries. This riot was emblematic of the wave of violence that surged at federal U.S. penitentiaries throughout 2008 (Sample 2008: 1–7).

In 2009, at the California Institution for Men, located in Chino, a riot involving approximately 1,400 inmates broke out. Fires were set. Inmates were stabbed. Others were slashed with pieces of broken glass. Yet others experienced traumatic blows to the head.

Officers from nearby police departments assembled outside the prison. Using pepper spray, less-than-lethal force as well as lethal-force options, the assembled force stormed and regained control of the prison. Hundreds of inmates had been injured. Fifty-five required hospitalization. No prison employees or police officers reported having been injured. It is noteworthy that, in 2006, this same prison had erupted in widespread violence (Castillo 2009: 1–2).

In 2012, at a 2,500-bed Corrections Corporation of America facility in Natchez, Mississippi, a fight broke out, possibly between rival gangs. The violence quickly spread throughout the prison and soon involved as many as 300 combatants. Inmates employed the usual array of weapons including shanks, clubs, broken glass, as well as mop and broom handles. Fires were set. A number of hostages were taken. Outside the prison, local and state police officers, as well as some officers from the FBI, assembled alongside prison staff. Using mostly pepper balls fired from "paint ball guns" that, to many inmates, look like shotguns, the assembled force retook the prison. One guard had been killed by a blow to the head. As many as 16 prison employees received treatment for injuries (Botelho & Gallman 2012: 1–4).

On September 19, 2012, a riot involving about 60 inmates broke out at the "New Folsom" prison in Folsom, California. New Folsom holds over 2,500 hardened inmates. New Folsom houses scores of inmates who could not get along in other California prisons. Guards used "blast dispersion rounds," as well as six bullets fired from a rifle, to break up the fighting. One inmate was wounded by the gunfire and required hospitalization. Twelve inmates, who had been stabbed, slashed or hit in the head, required hospitalization. A number of inmates received medical treatment at the prison for injuries incurred during the riot. This riot occurred at a time when thousands of California prisoners were taking part in rolling hunger strikes, in order to protest a number of ways they are treated (NBC News 2012: 1–2).

In 2015, at the Arizona State Prison – Kingman, run by the for-profit Management and Training Corporation, a riot broke out, sparked by a guard struggling with an inmate. Fires were set. A number of buildings at the Arizona prison were so badly damaged that they could no longer house inmates. Local and state police assembled at the prison. Working alongside the for-profit guards, the police regained control of the prison. Nine guards and four inmates were injured during the riot. However, due to the physical damage at the prison, over 1,000 inmates had to be transferred to other prisons (Christie 2015: 1–3).

The Federal Bureau of Prisons operates 13 Criminal Alien Requirement (CAR) prisons. These prisons are for over 25,000 aliens serving criminal sentences in the United States, before they will be deported. In 2015, a riot broke out at a CAR prison located in Raymondville, Texas. This 2,658-bed facility named the Willacy County Correctional Center was run by the for-profit Management and Training Corporation. Most inmates slept in 10 Kevlar tents, each housing 200 men sleeping in 100 bunkbeds. Another 800 men were kept in a building, separated into 4 dorms housing 200 men each. About 75 inmates were locked up in isolation cells due to overcrowding, not to misbehavior. The altercation began as a peaceful work strike on the part of inmates protesting the conditions of their confinement. Correctional officers, working for the Management and Training Corporation, donned riot gear and formed into "Disturbance Control Teams." The Teams approached inmate pods armed with guns loaded with rubber bullets, with tear gas canisters and with BB-filled grenades (Wessler 2015: 11). When some inmates refused to leave their pods, violence ensued. Soon thereafter, a full-blown riot was under way. Officers shot rubber bullets and threw BB-filled grenades at inmates. Inmates threw rocks and pieces of broken pipe at officers. Broom and mop handles were used as weapons. Inmates, trying to escape, cut holes in the Kevlar tents. Fires were set. Busting through doors and fences, inmates freed those confined to solitary. Police from local agencies, as well as federal officers, assembled outside the prison. In this case, negotiators were able to arrange for a peaceful takeover of the prison by guaranteeing that all inmates would be transferred to other prisons (18). Injured officers and inmates apparently received medical treatment at the prison. After the riot, the Federal Bureau of Prisons (FBOP) decided that the Correctional Center was uninhabitable. All inmates were transferred to other FBOP prisons. Almost all of the Correctional Center's employees lost their jobs (1).

In Alabama, at the William C. Holman Correctional Facility, an officer was stabbed while trying to break up a fight between two inmates. When the warden and other officers arrived, violence spread to other combatants. In the melee that followed, the warden was stabbed. A fire was set. About 100 inmates took part in the riot. Emergency Response Teams were assembled, and after a few hours, officers were able to take back control of the prison. Perhaps most notable about this prison riot was the fact that inmates, using cellular telephones and social media, were able to post pictures of the riot for others outside the prison walls to see while the riot was still under way. The existing criminal laws prohibiting inmates from possessing cellular telephones and from using social media apparently did not serve as an adequate deterrent (Hanna 2016: 1–4).

Officials have taken a number of steps to combat prison riots. Thousands of American inmates now reside in Secure Housing Units (SHUs) where they are locked down 23 hours per day, where they shower and exercise alone. When moved from their cells, SHU occupants are chained, hand and foot, and usually accompanied by at least two correctional officers. SHUs make it impossible for inmates to assemble in significant numbers, thus eliminating much of the risk of a riot. Most states and the federal government have built super-maximum-security prisons that typically hold only one prisoner per cell and keep inmates locked down in their cells 23 hours per day. The authors spent a day in an Indiana super-maximum-security prison where inmates were moved about, handcuffed and shackled, one at a time. When officers approached with an inmate, flashing lights went off in the ceiling of hallways, signaling that all persons must vacate the hallway. In this prison, a riot would be nearly impossible. Unfortunately, research indicates that holding inmates in isolation for extended periods causes mental illness and worsens existing mental illness (Grassian 1994).

Prison riots have spawned a new industry. Led by the Department of Justice's Office of Law Enforcement Technology Commercialization (OLETC), corrections officials and officers are learning how to combat inmates by using high technology. A featured event of this movement occurs at a Civil

War–era prison, now inoperative, near Moundsville, West Virginia. Each year, OLETC personnel bring together hundreds of corrections officers and officials with technologists, inventors and vendors who have high-technology riot fighting equipment and services for sale. For 4 days, they participate in equipment demonstrations, training programs and mock prison riots, staged by crack troops representing a number of the nation's corrections systems. In 1997, 107 persons showed up for the first Riot Academy. By 2001, 1,315 participants from 25 states were in attendance, and according to OLETC, the law enforcement technology industry had broken the $1 billion per year sales barrier (Gonnerman 2001). In 2004, the Moundsville Riot Academy featured "wall-climbing reconnaissance robots, rolling bullet-proof barriers, sound cannon, Pepper-Ball fusillades, and Hydro-Force foggers, as well as protective gear" (Hayden 2004: 72). Today, the U.S. Department of Justice operates the National Law Enforcement and Corrections Technology Center (NLECTC) system, an agency that carries forward matchmaking between prison officials and manufacturers of high-technology "inmate management equipment" (National Institute of Justice 2016: 1).

Prisons and disease

American prisons are incubators for disease (Nolan 2012: 1–3; Bingswanger 2010: 1–3). AIDS, hepatitis B and C, syphilis, gonorrhea, chlamydia, herpes, drug-resistant strains of tuberculosis, meningitis and treatment-resistant skin infections are diseases commonly found among American inmates:

> In any given year, 35 percent of people with tuberculosis, nearly a third of those with hepatitis C and 17 percent of the people with AIDS pass through jails and prisons. Faced with budget crises, many correctional facilities back away from testing inmates, fearing they will be required to pay for expensive treatments.
>
> (Staples 2004: 1)

About 95 percent of all prisoners will eventually be released (Mitchell 2002). In fact, each year, approximately 600,000 inmates are released from U.S. prisons. When we add jails to our count, released inmates bring with them back into American communities and cities an estimated 39,000 cases of AIDS; 98,000–145,000 HIV infections; 155,000 hepatitis B cases; 1,300,000–1,400,000 hepatitis C cases; and 12,000 cases of tuberculosis (Zack 2004: 7). America's prisons boast an HIV infection rate that is almost five times that of U.S. residents not serving prison sentences (New York Times 2006: 1). At the end of 2005, 20,888 state prison inmates and 1,592 federal prison inmates were either infected with the HIV virus or were confirmed to be suffering with AIDS (Maruschak 2007: 1; see also Centers for Disease Control and Prevention 2015: 1–2):

> "Tuberculosis ... infects 1 in 4 people in some prisons, compared to fewer than 1 in 10,000 in the general population. Hepatitis C infects an estimated 41 percent of inmates just in California prisons, compared to less than 2 percent of the population at large"
>
> (Weed 2001: 2–3)

Sovaldi is the current drug of choice for treating hepatitis C. Sovaldi costs $1,000 per pill (Denver Post 2014c: 12A). It is estimated that, in 1997, 250,000 inmates who were infected with syphilis, 77,000 with gonorrhea and 186,000 with chlamydia were released from U.S. jails and prisons (Stop Prisoner Rape 2004b: 1). Government estimates of disease among inmates are considerably lower, largely because many jails and prison systems do not test inmates for infectious diseases, and many jail and prison medical practitioners fail to correctly diagnose such ailments when confronted with them (Reiterman 2004; Yee 2003; Starchild 2001). Disease in prison is spread through fighting, rape, injection drug use, tattooing/piercing, skin contact, sharing towels and soap and breathing infected air.

AIDS

The incidence of AIDS is 10 to 14 times higher in state and federal prisons than in the general U.S. population. For most inmates who contract AIDS, it becomes an unadjudicated death sentence (Mitchell 2002). AIDS is the second most common cause of death among American inmates. AIDS is the cause of death for one in three California prisoners (Stop Prisoner Rape 2004b: 1): "HIV testing, emotional support, prevention education, and proper medical care are often not readily available in prison environments" (American Association for World Health 1999: 3). The U.S. Department of Justice conservatively estimates that, in 1991, there were 17,551 HIV-positive inmates in state and federal prisons (Maruschak 1997: 1). By 2002, the number of HIV-positive inmates had increased to 23,864 (Maruschak 2004: 1). One of the most effective ways to abate the spread of AIDS among men in prison would be through the distribution of condoms. Unfortunately, "condoms are banned or simply unavailable in more than 95 percent of the nation's prisons (Staples 2004: 1).

Tuberculosis

Tuberculosis (TB) is a lung disease that spreads quickly through the air, especially in enclosed places. Tuberculosis can cause death. In 1990, New York's prison system was besieged with a virulent strain of tuberculosis. Thirty-nine inmates and two correctional officers contracted the disease. A child of one correctional officer was struck by TB. Tuberculosis claimed the life of the other correctional officer. Thirty-five of the stricken inmates perished. As this strain of TB passed from New York prisons into New York communities and cities, another 1,000 persons contracted TB. In 1999, tuberculosis hit a South Carolina prison, first infecting a single inmate. The disease quickly spread among HIV-positive inmates, housed together in a special living unit. In just a few months, 31 inmates and 1 medical student were infected (Weed 2001). In 1997, the latest year for which data were available, government sources reported 729 new cases of tuberculosis in U.S. prisons (Hammett et al., 1999: 85). We suspect that this estimate is exceedingly low.

Hepatitis

Hepatitis C is an infection of the liver that kills approximately 5 percent of its victims. There is no certain cure for hepatitis C, and treatment is almost always problematic. Hepatitis C attacks the liver and can result in cirrhosis or liver cancer. The cost of medical treatment for liver failure can range from $50,000 to $250,000 per patient (Fazlollah & Lin 2002). Hepatitis C symptoms include fatigue, jaundice, vomiting and intense pain. In 2001, it was estimated that approximately 360,000 inmates were infected with hepatitis C. Drugs to treat hepatitis C cost between $12,000 and $14,000 per person per year. Side effects include flu-like symptoms and severe suicidal inclinations (Mandak 2001). Available drugs produce a "cure rate" of about 25 percent. Data available from corrections systems that test for it, suggest that, nationally, about 18–25 percent of all inmates are infected with hepatitis C (Fazlollah & Lin 2002; Lezin Jones & Smothers 2002). A massive hidden cost of hepatitis C is likely to come from the many inmate lawsuits being filed against corrections officials, contract medical providers and state departments of correction alleging that, while imprisoned, those infected were not given adequate medical treatment (Abbott 2002: 5A; Lezin Jones & Smothers 2002; Stewart 2002).

Skin infections

According to the Centers for Disease Control and Prevention, treatment-resistant skin infections are increasing among jail and prison inmates. Particularly troublesome is staphylococcus aureus, a staph infection that is difficult to accurately diagnose, that is highly contagious and that defies available drugs. Mild staph infections manifest themselves as rashes, boils or wounds. Left untreated, or incorrectly treated, staph infections become life-threatening, as they contaminate blood and bones (Yee 2003). Florida, Georgia, Mississippi and New Jersey prisons have been particularly hard-hit by such infections (Hartz 2003; Lee 2003). Most medical doctors diagnose staphylococcus aureus infections as spider or insect bites and attempt to treat the problem with spider and insect control regimens. Such treatment attempts ultimately fail, but do allow the staph infection additional time to spread (Rieger 2005).

Recommended procedures for reducing transmission of staphylococcus aureus – reducing the bacterial load in the environment, eliminating the sharing of towels and soap, disinfecting toilets and shower areas after each use, disinfecting work areas as one inmate leaves and before another enters, etc. – are nearly impossible to achieve in jail and prison settings. Since drug-resistant staph infections are highly contagious, the potential for their spread from inmates, through contact with correctional officers and visitors, to persons outside of prison is alarmingly high. In this way, through direct or indirect contact with inmates, law-abiding citizens of American communities and cities become part of this nation's ever-growing prison disease problem.

Phantom illnesses

U.S. prison inmates are, from time to time, subject to illnesses and infections that defy simple diagnosis. For example, at the Pleasant Valley State Prison in Coalinga, California, over a 3-year period, over 900 inmates and 80 employees have been stricken with what is called "valley fever." Valley fever mimics the symptoms of a cold or the flu. However, it is a far more serious infection that has resulted in 12 deaths. Other stricken inmates have experienced permanent disability, confinement to a wheelchair and long, expensive visits to hospitals (McKinley 2007: 1). Similarly, in Colorado, due to "virus outbreaks," four prisons were closed to visitors when 244 inmates experienced vomiting, diarrhea and nausea (Mitchell 2014: 6A).

Summary

In this chapter, we've examined what American sociologist, Robert Merton, would have termed "latent functions" of the U.S. prison system, consequences not intended and, often, not recognized. Rape is the raw underbelly of American imprisonment. Men and women raped in prison are scarred for life. They bring with them to their after-prison lives unreconciled pain and inability to trust. Somehow, prison rape victims must find ways to be loving spouses, loving, caring parents and dependable employees while hosting such demons from their past. The prison rapist, when released from prison, most likely takes his or her style of comportment into new relationships, thus creating much pain in U.S. cities and communities and much new work for police and courts.

As we have seen, prison violence impacts the lives of most inmates in the United States. We must remember that violence is a powerful language and can be used by practitioners to solve problems. Whether in the form of inmate-on-inmate violence, inmate-on-correctional officer violence, correctional officer-on-inmate violence or a prison riot, violence teaches inmates that rehabilitation is not the language of corrections. By operating prisons where persons are immersed in violence, we are inadvertently teaching inmates the value of this problem-solving strategy for use in their after-prison lives. In this sense, rampant prison violence dilutes, possibly extinguishes, most attempts at rehabilitation.

Disease, in all of its manifestations, has always been a problem in prisons. Prisons are places where men and women are kept in close proximity to one another and are frequently without the benefits of adequate hygiene and sanitation. However, as many U.S. prisons morphed into overcrowded warehouses, the disease problem has grown more threatening and serious. The cost of treating diseased inmates in prison is high, with no relief in sight. Inmates with contagious diseases, who are released from prison are likely to spread disease in the cities and communities to which they return.

Unfortunately, it is possible that for many inmates after-effects of rape, other violence and disease may become the most lasting legacy of their time spent in a U.S. prison. For most corrections officers and other prison workers, rape, other violence and disease pose an ever-present threat to their well-being as well as to the well-being of their families. Through corrections officers and other prison employees, violence and disease can move out of a prison and into the neighborhoods where prison workers live.

The future of prisons in the United States

Introduction

The U.S. prison system has become big business. The U.S. incarceration rate of over 700 inmates per 100,000 U.S. population competes for highest in the world. This loosely connected system, holding approximately 1.5 million inmates on any given day, encompasses hundreds of state and federal prisons spread throughout the United States. Corporate prisons compete alongside publicly run prisons to fill inmate beds. Running parallel to this system of prisons for common criminals is a rapidly growing network of federally financed prisons designed to hold men, women and children who illegally enter the United States, mostly along its Southern border. What social forces led to the creation and maintenance of this vast network of lock-ups? What factors, woven into U.S. culture, combine to suggest a healthy future for U.S. prisons?

Factors favoring growth

As a starting point, we look at stratification in the United States. Instead of favoring W. Lloyd Warner's dated "Yankee City" model of upper, middle and lower classes in the United States, we prefer a hybrid depiction that allows input from Marx and Veblen. Today, at the top of American society we find a class of wealthy, powerful humans who are varietal in nature. Some at the top are good-hearted folks who use their wealth and power to promote the general well-being of the citizenry. All too many other Americans at the top justify Veblen's label as the "Predatory Class," for their insatiable greed and for their disinterest in the welfare of others. Herein, borrowing from Marx, we label predators in the U.S. upper-class "LumpenOnePercenters." LumpenOnePercenters are persons possessing considerable wealth and power who, lacking humane consciousness, choose to oppress and exploit others in order to acquire ever more resources and power. LumpenOnePer- centers are, for the most part, immune from prosecution and imprisonment.

Next in line we find the American middle class. Most of us in the U.S. were taught that this was the large class, that middle-class Americans and their prosperity were the bedrock of a great civilization. Then, sometime back in the 1970s, the middle class started shrinking. As predators took more and more of America's wealth, many in the middle class couldn't keep up. In economic terms, they slipped downward.

At the bottom of U.S. stratification is the lower class, or the prole- tariat in Marxist terms. This class is a vast, and growing, segment of the U.S. population. Many at the bottom of U.S. stratification are law-abiding persons who work for a wage, a wage that sorely limits their opportuni- ties to rise from the bottom. Many others at the bottom of U.S. stratifica- tion are dispossessed or unemployed workers. A number of such persons must depend upon public assistance and charity for subsistence. Also at the bottom of American society, again using imagery developed by Marx, are the lumpenproletariat, persons of limited means who, lacking humane consciousness, choose to oppress and exploit others in order to acquire resources and power. Growth in the size of the U.S. lower class and consequently in the lumpenproletariat, promises an unending sup- ply of common criminals for police attention, for prosecution and for imprisonment.

In school, most U.S. citizens were taught that, through evolving public consensus, a common need was recognized for the development of formal means to manage, and otherwise control, the lumpenproletariat. In turn, the vast network of police, criminal courts, jails and prisons in the United States was created as the mechanism used to control members of the criminal underclass. From this perspective, by developing and maintaining a "justice" system that leads to mass incarceration, U.S. cities and communities are somewhat pacified, as many of the "worst-of-the-worst" common criminals are placed behind bars. However, there is another way to look at criminal justice in the United States. From this perspective, the rich and powerful, especially the LumpenOnePercenters, operate police, criminal courts, jails and prisons in order to maintain an effective defensive buffer between their excessive wealth and other members of society who are in need.

Beyond stratification, there is another cultural factor that seems to portend a healthy future for prisons in the United States. From early on, this country was founded upon racist ideas and practices. In simple terms, European Americans, through a series of cultural and structural iterations, created and maintained a belief system whereby whites were superior to blacks, reds, yellows and browns. Whites dictated the structure and function of criminal law. Persons of color were the subjects of criminal law. Little has changed in American society. At some point while they are alive, African American males have a 32 percent chance of imprisonment, and Hispanic American males have a 17 percent chance of imprisonment, whereas European American males have a 6 percent chance of imprisonment. In contrast, a large proportion of persons in the dwindling middle class, as well as rich and powerful Americans, would have to put forth great effort in order to be sent to prison.

In the sense that Du Bois meant, we Americans see each other through colored lenses. Many Americans looking through the white lens, see color as dangerous and innately criminal. Americans looking through colored lenses see a system of "criminal justice" rigged against them, a system designed to sweep them into jail, then into prison. In this sense, the War Between the States never ended. As de Tocqueville predicted, the war over race and racism rages onward in the streets of our cities and communities and behind the walls of our prisons. Americans who no longer see color as an important factor are, unfortunately, greatly outnumbered by Americans practicing one or another form of racism. Racism in the United States has mutated into a range of behaviors. On the soft side, most racist Americans today follow former U.S. Senator Daniel Moynihan's advice to then President Richard Nixon, to adopt a policy of "benign neglect" toward race-related issues. In other words, just ignore them and maybe they will go away. On the hard side of contemporary racism in the United States, we find numerous well-organized and well-funded hate groups, like the Ku

Klux Klan and their like. Hard haters practice aggressive, violent racism. In sum, it appears that racist ideas and practices woven into U.S. culture are likely to ensure a large, steady supply of minority inmates, as well as a good number of violent haters, for the U.S. prison system. As we have noted elsewhere, should U.S. police, prosecutors, judges and juries ever develop an appetite for tackling middle-class and upper-class crime, the need for prisons would likely increase considerably.

In the last three decades of the twentieth century, as a majority of U.S. mental institutions were closed, and as dispossessed mental patients were placed back into America's cities and communities, a new demand for prison space was created. In the years that followed, as America's mentally ill came into contact with the police, many arrests were made. Many imprisonments occurred. The net effect is that, today, jails and prisons in the United States on any given day house approximately 350,000 persons who are severely mentally ill. In contrast, psychiatric hospitals that remain open in the United States provide in-patient services for about 35,000 severely mentally ill persons. Housing such large numbers of severely mentally ill persons in U.S. prisons has become costly. Taxpayers in the United States are financing the equivalent of 100 prisons, each with 3,500 beds, full of severely mentally ill persons. Given current levels of economic distress in the middle and at the bottom of the stratification system and given participation of thousands of American soldiers in foreign combat, we see no looming shortage of severely mentally ill persons in the United States. Consequently, demand for prison space should be boosted by a steady supply of severely mentally ill criminal-law violators, well into the future.

Yet another social factor characteristic of contemporary culture seems to point toward a bright future for prisons in the United States. For the past 20 years, or so, Big Money, in the form of private equity firms, has been sifting through U.S. industries, looking for properties that could be acquired cheaply, then manipulated, in order to achieve large, quick profits. As we described in Chapter 5, Big Money found the U.S. prison industry and invested heavily. With Big Money as a player in the prison game, effective lobbying of politicians and prison officials heightens considerably. Big Money recruits and employs former politicians and policymakers, who then lobby their buddies in Congress and the executive branch for prison contracts of various types. With a powerful force like Big Money pushing for more and more imprisonment, continued growth in the prison industry would seem likely.

Factors favoring shrinkage

What factors, now woven into the culture, combine to suggest a less promising future for prisons in the United States? As a starting point, we look at the U.S. economy, a system seriously damaged by impacts related to the Great Recession of 2008. Many workers in the United States lost their jobs. Many lost their homes. LumpenOnePercenters jumped in and bought large quantities of the repossessed homes, often in batches of 100 or more. Some dispossessed workers found new homes, all too often as tenants paying rent to companies owned by LumpenOnePercenters. Many dispossessed workers remain homeless. Others found temporary quarters, usually with a relative. Some workers found new jobs, usually for less pay. Many have not. The net effect of this recent shift downward in the well-being of U.S. wage earners is a base of taxpayers who cannot afford to continue underwriting an ever-more-expensive system of mass incarceration.

We must also look at the increasing costs of keeping masses of humans locked up. As we have noted elsewhere, many taxpayers now find themselves paying more of their tax dollars for imprisonment than for higher education or for the maintenance of infrastructure (roads, bridges, railways, etc.). As the U.S. prison population grays, hospital prisons will be necessary, and inmate medical costs will shoot upward. As the U.S. prison population becomes more diverse, new, somewhat shocking medical costs will emerge. For example, in 2015, U.S. District Court Judge, Jon Tigar, ruled that a California inmate be allowed to undergo a sex change operation that will cost California taxpayers as much as $100,000. Increased needs for hip and knee replacements, for treatment of heart conditions, as well as for treatment for communicable diseases will significantly push the cost of imprisonment upward. Politicians have been responding by closing prisons and by releasing inmates. For example, in 2015, the U.S. Department of Justice announced that it would release early approximately 6,000 inmates from federal prisons. In 2016, the U.S. Bureau of Prisons announced that they had created enough space in federal prisons to allow all federal inmates to be transferred out of for-profit prisons. These steps towards shrinking prison populations are encouraging. But, they should be viewed with a grain of skepticism. If the past provides a glimpse of the future, then a majority of inmates released early from prison will be caught within 3 years of release and will again be imprisoned for commission of a crime. If this is the case, policymakers and prison officials are simply pushing the prison overcrowding problem out onto the streets and into the future. In another sign of contraction, in July 2016, like a number of other state departments of correction, the Colorado Department of Corrections announced the closing of a prison located in Burlington, Colorado. This closing, however, still leaves Colorado with 19 other costly prisons in their system.

About the death penalty and executions

As with other race-related issues, the War Between the States lingers when the death penalty and executions are brought to the forefront. A majority of the United States still favors use of the death penalty and executions. A growing minority of the United States, in legal terms, has turned away from the death penalty and executions. In Chapter 6, we described significant recent downturns in death sentences handed down by U.S. judges and juries, as well as in numbers of executions successfully undertaken. There are, however, approximately 3,000 inmates sitting on death rows spread throughout the death-belt states. Executions have slowed partly because a number of recent attempts were horribly botched. Executions have also slowed because a few pharmaceutical corporations quit manufacturing a drug deemed an essential part of the death-causing process used by executioners. As departments of correction used up their supplies of the drug, it seemed that execution, at least in the form of the preferred three-drug injection series, would end. However, capitalism seems to be prevailing. At least one department of correction found a boutique pharmacy (a legal pharmacy specializing in high-priced, small-batch production of pharmaceutical products), located in the United States, that will manufacture the drug for use in executions. With this development, it would appear that America's executioners have found a new source for their preferred drug.

What about the future of capital punishment in the United States? Capital punishment and executions are part of the fabric of American society. They are, therefore, likely here to stay. Only the U.S. Supreme Court seems to be positioned to expunge the death penalty. So far, the Supreme Court has not done so. As we surrender this manuscript to our patient publisher, a new President is preparing to take office. The President-elect will appoint at least one new justice to the U.S. Supreme Court. Should he stay in office for a full term, the President-elect will likely appoint two new justices. Should the President-elect serve for two terms, he could appoint as many as four new justices. Consequently, we see little chance, at least in the foreseeable future, that the U.S. Supreme Court would rule against the death penalty. Similarly, the U.S. Supreme Court is likely to support some form of execution protocol, perhaps old-school approaches like hanging and the electric chair or perhaps a more modern technique, like a one-drug, lethal injection approach.

What can be done?

We understand that prisons are a necessary part of any large civilization, that some humans are so dangerous, so exploitive that they must be locked up. This is an essential societal imperative. We do, however, believe that prisons are overused in the United States and that modern warehouse prisons are inappropriate placements for many inmates. The modern American warehouse prison is almost all about punishment. Only approximately 10 to 15 percent of inmates in a warehouse prison are enrolled in academic or rehabilitation classes. The experiences of the other 85 out of every 100 inmates are strongly influenced by state-raised convicts and by the inmate subculture. Because of this dynamic, most attempts at rehabilitation inside a warehouse prison are smothered under the weight of violence and gang-related pressure.

To maintain the status quo is lunacy. The United States hosts about 5 percent of the world's population. Yet United States taxpayers finance about 25 percent of the world's prison cells. Warehouse prisons help us handle the large numbers. But warehouse prisons infrequently rehabilitate. Warehouse prisons, for the most part, do not help inmates become taxpayers, good parents and loving spouses. Instead, warehouse prisons expose inmates to gratuitous violence, disease and forced sex. As inmates leave prison – and most inmates will get out of prison – they bring with them, back to U.S. cities and communities harmful by-products of inmate life. In this sense, imprisonment keeps on giving, well after the sentence has been completed.

As a starting point for moving beyond warehouse prisons, we suggest a two-tier system of imprisonment that physically separates punishment from rehabilitation. Our plan is simple. All persons living in the United States who are convicted of a crime that warrants imprisonment, as a first step, would be sentenced to incarceration in a "Punishment Prison." While serving time at the punishment prison, inmates would pay their debt to society by working at jobs created by the state. Treatment of inmates in punishment prisons would be much the same as it is today in warehouse prisons. In this way, the American need will be met to see criminals punished. Over time, as inmates demonstrate peaceful behavior, respect for others and a willingness to learn, they can become eligible to apply for transfer to the second tier of incarceration. The second tier of incarceration, called the "Rehabilitation Prison," is physically separate from the punishment prison. At the rehabilitation prison, primary focus turns to helping each inmate become a law-abiding, taxpaying member of society, when she or he is released. In order to help in creating law-abiding, respectful taxpayers out of inmates, partnerships can be formed with American businesses to create jobs that pay a fair wage and that will help inmates pay their bills. If, while at a rehabilitation prison, an inmate engages in violence, commits a new crime, or attempts to escape, then the inmate is returned to a punishment prison. We believe that this simple transformation within the U.S. prison system would begin the process of reform that is sorely needed. We understand that no single solution will solve all of the problems found in U.S. prisons. Maintaining the status quo, however, could lead to disaster of significant proportions.

Bibliography

Abbott, J. (1981). *In the belly of the beast.* New York: Vintage.

Abbott, K. (2002, February 28). Lawyer: infected inmates not treated. *Rocky Mountain News.*

ABCNews (2001, July 18). New prison diet aims to reduce violence [Online]. Available: www.abcnews.com.

ABCNews.com (1999). John Gotti on tape [Online]. Available: http://abcnews.go.com/topics/news/john-gotti-jr.htm.

Abramsky, S. (2001, July). Breeding violence: locking people up is supposed to make our streets safer, but it may be doing the opposite [Online]. Available: www.sashaabramsky.com/articles.html.

———. (1998). Slouching toward barbarism: wanton cruelty and private profit in the new US gulag [Online]. Available: www.sashaabramsky.com/articles.html.

Abramsky, S. & Fellner, J. (2004). The nation's mentally ill used to be locked in asylums: now they're stowed in prisons [Online]. Available: www.prospect.org.

Adamson, C. (1983). "Punishment after slavery: southern state penal systems, 1865–1890." *Social Problems*, 30, 555–569.

Aday, R. (2003). *Aging prisoners: crisis in American corrections.* Westport, CT: Praeger Publishers.

Aday, R. & J. Kabrill. (2011). *Cold comfort: women aging in prison.* Boulder, CO: Lynne Reinner Publishers.

Allard, J. (1998). Teens claim abuse at prison [Online]. Available: www.corpwatch.org/article.php?id=866.

Allen, H. & Simonsen, C. (1998). *Corrections in America*, 8th edition, Upper Saddle River, NJ: Prentice Hall.

Allen, W. & Bell, K. (1998). Death, neglect and the bottom line: push to cut costs poses risks [Online]. Available: www.corpwatch.org/article.php?id=858.

American Academy of Child & Adolescent Psychiatry (2000, October 24). Policy statement: juvenile death sentences [Online]. Available: www.aacap.org/aacap/policy_statements/2000/Juvenile_Death_Sentences.aspx.

American Association for World Health (1999, December 1). Fact sheets: HIV in specific populations [Online]. Available: www.thebody.com/content/art33129.html.

American Civil Liberties Union (2011, November). Banking on bondage: private prisons and mass incarceration [Online]. Available: https://www.aclu.org/banking-bondage-private-prisons-and-mass-incarceration.

———. (1999). ACLU sues private extradition company over guard's sexual assault of prisoner [Online]. Available: www.corpwatch.org/article.php?id=3290.

American Civil Liberties Union of Tennessee (2015). Who is CCA? What goes wrong at CCA prisons? [Online]. Available: www.aclu-tn.org/wp-content/uploads/2016/05/Who-is-CCA-Infographic-source-page.pdf.

American Correctional Association (1993). *Gangs in correctional facilities*, Laurel, MD: American Correctional Association.

American Friends Service Committee (1971). *Struggle for justice.* New York: Hill and Wang.

Ammon, D., Campbell, R. & Somoza, S. (1992). *The option of prison privatization: a guide for community deliberations.* Athens, GA: University of Georgia Press.

Amnesty International (2015, March 31). Death sentences and executions 2014 [Online]. Available: www.amnestyusa.org/research/reports/death-sentences-and-executions-2014.

———. (2012). Death penalty cost. [Online]. Available: www.amnestyusa.org/our-work/issues/death-penalty/us-death-penalty-facts/death-penalty-cost.

———. (2011a). The use of the death penalty in 2010: the global picture [Online]. Available: https://www.amnesty.org/download/Documents/24000/act500012011en.pdf.

———. (2011b). Death sentences and executions 2010 [Online]. Available: https://www.amnesty.org/en/documents/ACT50/001/2011/en/.

———. (2011c). Stop the trade in torture and death penalty equipment [Online]. Available: www.amnesty.eu/en/news/press-releases/eu/death-penalty/0532-0532/.

———. (2004a). Facts and figures on the death penalty [Online]. Available: https://www.amnesty.org/download/Documents/80000/act500062005en.pdf.

———. (2004b). The death penalty [Online]. Available: www.amnestyusa.org/sites/default/files/pdfs/deathpenaltyfacts.pdf.

———. (2004c). Women in prison: a fact sheet [Online]. Available: https://www.prisonpolicy.org/scans/women_prison.pdf.

———. (2003). Abuse of women in custody: sexual misconduct and shackling of pregnant women [Online]. Available: http://womenprisoners.org/?p=973.

———. (2001). Human rights in Oklahoma [Online]. Available: www.amnestyokc.org.

Anand, P. (2012, September 5). Winners and losers: corrections and higher education in California [Online]. Available: http://uscommonsense.org/research/winners-and-losers-corrections-and-higher-education-in-california/.

Ananova (2001, December 21). Prisoners riot at California jail [Online]. Available: www.ananova.com.

Anderson, A. (2008, October 22). Hiding out in prison bonds [Online]. Available: www.forbes.com/2008/10/22/prison-correctional-bonds-pf-ii-in_aa_1022fixedincome_inl.html.

Angelfire (2004). *Female corrections officers v. Dept. of Corrections (DOC)*: inmates gunning female nurses [Online]. Available: www.angelfire.com.

Annin, P. (1998, July 13). "Inside the new Alcatraz: the ADX 'Supermax' prison redefines hard time." *Newsweek*: 52B.

Arax, M. & Gladstone, M. (2004). Prison discipline [Online]. Available: www.worldfreeinternet.us/news/nws153.htm.

———. (1998, December 16). Keeping justice at bay [Online]. Available: http://articles.latimes.com/1998/dec/16/news/mn-54619.

Ashton, P. & Petteruti, A. (2011, June). Gaming the system: how the political strategies of private prison companies promote ineffective incarceration policies. Washington, DC: Justice Policy Institute.

Associated Press (2016, August 18). Obama administration to phase out some private prison use [Online]. Available: www.bigstory.ap.org/article/567c4b8693044e2c98e3d6fb81682c1f/obama-administration-end-use-private-prisons.

———. (2009, August 12). California struggles to desegregate prison inmates [Online]. Available: www.nbcnews.com/id/32382976/ns/us_news-life/t/calif-struggles-desegregate-prison-inmates/#.WFXdPyIzWAY.

———. (2007a). Official: guards made inmates lick toilets clean [Online]. Available: www.prisontalk.com/forums/archive/index.php/t-267934.html.

———. (2007b, April 25). Indiana prison riot quelled [Online]. Available: http://usatoday30.usatoday.com/news/nation/2007-04-24-prison-riot_N.htm.

———. (2006, September 28). State's expert: lethal injection is painless [Online]. Available: www.cbs13.com.

———. (2004, February 28). Elderly inmates burden U.S. prisons [Online]. Available: www.pewtrusts.org/en/research-and-analysis/blogs/stateline/2016/03/17/elderly-inmates-burden-state-prisons.

———. (2003a, January 3). Lockdown at Pelican bay after fight [Online]. Available: www.sfgate.com.

———. (2003b, December 3). At least 19 hurt in California prison riot [Online]. Available: www.nytimes.com/2003/12/03/us/at-least-19-hurt-in-california-prison-riot.html.

———. (2002a, June 9). California struggling with growing numbers of elderly prisoners [Online]. Available: http://globalag.igc.org/elderrights/us/CAprisons.htm.

———. (2002b, October 29). State adds more guards at Limon prison in wake of slaying. *Rocky Mountain News*.

———. (2000, July 24). Ex-guard to help with prison inquiry. *Rocky Mountain News*.

———. (1999, July 27). Prison captain twice arrested on the outside [Online]. Available: www.sunone.com.

Austin, J. & Coventry, G. (February, 2001). *Emerging issues on privatized prisons*. Washington, DC: National Council on Crime and Delinquency.

Austin, J., Johnson, K. & Gregoriou, M. (2000, October). *Juveniles in adult prisons and jails: a national assessment.* Washington, DC: U.S. Department of Justice (NCJ-182503).

Ayers, E. (1984). *Vengeance and justice: crime and punishment in the 19th-century American South.* New York: Oxford University Press.

Bailey, W.C. & Peterson, R.D. (1997). Murder, capital punishment and deterrence: a review of the literature. In H.A. Bedau (Ed.). *The death penalty in America: current controversies* (pp. 135–161). New York: Oxford University Press.

Barrett, B. & Kandel, J. (2004). L.A. gang history runs deep [Online]. Available: http://lang.dailynews.com/socal/gangs/articles/ALL_p1side1.asp.

Bates, E. (1998). Prisons for profit, cont [Online]. Available: www.corpwatch.org/article.php?id=850.

———. (1997). Private prisons [Online]. Available: www.prop1.org/legal/prisons/980105.htm.

Bates, S. (1936). *Prisons and beyond.* New York: The Macmillan Company.

Baumgartner, F. & Dietrich, A. (2015, March 17). Most death penalty sentences are overturned: here's why that matters [Online]. Available: https://www.washingtonpost.com/news/monkey-cage/wp/2015/03/17/most-death-penalty-sentences-are-overturned-heres-why-that-matters/?utm_term=.09a1bfe4a403.

Beard, J., Toche, D. & B. Beyer (2014, November). *Fall 2014 population projections.* Sacramento, CA: California Department of Corrections and Rehabilitation.

Beck, A. & Gilliard, D. (1995, August). *Prisoners in 1994* (NCJ 151654). Washington, DC: U.S. Department of Justice.

Beck, A. & Harrison, P. (2007). Sexual victimization in state and federal prisons reported by inmates, 2007. Washington, DC: Bureau of Justice Statistics (NCJ 219414).

Beck, A. & Johnson, C. (2012, May). Sexual victimization reported by former state prisoners, 2008 [Online]. Available: https://www.bjs.gov/content/pub/pdf/svrfsp08.pdf.

Beck, A. & Karberg, J. (2001, March). *Prison and jail inmates at midyear 2000.* (NCJ 185989). Washington, DC: U.S. Department of Justice.

Beiser, V. (2001, July). How we got to two million: how did the land of the free become the world's leading jailer? [Online]. Available: www.andosciasociology.net/app/download/7121535361/Debt%2BTo%2BSociety.pdf.

Bennett, J. (1970). *I chose prison.* New York: Alfred A. Knopf, Inc.

Berkowitz, B. (2001). Murder incorporated: profits from privatized prison health care [Online]. Available: http://www3.alternet.org/story/11870/murder_incorporated%3A_profits_from_privatized_prison_health_care.

Bernard, T. & McCleary, R. (Eds.). 1996. *Life without parole.* Los Angeles: Roxbury Publishing Company.

Bervera, X. (2004, Summer). The death of Tallulah Prison [Online]. Available: www.alternet.org/story/19040/the_death_of_tallulah_prison.

Bicknell, C. (1997, December). Searching for humane execution machines [Online]. Available: https://www.wired.com/1997/12/searching-for-humane-execution-machines/.

Binelli, M. (2015, March 29). A landmark lawsuit reaches inside the walls of America's toughest federal prison. *The New York Times Magazine*: 36–41.

Bingswanger, I. (2010, October 25). Chronic medical diseases among jail and prison inmates [Online]. Available: http://societyofcorrectionalphysicians.org/corrdocs/corrdocs-archives/winter-2010/chronic-medical-diseases-among-jail-and-prison-inmates.

Black, A. (2015, February 21). Here are 6 companies that get rich off prisoners [Online]. Available: www.attn.com/stories/941/who-profits-from-prisoners.

Bloomer, K. (1997, March 17). Prisons – America's newest growth industry [Online]. Available: http://prop1.org/legal/prisons/970317itt.htm.

Blumberg, P. (1999). Prisoners who speak out receive punishment, suit says [Online]. Available: www.corpwatch.org/article.php?id=3291.

Bohm, R. (2012). *DeathQuest: an introduction to the theory and practice of capital punishment in the United States*, 4th edition, New York: Elsevier.

Bonner, R. (2001a, August 30). Death sentence voided for withheld evidence [Online]. Available: www.nytimes.com.

———. (2001b, August 24). Death row inmate is freed after DNA test clears him [Online]. Available: www.nytimes.com/2001/08/24/us/death-row-inmate-is-freed-after-dna-test-clears-him.html.

Boone, R. (2011, October 10). CCA-run prison remains Idaho's most violent lock-up [Online]. Available: https://www.yahoo.com/news/cca-run-prison-remains-idahos-most-violent-lockup-153137051.html.

Botelho, G. & Gallman, S. (2012, May 21). Sheriff: anxiety ran high before Mississippi prison riot was quashed [Online]. Available: www.cnn.com/2012/05/21/us/mississippi-prison-disturbance/.

Bowers, K. (1996, August 1). Stealing time: as its inmate population ages, the Colorado prison system discovers there's no con like an old con [Online]. Available: www.westword.com/news/stealing-time-5056532.

Bowker, L. (1980). *Prison victimization*. New York: Elsevier.

Britton, D.M. (2003). *At work in the iron cage: the prison as gendered organization*. New York: New York University Press.

Brown, K. (2008). Residential facilities: State and federal oversight gaps may increase risk to youth well-being. Washington, DC: United States Government Accountability Office (GAO-08-696T).

Brown, R. & Severson, K. (2011, February 24). Enlisting prison labor to close budget gaps [Online]. Available: www.nytimes.com/2011/02/25/us/25inmates.html.

Browne, J. (1996). The labor of doing time. In Rosenblatt, E. (Ed.). *Criminal justice: confronting the prison crisis* (pp. 61–72). Boston, MA: South End Press.

Burton-Rose, D., Pens, D. & Wright, P. (Eds.) (1998). *The celling of America: an inside look at the U.S. prison industry*. Monroe, ME: Common Courage Press.

Butler, A.M. (1997). *Gendered justice in the American west: women prisoners in men's penitentiaries*. Urbana, IL: University of Illinois Press.

Butterfield, F. (2004, May 8). Mistreatment of prisoners is called routine in U.S. [Online]. Available: www.nytimes.com/2004/05/08/world/struggle-for-iraq-prisoners-mistreatment-prisoners-called-routine-us.html.

———. (2003, December 29). Women find a new arena for equality: prisons [Online]. Available: www.nytimes.com/2003/12/29/us/women-find-a-new-arena-for-equality-prison.html.

———. (2001a, August 13). Number of people in state prisons declines slightly [Online]. Available: www.nytimes.com/2001/08/13/us/number-of-people-in-state-prisons-declines-slightly.html.

———. (2001b, September 2). States ease laws on time in prison [Online]. Available: www.nytimes.com/2001/09/02/us/states-ease-laws-on-time-in-prison. html.

Cabana, D.A. (1996). *Death at midnight: the confession of an executioner.* Boston, MA: Northeastern University Press.

Cahalan, M. & Parsons, L. (1986). *Historical corrections statistics in the United States, 1850–1984.* Rockville, MD: Westat, Inc.

Caldwell, C., Jarvis, M. & Rosefield, H. (2001). "Issues impacting today's geriatric female offenders." *Corrections Today,* 65 (5), 110–113.

California Department of Corrections (2015). San Quentin State Prison [Online]. Available: www.cdcr.ca.gov/Facilities_Locator/SQ.html.

———. (2011). New internet resource for California's joint venture program [Online]. Available: http://calpia.ca.gov/JVP/7.4.11JVPRelease.pdf.

———. (2001a). Folsom State Prison [Online]. Available: www.cdcr.ca.gov.

———. (2001b). Correctional facilities [Online]. Available: www.cdcr.ca.gov.

———. (2001c). Spring 2001 population projections [Online]. Available: www.cdcr. ca.gov.

———. (2001d). San Quentin State Prison (SQ) [Online]. Available: www.cdcr.ca.gov.

———. (2001e). Pelican Bay State Prison: security housing unit [Online]. Available: www.cdcr.ca.gov.

———. (2001f). Women's institution profiles [Online]. Available: www.cdcr.ca.gov.

California Department of Corrections and Rehabilitation (2016). *Spring, 2016 population projections.* Sacramento, CA: California Department of Corrections and Rehabilitation.

California State Auditor (2011, May). Report 2010-118: California Prison Industry Authority [Online]. Available: https://www.bsa.ca.gov/reports/summary/2010-118.

Californians United for a Responsible Budget (2008, May). AB900 borrows $7.5 billion to build new prisons [Online]. Available: http://curbprisonspending.org/wp-content/uploads/2010/05/Fact-Sheet-on-Lease-Revenue-Bonds-Updated-May-08.pdf.

Camp, C. & Camp, G. (1995). *The corrections yearbook 1995.* South Salem, NY: Criminal Justice Institute.

Campaign for Youth Justice (2014). Key Facts: Youth in the justice system [Online]. Available: https://www.campaignforyouthjustice.org/documents/KeyYouthCrimeFacts.pdf.

Canadian Coalition Against the Death Penalty (2010, December 28). Death penalty for juveniles ruled unconstitutional by Supreme Court [Online]. Available: www. deathpenaltyinfo.org/juveniles-and-death-penalty.

Cannon, G. (2015, June 17). Here's the latest evidence of how private prisons are exploiting inmates [Online]. Available: www.motherjones.com/mojo/2015/06/private-prisons-profit.

Carelli, R. (1997, February 3). ABA doubts fairness, may urge moratorium on death penalty. *Daily Camera.*

Carleton, M. (1971). *Politics and punishment.* Baton Rouge, LA: Louisiana University Press.

Carnell, B. (2003). Prison rape elimination act of 2003 [Online]. Available: http://nicic.gov/prea.

Carson, E. (2014, September). *Prisoners in 2013.* Washington, DC: U.S. Department of Justice NCJ 247282.

Carter, K. (1994). Prison officers and their strategies. In Coffey, A. & Atkinson, P. (Eds.). *Occupational socialization and working lives* (pp. 41–57). Brookfield, VT: Ashgate.

Castillo, J. (2009, August 9). 250 inmates hurt, 55 hospitalized after California prison riot [Online]. Available: www.cnn.com/2009/US/08/09/california.prison.riot/.

CBS News (2001, January 8). 60ll classic: a brutal prison [Online]. Available: www.cbsnews.com/news/60ii-classic-a-brutal-prison/.

Center for Children of Incarcerated Parents (2003). Where's mommy? Mothers in the California prison system in 2003 [Online]. Available: http://e-ccip.org.

Centers for Disease Control and Prevention (2015, July). HIV among incarcerated populations [Online]. Available: www.cdc.gov/hiv/group/correctional.html.

Champion, D. (2001). *The American dictionary of criminal justice,* 2nd edition, Los Angeles, CA: Roxbury.

Chetttiar, I., Bunting, W., & Schotter, G. (2012). At America's expense: the mass incarceration of the elderly [Online]. Available: https://www.aclu.org/files/assets/elderlyprisonreport_20120613_1.pdf.

Chicago Gang History Project (2005). Chicago gangs [Online]. Available: www.uic.edu.

Chonco, N. (1989). Sexual assaults among male inmates: a descriptive study. *The Prison Journal,* 69 (1), 72–82.

Christianson, S. (1998). *With liberty for some: 500 years of imprisonment in America.* Boston, MA: Northeastern University Press.

Christie, B. (2015, July 6). New pictures show Arizona prison riot damage [Online]. Available: www.cbs46.com/story/29485786/arizona-governor-calls-for-probe-of-private-prison-unrest.

Clark County Prosecutor (2006). Brandon Hedrick executed by electric chair in Virginia [Online]. Available: www.clarkprosecutor.org/html/death/US/hedrick1035.htm.

Clear, T. (1994). *Harm in American penology: offenders, victims, and their communities.* Albany, NY: State University of New York Press.

Clear, T. & Cole, G. (2000). *American corrections,* 5th edition, Belmont, CA: West/Wadsworth.

Clements, C. (1996, March). Offender classification: two decades of progress. *Criminal Justice and Behavior,* 23 (1), 121–143.

Cockburn, A. (2001, July 18). Going insane inside the SHU box [Online]. Available: Prisonact-list digest, 1 (236), http://articles.latimes.com/2001/jul/15/opinion/op-22578.

Columbia Law School (2000). A broken system: error rates in capital cases 1973–1995 [Online]. Available: http://www2.law.columbia.edu/instructionalservices/liebman/liebman_final.pdf.

Committee on Criminal Justice – The Florida Senate (2002). A monitor: methods of execution & protocols [Online]. Available: www.helsinki.fi/~tuschano/cp/.

Committee to End the Marion Lockdown (1992). From Alcatraz to Marion to Florence – control unit prisons in the United States [Online]. Available: http://people.umass.edu/~kastor/ceml_articles/cu_in_us.html.

Conley, J. (1980). "Prisons, production and profit: reconsidering the importance of prison industries." *Journal of Social History*, 257–275.

Coordinating Council on Juvenile Justice and Delinquency Prevention (2000, November). *Juveniles and the death penalty*. Washington, DC: U.S. Department of Justice (NCJ-184748).

Corizon Health (2015). About Corizon Health [Online]. Available: www.corizon-health.com/index.php/S=0/About-Corizon/Who-We-Are-History-and-Today.

Correction Connection (2016). How Correction Connection and Prison Blues work together. [Online]. Available: www.prisonblues.net/product/1201111.

Correctional Service of Canada (2004). Institutional violence: how do inmates respond? [Online]. Available: www.csc-scc.gc.ca/research/forum/e043/e043f-eng.shtml.

Corrections Corporation of America (2015). CCA Resource Center. Available: www.cca.com/cca-resource-center.

———. (2002). Frequently asked questions [Online]. Available: www.correction scorp.com.

———. (2000). CCA completes annual summary of offender rehabilitation program results for 2000 [Online]. Available: www.correctionscorp.com.

Corrections USA (2001). Prison privatization resolution [Online]. Available: www.cusa.org.

Corwin, P. (2001). Senioritis: why elderly federal inmates are literally dying to get out of prison [Online]. Available: http://scholarship.law.edu/cgi/viewcontent.cgi?article=1244&context=jchlp.

Cowan, A. (2004, May 9). Costs and claims of cronyism besiege youth home [Online]. Available: www.nytimes.com.

Cowell, A. (2004, March 24). Swedish court sentences foreign minister's killer to life [Online]. Available: www.nytimes.com.

Cowles, E. & Sabath, M. (1996). Changes in the nature and perception of the long-term inmate population: some implications for prison management and research. *Criminal Justice Review*, 21 (1), 44–61.

Crouch, B. & Marquart, J. (1989). *An appeal to justice: litigated reforms of Texas prisons*. Austin, TX: University of Texas Press.

Currie, E. (1998). *Crime and punishment in America: why the solutions to America's most stubborn social crisis have not worked – and what will*. New York: Metropolitan Books.

Curtis, H. (2015, May 4). Feds: prison-transport driver was felon who plied inmates with booze, drugs for sex [Online]. Available: www.orlandosentinel.com/news/breaking-news/os-sex-drugs-prison-transport-bust-20150504-story.html.

Daily Camera (2000, August 31). Guard suspended over report of sex. *Daily Camera*.

Daily Times-Call (2001, May 19). 9 Saudis beheaded for rape, drugs, shooting. *Longmont Times-Call*.

Daniels, C. (2001, July 17). The big house vs. small business [Online]. Available: www.businessweek.com.

Davis, A. (1998). Masked racism: reflections on the prison industrial complex [Online]. Available: www.corpwatch.org/article.php?id=849.

Davis, B. (2016, October 28). Corrections Corporation of America rebrands as CoreCivic [Online]. Available: www.cca.com/insidecca/corrections-corporation-of-America-rebrands-as-corecivic.

Death By Lethal Injection (2001). What really happens [Online]. Available: www.cdinet.demon.co.uk.

Death Penalty Focus of California (1996). Death penalty facts and figures: exploding the myths. In Rosenblatt, E. (Ed.). *Criminal justice: confronting the prison crisis* (pp. 198–208). Boston, MA: South End Press.

Death Penalty Information Center (2016). State by state lethal injection [Online]. Available: www.deathpenaltyinfo.org/state-lethal-injection.

———. (2015). Death sentences in the United States from 1977 by state and by year [Online]. Available: www.deathpenaltyinfo.org/death-sentences-united-states-1977-present.

———. (2015a). Executions by year since 1976 [Online]. Available: www.deathpenaltyinfo.org/executions-year.

———. (2015b). Size of death row by year – (1968–present) [Online]. Available: www.deathpenaltyinfo.org/death-row-inmates-state-and-size-death-row-year#year.

———. (2015c). Number of executions by state and region since 1976 [Online]. Available: www.deathpenaltyinfo.org/number-executions-state-and-region-1976.

———. (2015d). State by state lethal injection [Online]. Available: www.deathpenaltyinfo.org/state-lethal-injection.

———. (2013). Information on defendants who were executed since 1976 and designated as "volunteers." [Online]. Available: www.deathpenaltyinfo.org/information-defendants-who-were-executed-1976-and-designated-volunteers.

———. (2012a). Facts about the death penalty [Online]. Available: www.deathpenaltyinfo.org.

———. (2012b). Executions by county [Online]. Available: www.deathpenaltyinfo.org/executions-county.

———. (2012c). Costs of the death penalty [Online]. Available: www.deathpenaltyinfo.org/costs-death-penalty.

———. (2012d). The innocence list [Online]. Available: www.deathpenaltyinfo.org/innocence-list-those-freed-death-row.

———. (2011). Lethal injection [Online]. Available: www.deathpenaltyinfo.org/lethal-injection.

———. (2004a). Executions in the U.S. 1608–1987: the Espy file [Online]. Available: www.deathpenaltyinfo.org.

———. (2004b). Searchable execution database [Online]. Available: www.deathpenaltyinfo.org/views-executions.

———. (2004c). Death sentences by year [Online]. Available: www.deathpenaltyinfo.org/death-sentences-year-1977-present.

———. (2004d). Size of death row by year – 1968–present [Online]. Available: www.deathpenaltyinfo.org.

———. (2004e). Costs of the death penalty [Online]. Available: www.deathpenaltyinfo.org/costs-death-penalty.

————. (2001). Executions in the U.S. 2000 [Online]. Available: www.deathpenalty info.org/executions-us-2000.

Deathpenalty.org (2000). The high cost of the death penalty to taxpayers [Online]. Available: www.deathpenalty.org.

deBeaumont, G. & deTocqueville, A. (1979). *On the penitentiary system in the United States and its application in France.* Carbondale and Edwardsville, IL: Southern Illinois University Press. (Originally published in 1833).

DeMause, L. (Ed.). (1974), *The history of childhood.* New York: Psychohistory Press.

Denver Post (2015a, January 29). Supreme Court puts Oklahoma executions on hold. *Denver Post.*

————. (2015b, February 14). Utah, Wyoming advance firing squad bills. *Denver Post.*

————. (2015c, October 23). FCC cuts cost of phone calls by inmate. *Denver Post.*

————. (2014a, May 1). Another blow to the death penalty. *Denver Post.*

————. (2014b, March 20). Texas finds new supplier for execution drugs. *Denver Post.*

————. (2014c, July 30). At $1,000 per pill, Sovaldi is hepatitis medicine of choice. Available: www.denverpost.com/2014/07/29/at-1000-per-pill-sovaldi-is-hepatitis-medicine-of-choice/.

————. (2004, January 4). Utah lawmakers to consider ban on death-row firing squads. *Denver Post,* 5A.

Dickey, F. (2002) Rape, how funny is it? [Online]. Available: www.pqarchiver.com.

Dilulio, J., Jr. (1994). The evolution of executive management in the Federal Bureau of Prisons. In Roberts, J. (Ed.), *Escaping prison myths* (pp.159–174). Washington, DC: The American University Press.

Dober, G. (2014, March 15). Corizon needs a checkup: problems with privatized correctional healthcare [Online]. Available: https://www.prisonlegalnews.org/news/2014/mar/15/corizon-needs-a-checkup-problems-with-privatized-correctional-healthcare/.

Donaldson, G. (2002). Gang busters: so where are today's gangs of New York? Turns out they're on the verge of extinction [Online]. Available: www.NewYorkmetro.com.

Dow, D. (2011, July 9). Death penalty, still racist and arbitrary [Online]. Available: www.nytimes.com/2011/07/09/opinion/09dow.html.

Dowdy, Z. (2002). Prison sued in 'sex slave' case [Online]. Available: www.newsday.com.

Dumond, R. & Dumond, D. (2002). Training staff on inmate sexual assault. In Hensley, C. (Ed.). *Prison sex: practice & policy* (pp. 89–100). Boulder, CO: Lynne Rienner Publishers.

Dyer, J. (2000). *The perpetual prisoner machine: how America profits from crime.* Boulder, CO: Westview Press.

Eckholm, E. (2014, December 14). Grisly execution detailed in court brief. *New York Times.*

Edwards, J. (2015, June 29). Most people don't know America's system for carrying out the death penalty was designed by a Holocaust denier [Online]. Available: www.businessinsider.com/fred-leuchter-and-whether-lethal-injection-is-cruel-or-unusual-2015-6.

Egelko, B. (2012, September 6) Prison sex requires consent, court says [Online]. Available: http://blog.sfgate.com/crime/2012/09/06/prison-sex-requires-consent-court-says/.

Elliott, D. (2013, May 22). Governor Hickenlooper delays Nathan Dunlap's execution. Available: http://denver.cbslocal.com/2013/05/22/gov-hickenlooper-delays-nathan-dunlaps-execution/.

Equal Justice Initiative (2014). Children in prison. [Online]. Available: http://eji.org/children-prison.

Ethridge, P. & Marquart, J. (1993). "Private prisons in Texas: the new penology for profit." *Justice Quarterly*, 10 (1), 29–48.

European Union (2005). Ban on trade in instruments of torture [Online]. Available: http://europa.eu.

Farmer v. Brennan, U.S. S. Ct., No. 92-7247 (1994).

Farrell, M. (2000). McAlester [Online]. Available: www.geocities.com.

Fazlollah, M. & Lin, J. (2002, July 21). New Jersey prisons fail to treat an epidemic [Online]. Available: www.philly.com.

Federal Bureau of Investigation (2015). Crime in the United States 2013, Table 32, ten-year arrest trends [Online]. Available: https://ucr.fbi.gov/crime-in-the-u.s/2013/crime-in-the-u.s.-2013/tables/table-32/table_32_ten_year_arrest_trends_totals_2013.xls.

Federal Bureau of Prisons (2015a). About our facilities [Online]. Available: www.bop.gov.

———. (2015b). About our agency [Online]. Available: www.bop.gov.

———. (2004). BOP/NIC Directory [Online]. Available: www.bop.gov.

———. (2001a, January). About the Federal Bureau of Prisons. Washington, DC: Federal Bureau of Prisons.

———. (2001b, August). Federal Bureau of Prisons: quick facts [Online]. Available: www.bop.gov.

———. (2001c, September). The Bureau in brief [Online]. Available: www.bop.gov.

———. (2001d). Executive order: creating a body corporate to be known as Federal Prison Industries, Inc. [Online]. Available: www.bop.gov.

———. (2001e, October 4). Weekly population report [Online]. Available: www.bop.gov.

———. (2001f). A brief history of Alcatraz [Online]. Available: www.bop.gov.

———. (2001g). Acquisition [Online]. Available: www.bop.gov.

———. (2001h). What we buy [Online]. Available: www.bop.gov.

———. (2000a, June 9). Notice of contract award for the management and operation of private correctional institutions [Online]. Available: www.bop.gov.

———. (2000b, March 7). Notice of contract award for the management and operation of a private correctional institution [Online]. Available: www.bop.gov.

———. (1999, April 2). Notice of contract award for the management and operation of a private correctional institution to house District of Columbia sentenced felons transferred to the Federal Bureau of Prisons [Online]. Available: www.bop.gov.

———. (1998, June 19). Notice of contract award for the management and operation of the southwest detention facility [Online]. Available: www.bop.gov.

Federal Prison Industries, Inc. (2001). What is Unicor? [Online]. Available: www.unicor.gov.

Feeler, M. (1991). "The privatization of prisons in historical perspective." *Criminal Justice Research Bulletin*, 6 (2), 1–10.

Fellner, J. (2000). Supermax prisons: an overview [Online]. Available: https://www.hrw.org/reports/2000/supermax/Sprmx002.htm.

———. (1999, April). Red Onion State Prison: super-maximum security confinement in Virginia [Online]. Available: https://www.hrw.org/reports/1999/redonion/.

FindLaw (2001, November 27). Supreme Court: prison firms can't be sued [Online]. Available: www.findlaw.com.

Fischer, B. (2013, September 26). Violence, abuse and death at for-profit prisons: a GEO Group rap sheet [Online]. Available: www.prwatch.org/news/2013/09/12255/violence-abuse-and-death-profit-prisons-geo-group-rap-sheet.

Fisher, C. (2001). Summary: principles of prison discipline suggested for consideration by the 1870 National Prison Congress [Online]. Available: www.ccpl.lib.co.us.

Fletcher, H. (2000, October 5-11). The oldest lifer in Colorado prisons is dying to be anywhere but here. *Westword.*

Florida Department of Corrections (2005) Gangs in Florida [Online]. Available: www.dc.state.fl.us.

———. (2004). Number of younger inmates declining as number of older inmates increases [Online]. Available: www.dc.state.fl.us/pub/annual/0405/stats/ip_age.html.

———. (2003a). American Correctional Association awards medal of valor to Florida sergeant Russell Bourgault [Online]. Available: www.dc.state.fl.us.

———. (2003b). Assault advisory: two inmates attack correctional officers at Washington Correctional Institution [Online]. Available: www.dc.state.fl.us/secretary/press/2003/assault01.html.

Floridians for Alternatives to the Death Penalty. (2004a). Why should Floridians support alternatives to the death penalty? [Online]. Available: www.fadp.org.

———. (2004b). Do we have a problem in Florida? [Online]. Available: www.fadp.org.

Foster, B. (2001). How to abolish the death penalty [Online]. Available: www.burkfoster.com.

Foucault, M. (1977). *Discipline and punish: the birth of the prison.* New York: Pantheon.

Frieden, T. (2012, May 17). Study finds nearly 1 in 10 state prisoners is sexually abused while incarcerated [Online]. Available: www.cnn.com/2012/05/17/us/us-state-prisons-abuse/.

Friedmann, A. (1999a). Prison privatization: the bottom line [Online]. Available: www.corpwatch.org/article.php?id=851.

———. (1999b). Corporate prison spin doctor faces ethics charges [Online]. Available: www.corpwatch.org.

———. (1998). Juvenile crime pays [Online]. Available: http://corpwatch.org/article.php?id=865.

———. (1997a). Strange bedfellows: Corrections Corporation of America's political connections [Online]. Available: www.corpwatch.org/article.php?id=869.

———. (1997b). Private transportation firms take prisoners for a ride [Online]. Available: www.corpwatch.org/article.php?id=863.

Friel, B. (1999, April 22). Critics question federal prisons' business plans [Online]. Available: www.govexec.com/federal-news/1999/04/critics-question-federal-prisons-business-plans/2821/.

Fusfeld, D. (1972, March). "The rise of the corporate state in America." *Journal of Economic Issues*, 6, 1–23.

Gaes, G., Wallace, S., Gilman, E., Klein-Saffran, J. & Suppa, S. (2001, March 9). The influence of prison gang affiliation on violence and other prison misconduct. Washington, DC: Federal Bureau of Prisons.

Gallagher, M. (1999, September 19). 1980 prison riot a black mark on state's history [Online]. Available: https://www.abqjournal.com/2000/nm/future/9futo9-19-99.htm.

Galvan, A. (2014, August 2). Inmate injected 15 times in execution in Arizona. *Denver Post*.

Gardner, G. (1987). "The emergence of the New York state prison system: a critique of the Rusch-Kirchheimer model." *Crime and Social Justice*, 29, 88–109.

Genders, E. & Player, E. (1990). "Women lifers: assessing the experience." *Prison Journal*. 80 (1), 46–57.

Gendreau, P. (1996, March). Offender rehabilitation: what we know and what needs to be done. *Criminal Justice and Behavior*, 23 (1), 144–161.

Geniella, M. (2001, April 22). Inside Pelican Bay [Online]. Available: www.mapinc.org/drugnews/v01/n707/a04.html.

Giallambardo, R. (1966). *Society of women: a study of women's prison*. New York: Wiley.

Ginzburg, R. (1962). *100 years of lynchings*. Baltimore, MD: Black Classic Press.

Glaberson, W. (2003, February 1). Ashcroft's push for execution voids plea deal [Online]. Available: www.nytimes.com/2003/02/01/nyregion/ashcroft-s-push-for-execution-voids-plea-deal.html.

Glave, J. (1997, December 1). Prisons aim to keep, and keep ahead of, convicts [Online]. Available: http://archive.wired.com/science/discoveries/news/1997/12/8583.

Glaze, L. & Kaeble, D. (2014, December) *Correctional populations in the United States, 2013*. Washington, DC: U.S. Department of Justice (NCJ 248479).

Glaze, L. & Maruschak, L. (2008, August, revised 3/30/2010). *Parents in prison and their minor children*. Washington, DC: U.S. Department of Justice (NCJ 222984).

Goldberg, E. & Evans, L. (2001). The prison industrial complex and the global economy [Online]. Available: www.globalexchange.org.

Gonnerman, J. (2001, May 30). The Riot Academy [Online]. Available: http://www3.alternet.org/story/9234/the_riot_academy.

Gonzales, M., Emery, E. & Mitchell, K. (2004, July 22). Prison back under control. *The Denver Post*.

Gottesdiener, L. (2011, June 3). California women prisons: inmates face sexual abuse, lack of medical care and unsanitary conditions [Online]. Available: www.huffingtonpost.com/2011/06/03/california-women-prisons_n_871125.html.

Governing the States and Localities (2016). State government employment: totals by job type: 1960–2012 [Online]. Available: www.governing.com/gov-data/state-government-employment-by-agency-job-type-current-historical-data.html.

Graczyk, M. (2015, March 10). Texas prison agency seeks to restock execution drug. *Denver Post*.

Grady, D. (2006, June 23). Doctors see way to cut suffering in executions [Online]. Available: www.nytimes.com/2006/06/23/us/23inject.html.

Graham, R. & DeGraff, M. (2015, August 12). Massive 70-inmate riot breaks out in California prison sparked by stabbing death of infamous 'San Quentin 6' member [Online]. Available: www.dailymail.co.uk/news/article-3195869/Slaying-infamous-San-Quentin-6-member-triggers-massive-70-inmate-riot-New-Folsom-Prison-11-convicts-stabbed.html.

Grann, D. (2004, February 16 & 23). The Brand: how the Aryan Brotherhood became the most murderous prison gang in America. *The New Yorker*.

Grassian, S. (1994). *Amended declaration regarding the incarceration of mentally ill persons in the California State Prison at Pelican Bay*. U.S. District Court case No. C-90-3094 TEH.

Greene, J. (2000). Prison privatization: recent developments in the United States [Online]. Available: www.oregonafscme.com.

Greenfield, L., Beck, A. & Gilliard, D. (1996). "Prisons: population trends and key issues for management." *Criminal Justice Review*, 21(1), 4–20.

Greenhouse, L. (2004, January 27). Supreme Court to review using execution in juvenile cases, *New York Times*: A1.

———. (2001, October 2). In a new term's somber first day, justices hear arguments on inmate rights [Online]. Available: www.nytimes.com/2001/10/02/us/supreme-court-roundup-new-term-s-somber-first-day-justices-hear-arguments-inmate.html.

Greenspan, J. (2003, October). New invasive pat search policy at women's prison in Chowchilla violates prisoner's human rights. San Francisco: California Prison Focus.

Griffin, P., Addie, S., Adams, B. & Firedtine, K. (2011, September). Trying juveniles as adults: an analysis of state transfer laws and reporting. [Online]. Available: https://www.ncjrs.gov/pdffiles1/ojjdp/232434.pdf.

Grondahl, P. (2000, March 26). Sensible control or senseless cruelty? [Online]. Available: www.mhanys.org.

Groner, J. (2002, November). Lethal injection: a stain on the face of medicine [Online]. Available: www.bmj.com/content/325/7371/1026.

Groth, A., Burgess, A. & Holmstrom, L. (1977). Rape: power, rage and sexuality. *American Journal of Psychiatry*, 134 (11), 1239–1243.

Gruley, B. (2001, September 6). Wanted: criminals: why did Mississippi agree to pay for cells for 'ghost inmates'? – prison-building spree creates oversupply of lockups, competition for convicts – Wackenhut seeks its share. *The Wall Street Journal*.

Gustin, S. (2014, February 12). Prison phone calls will no longer cost a fortune [Online]. Available: www.time.com.

Haberman, C. (2002, May 11). The specter of Attica, restless still [Online]. Available: www.nytimes.com.

Hallinan, J. (2001). *Going up the river: travels in a prison nation*. New York: Random House.

Hammett, T., Harmon, P. & Maruschak, L. (1999, July). *1996–1997 update: HIV/AIDS, STDs, and TB in correctional facilities*. Washington, DC: U.S. Department of Justice (NCJ 176344).

Hanna, J. (2016, March 12). Warden, officer stabbed in Alabama prison riot [Online]. Available: www.cnn.com.

Harer, M. & Langan, N. (2001, October). "Gender differences in predictors of prison violence: assessing the predictive validity of a risk classification system." *Crime and Delinquency*, 47 (4), 513–536.

Harer, M. & Steffensmeier, D. (1996). Race and prison violence. *Criminology*, 34 (3), 323–355.

Harris, D. (2013, March). Prison rape called common, but inmates' complaints often ignored. ABC News [Online]. Available: http://abcnews.go.com.

Harris, S. (1995, November 4). Plethora of prisoner lawsuits clog courts. *Daily Camera*.

Harrison, P. & Beck, A. (2003, July). *Prisoners in 2002*. Washington, DC: U.S. Department of Justice (NCJ-200248).

Harrison, P. & Karberg, J. (2004, May). *Prison and jail inmates at midyear 2003*. Washington, DC: U.S. Department of Justice (NCJ-203947). Note: Revised July 14, 2004.

Hartz, L. (2003, November 13). Staph infections in prisons, Inmates Contagious [Online]. Available: www.suite101.com.

Hastings, D. (2001, September 1). Slide retests cast doubt on testimony that led to Oklahoma Execution [Online]. Available: www.dallasnews.com.

Hayden, T. (2004, June 14). "Putting down a riot." *U.S. News & World Report*.

Heinzl, T. (2003, June 4). Rape victim wins suit against prison guard [Online]. Available: www.corrections.com/news/article/10908.

Henrichson, C. & Delaney, R. (2012, January, updated July 20, 2012). The price of prisons: what incarceration costs taxpayers. New York: The Vera Institute.

Henry, J. (2014, September 29) When prison guards kill inmates: Florida's Prison Massacre Revealed [Online]. Available: www.huffingtonpost.com/jessica-s-henry/when-prison-guards-kill-i_b_5897486.html.

Hensley, C. (2002a). Life and sex in prison. In Hensley, C. (Ed.). *Prison sex: practice & policy* (pp. 1–11). Boulder, CO: Lynne Rienner Publishers.

———. (Ed.). (2002b). *Prison sex: practice & policy*. Boulder, CO: Lynne Rienner Publishers.

Hensley, D. & Tewksbury, R. (2005, June). Wardens' perceptions of prison sex. *The Prison Journal*, 85 (2), 186–197.

Herbert, B. (2003, August 6) Tainted justice [Online]. Available: www.nytimes.com.

———. (2002, February 11). The fatal flaws [Online]. Available: www.nytimes.com.

Hertzberg, H. (2007, January 15) Desolation rows. *The New Yorker*, 21.

HM Prison Service (2005). New toolkit helps staff tackle violence in prison [Online]. Available: www.hmprisonservice.gov.uk.

Hockenberry, S. Sickmund, M. & Sladky, A. (2013, September). *Juvenile residential facility census, 2010: selected findings*, Washington, DC: U.S. Department of Justice, Office of Justice Programs.

Holland, G. (2004, April 19) Death sentences hinge on Supreme Court [Online]. Available: www.newsobserver.com.

Home Box Office (1991). *Doing time: life inside the big house*. (Cassette Recording). New York: Home Box Office.

Hood, R. (2002). *The death penalty: a worldwide perspective*, 3rd edition, New York: Oxford University Press.

Hoover's Online (2002a). Corrections Corporation of America [Online]. Available: www.hoovers.com.

———. (2002b). Wackenhut Corrections Corporation [Online]. Available: www.hoovers.com.

———. (2002c). Cornell Companies, Inc. [Online]. Available: www.hoovers.com/company-information/cs/company-profile.cornell_companies_inc.47ocad1278fcb3d1.html.

House, H.W. (1997). The new testament and moral arguments for capital punishment. In H.A. Bedau (Ed.). *The death penalty in America: current controversies*. New York: Oxford University Press.

Huff, R. & Meyer, M. (1997). "Managing prison gangs and other security threat groups." *Corrections Management Quarterly*, 1, 10–18.

Hughes, J. (2002, November 24). Aryan Brotherhood makes home in state: Florence prison now its headquarters. *Denver Post*.

Human Rights Watch (1995). Children in confinement in Louisiana [Online]. Available: https://www.hrw.org/reports/1995/Us3.htm.

Human Rights Watch (2000, May). Punishment and prejudice: racial disparities in the War on Drugs. Vol.12, No. 2 (G). New York: Human Rights Watch.

———. (1999, June). *U.S. Department of Justice bargains away rights of women prisoners*. New York: Human Rights Watch.

———. (1996). *All too familiar: sexual abuse of women in U.S. state prisons*. New York: Human Rights Watch.

Inciardi, J. (1986). *The war on drugs*. Palo Alto, CA: Mayfield Publishing Company.

Indiana Department of Correction (2001). Maximum control facility [Online]. Available: www.ai.org/indcorrection.

Ingold, C. (2011, February 7). Inmates claim abuse: 10 women in state prisons file lawsuit alleging sexual acts by guards. *Denver Post*: 11A.

Investigative Reports (1998). *The Farm: life inside Angola Prison*. (Cassette Recording). New York: A&E Network.

Irwin, J. (1980). *Prisons in turmoil*. Glenview, IL: Scott, Foresman and Company.

———. (1970). *The felon*. Englewood Cliffs, NJ: Prentice-Hall, Inc.

Irwin, J. & Austin, J. (1997). *It's about time: America's imprisonment binge*, 2nd edition, Belmont, CA: Wadsworth Publishing Company.

itvs (2004, July). When the bough breaks: mothers in prison [Online]. Available: https://itvs.org/films/when-the-bough-breaks.

Ivins, M. (2000, May 5). Prison riots wait for no candidate [Online]. Available: www.workingforchange.com.

Jacobs, D. & Helms, R. (2001). "Towards a political sociology of punishment: politics and changes in the incarcerated population." *Social Science Research*, 30, 171–194.

Jacobs, J. (1976). Prison violence and formal organization. In A. Cohen, G. Cole, & R. Bailey (Eds.). *Prison violence*. Lexington, MA: D.C. Heath and Company.

Jackson, A., Shuman, A. & G. Dayaneni (2006). Toxic sweatshops: how UNICOR prison recycling harms workers, communities, the environment and the recycling industry. Berkeley, CA: Center for Environmental Health.

Jackson, D., Marx, G. & Medill Watchdog (2014, December 8). Violence, runaways a problem at residential centers across the U.S. [Online]. Available: www.chi-cagotribune.com/news/watchdog/rtc/ct-youth-treatment-national-picture-met-20141209-story.html.

Jackson, J.L., Jackson, J.L. Jr. & Shapiro, B. (2001). *Legal lynching: the death penalty and America's future,* New York: Anchor Books.

Jackson, W. (2013, September 5). Prisons get a new way to stop inmates from using cell telephones [Online]. Available: https://gcn.com/articles/2013/09/05/prison-cell-phones.aspx.

Janofsky, M. (2003, May 29). Utah officials preparing for another firing squad, to be used as soon as next month [Online]. Available: www.nytimes.com/2003/05/29/us/utah-officials-preparing-for-another-firing-squad-be-used-soon-next-month.html.

Johnson, E. & Waldfogel, J. (2003). Where children live when parents are incarcer-ated. *JCPR Policy Briefs* 5 (4) [Online]. Available: www.jcpr.org.

Johnson, H. (2001). Prisons of profit: turning a buck on America's incarceration frenzy [Online]. Available: www.phillyimc.org.

Johnson, H. & Wolfe, N. (1996). *History of criminal justice,* 2nd edition, Cincinnati, OH: Anderson Publishing Company.

Johnson, R. (1990). *Death work: a study of the modern execution process.* Belmont, CA: Wadsworth.

———. (1987). *Hard time: understanding and reforming the prison.* Pacific Grove, CA: Brooks/Cole.

Justice Policy Institute (2014, April). *Billion dollar divide: Virginia's sentencing, cor-rections and criminal justice challenge.* Washington, DC: Justice Policy Institute.

Justice Strategies (2010, March 1). As N-Group scandal emerges in governor's race, have lessons been learned? [Online]. Available: www.texasprisonbidness.org/2010/03/n-group-scandal-emerges-governors-race-have-lessons-been-learned.

Justice Works (2004, July). Mothers in prison [Online]. Available: www.justiceworks.org.

Kappeler, V., Blumberg, M. & Potter, G. (1996). *The mythology of crime and criminal justice,* second edition, Prospect Heights, IL: Waveland Press, Inc.

Kershaw, S. (2002, June 24). Report shows serious crime rose in 2001 [Online]. Available: www.nytimes.com/2002/06/24/us/report-shows-serious-crime-rose-in-2001.html.

Keim, J. (2015, June 29). *Glossip v. Gross:* holding the line on lethal injection [Online]. Available: www.nationalreview.com/bench-memos/420493/glossip-v-gross-holding-line-lethal-injection-jonathan-keim.

Keve, P. (1994). At the mercy of the states. In Roberts, J. (Ed.). *Escaping prison myths: selected topics in the history of federal corrections* (pp. 25–35). Washington, DC: The American University Press.

———. (1991). *Prisons and the American conscience: a history of U.S. federal corrections.* Carbondale, IL: Southern Illinois University Press.

Khalek, R. (2011, July 21). 21st-century slaves: how corporations exploit prison labor [Online]. Available: www.alternet.org/story/151732/21st-century_slaves%3A_how_corporations_exploit_prison_labor.

Kilborn, P. (2001, August 1). Rural towns turn to prisons to reignite their economies. *New York Times*.

King, R. (1999). The rise and rise of supermax: an American solution in search of a problem? *Punishment & Society*. 1 (2), 163–186.

King, R. & Mauer, M. (2001, August). Aging behind bars: "three strikes" seven years later. Washington, DC: The Sentencing Project.

Kirkham, C. (2013, March 22). Lake Erie prison plagued by violence and drugs after corporate takeover [Online]. Available: www.huffingtonpost.com/2013/03/22/lake-erie-prison-violence_n_2925151.html.

Kleinsorge, T. & Zatlokal, B. (Eds.). (1999, May). *The death penalty: abolition in Europe*. Strasbourg, Germany: Council of Europe Publishing.

Knox, G. (1999). A national assessment of gangs and security threat groups (STGs) in adult correctional institutions: results of the 1999 adult corrections survey [Online]. Available: www.ngcrc.com/ngcrc/page7.htm.

Konda, S, Reichard, A. & Tiesman, H. (2012, July). Occupational injuries among U.S. correctional officers, 1999–2008 [Online]. Available: https://www.ncbi.nlm.nih.gov/pmc/articles/PMC4562411/pdf/nihms716793.pdf.

Koscheski, M., Hensley, C., Wright, J. & Tewksbury, R. (2002). Consensual sexual behavior. In Hensley, C. (Ed.). *Prison sex: practice & policy* (pp. 111–131). Boulder, CO: Lynne Rienner Publishers.

Krugman, P. (2012, June 21). Prisons privatization, patronage. [Online]. Available: www.nytimes.com/2012/06/22/opinion/krugman-prisons-privatization-patronage.html.

Kunselman, J. Tewksbury, R., Dumond, R. & Dumond, D. (2002). Nonconsensual Sexual Behavior. In Hensley, C. (Ed.). *Prison sex: practice & policy* (pp. 27–47). Boulder, CO: Lynne Rienner Publishers.

LaFree, G. & Drass, K.A. (1996).The effect of changes in intraracial income inequality and educational attainment on changes in arrest rates for African Americans and whites, 1957 to 1990. *American Sociological Review*, 61(4), 614–634.

Lamott, K. (1961). *Chronicles of San Quentin: the biography of a prison*. New York: David McKay Company.

LaMotte, G. (2000, June 10). Prison guards acquitted of staging gladiator-style prison fights [Online]. Available: www.archives.cnn.com.

Lavoie, D. (2015, June 26). Boston bomber in Colo. prison for temporary stay. *Denver Post*.

Lee, K. (2003, November 4). Letter to Florida Epidemic Intelligence Service regarding MRSA [Online]. Available: www.angelfire.com.

———. (2002). A crime in the name of God, the state, and Justice: Florida guards once again go unpunished [Online]. Available: www.angelfire.com.

Legislative Analyst's Office (2010, May 11). Elderly inmates in California prisons [Online]. Available: www.lao.ca.gov/handouts/crimjust/2010/Elderly_Inmates_05_11_10.pdf.

Lessing, B. (2016, September 30). Study shows prison gangs rule much more than penitentiaries [Online]. Available: www.insightcrime.org/news-analysis/study-shows-prison-gangs-rule-much-more-than-penitentiaries.

Levy, G. (1994). *To die in Chicago: Confederate prisoners at Camp Douglas, 1862–1865*. Evanston, IL: Evanston Publishing Company.

Lewin, T. (2001, August 24). 3-strikes law is overrated in California, study finds [Online]. Available: www.nytimes.com/2001/08/23/us/study-finds-3-strikes-measure-in-california-much-overrated.html.

Lewis, A. (2001, April 21). Abroad at home; a test of civilization [Online]. Available: www.nytimes.com/2001/04/21/opinion/abroad-at-home-a-test-of-civilization.html.

Lewis, N. (2003, October 7). Justices let stand ruling that allows forcibly drugging an inmate before execution [Online]. Available: www.nytimes.com/2003/10/07/us/justices-let-stand-ruling-that-allows-forcibly-drugging-inmate-before-execution.html.

Lewis, W. (1965). *From Newgate to Dannemora*. Ithaca, NY: Cornell University Press.

Lezin, K. (1999). *Finding life on death row: profiles of six inmates*. Boston, MA: Northeastern University Press.

Lezin Jones, R. & Smothers, R. (2002, November 28) Prisoners' suit says New Jersey ignored hepatitis to save money [Online]. Available: www.nytimes.com/2002/11/28/nyregion/prisoners-suit-says-new-jersey-ignored-hepatitis-to-save-money.html.

Lichtblau, E. (2001, August 21). DEA chief looks at California policy as blueprint for U.S. *Los Angeles Times*.

Lindsay, S. (2002, November 9). "Grandpa" sentenced in sex assault on girl, 8. *Rocky Mountain News*.

Liptak, A. (2008, February 9). Electrocution is banned in last state to rely on it [Online]. Available: www.nytimes.com/2008/02/09/us/09penalty.html.

———. (2004, February 14). Study revises Texas' standing as a death penalty leader [Online]. Available: www.nytimes.com/2004/02/14/us/study-revises-texas-standing-as-a-death-penalty-leader.html?_r=0.

———. (2003, October 7). Critics say execution drug may hide suffering [Online]. Available: www.nytimes.com/2003/10/07/us/critics-say-execution-drug-may-hide-suffering.html.

LIS, Inc. (2000, May). *Sexual misconduct in prisons: law, remedies, and incidence*. Longmont, Colorado: National Institute of Corrections.

———. (1998, September). *Hospice and palliative care in prisons*. Longmont, Colorado: National Institute of Corrections.

Locke, M. (2001, July 7). A big 'sayonara' to San Quentin? *Daily Camera*.

Logan, C. (2000). Private prisons: the prison privatization research site [Online]. Available: www.ucc.uconn.edu/~logan.

———. (1990). *Private prisons: cons and pros*. New York: Oxford University Press.

Loney, R. (2001). A dream of the tattered man: stories from Georgia's death row. Grand Rapids, MI: Wm. B. Eerdmans Publishing Company.

Long, P. (2001, October 9). In inmate death case, questions of fairness abound [Online]. Available: www.cgi.herald.com.

Lutheran Church in America (1991). A social statement on the death penalty [Online]. Available: http://download.elca.org/ELCA%20Resource%20Repository/Death_PenaltySS.pdf?_ga=1.210610390.2140995880.1481387985.

Maciag, M. (2014, March, 13). Where state government has dropped, climbed [Online]. Available: www.governing.com/news/headlines/state-government-employment-changes-since-recession-takeaways.html.

Macias Rojas, P. (1998). Prisons and poverty: a nation in crisis [Online]. Available: www.corpwatch.org.

Madrid v. Gomez, 889 F.Supp. 1146 (1995), 1181. (C-90-3094-TEH).

Maker, J. (2001, May). The quality of care of elderly inmates in prison [Online]. Available: www.keln.org.

Mandak, J. (2001, September 5). US: prisons see surge in cases of Hepatitis C [Online]. Available: www.mapinc.org.

Mariner, J. (2003, July 28). Stopping prison rape [Online]. Available: http://writ.findlaw.com.

———. (2001). *No escape: male rape in U.S. prisons*. New York: Human Rights Watch.

Marois, M. (2013, July 24). Brown scuttled prison bond haunts inmate release order [Online]. Available: https://www.bloomberg.com/news/articles/2013-07-25/brown-scuttled-prison-bond-haunts-inmate-release-order.

Martin, J. (2013, February 3). AT&T to pay Washington prisoners' families $45 million in telephone class action settlement [Online]. Available: http://blogs.seattletimes.com/opinionnw/2013/02/03/att-to-pay-washington-prisoners-families-45-million-in-telephone-class-action-settlement/.

Martinez, J. (2001, September 5). Prison vs. drug program weighed: treatment sentences would free up space. *Denver Post*.

Martinson, R. (1974, Spring). What works: questions and answers about prison reform. *Public Interest*. 35, 22–54.

Maruschak, L. (2007, September). *HIV in prisons, 2005*. Washington, DC: Bureau of Justice Statistics, U.S. Department of Justice. (NCJ218915).

———. (2004, December). *HIV in prisons and jails, 2002*. Washington, DC: U.S. Department of Justice (NCJ 205333).

———. (1997, August). *HIV in prisons and jails, 1995*. Washington, DC: U.S. Department of Justice (NCJ 164260).

Marvel, W. (1994). *Andersonville: the last depot*. Chapel Hill, NC: University of North Carolina Press.

Mason, C. (2012, January). Too good to be true: private prisons in America [Online]. Available: http://sentencingproject.org/wp-content/uploads/2016/01/Too-Good-to-be-True-Private-Prisons-in-America.pdf.

Massachusetts Department of Corrections (2005). Gang security threat group information [Online]. Available: www.mass.gov.

Mattera, P., Khan, M., LeRoy, G. & Davis, K. (2001). As states struggle with budget crises, governments spend huge sums on economic development subsidies for private prisons [Online]. Available: www.goodjobsfirst.org.

Mauer, M. (1999). *Race to incarcerate*. New York: The New Press.

McAfee, W. (1987). Tennessee's Private Prison Act of 1986: an historical perspective with special attention to California's experience. *Vanderbilt Law Review*, 40, 851–865.

McCombs, B. & Whitehurst, L. (2015). Utah vote may show execution frustration. *Denver Post*: 15A.

McCrie, R. (1992). "Three centuries of criminal justice privatization in the United States." in G. Bowman, Hakim, S. & Seidenstat, P. (Eds.). *Privatizing the United States Justice System*. Jefferson, NC: McFarland & Company, Inc.

McGaughey, D. & Tewksbury, R. (2002). Masturbation. In Hensley, C. (Ed.). *Prison sex: practice & policy* (pp. 1–11). Boulder, CO: Lynne Rienner Publishers.

McKelvey, B. (1936). *American prisons.* Chicago: University of Chicago Press.

McKinley, J. (2007, December 30). Infection hits a California Prison hard [Online]. Available: www.nytimes.com/2007/12/30/us/30inmates.html.

McMahon, P. (2003, August 11). Aging inmates present prison crisis [Online]. Available: http://usatoday30.usatoday.com/news/nation/2003-08-10-prison-inside-usat_x.htm.

Mears, M. (2001). Death by lethal injection or death by electrocution: and the difference is ???? [Online]. Available: www.gidc.com.

Melossi, D. & Pavarini, M. (1981). *The prisons and the factory: origins of the penitentiary system.* Totowa, NJ: Barnes and Noble.

Mendel, R. (2011). No place for kids. [Online]. Available: www.aecf.org/resources/no-place-for-kids-full-report.

Merriman, A. (2016, April 2). Corrections officer injured during assault by inmate, report says [Online]. Available: www.nj.com/mercer/index.ssf/2016/04/corrections_officer_injured_after_inmate_assault.html.

Metz, A. (1999, March 21). Life on the inside: the jailers. *Newsday.*

Mill, J.S. (2004). Speech in favor of capital punishment [Online]. Available: http://ethics.sandiego.edu/Books/Mill/Punishment/.

Mitchell, K. (2015, February 19). Inmate says he wants to stay in solitary. *Denver Post,* 8A.

———. (2014, April 19). Illness spurs four prisons to limit visits. *Denver Post,* 4A.

———. (2013, December 10). Transfers follow supermax lawsuit. *Denver Post,* 4A.

———. (2009, December 13). Inmate Relives Terror: raped in Prison. *Denver Post,* B1.

Mitchell, S. (2002, July 26). Prison rapes spreading deadly diseases [Online]. Available: www.upi.com/Prison-rapes-spreading-deadly-diseases/14231027722324/.

Montero, D. (2005, January 6). Grand jury indicts prison gangsters. *Rocky Mountain News.*

Moreno, I. (2015, July 10). Suit: immigrants got $1 a day for work at prison. *Longmont Times- Call.*

Morton, J. (1993, February). "Training staff to work with elderly and disabled inmates." *Corrections Today,* 55, 44–47.

———. (1992, August). *An administrative overview of the older inmate.* Washington, DC: U.S. Department of Justice.

Mother Jones (2002, May 13). 7-Up bubbles over prison rape [Online]. Available: www.motherjones.com.

———. (2001, July 23). The incarceration Index: prison's rising numbers in the land of the free [Online]. Available: www.alternet.org/story/11203/the_incarceration_index%3A_prison%27s_rising_numbers_in_the_land_of_the_free.

Moushey, B. (1990, October 19). Camp hill convicts tell of hard time. *Pittsburgh Post-Gazette.*

MSNBC (2000). *Lockup: inside Pelican Bay.* (Cassette Recording). New York: MSNBS.

Mumola, C. (2000, August). *Incarcerated parents and their children.* (NCJ-182335). Washington, DC: U.S. Department of Justice.

Murton, T. (1976). *The dilemma of prison reform*. New York: Holt, Rinehart and Winston.

Murton, T. & Hyams, J. (1967). *Accomplices to the crime: the Arkansas prison scandal*. New York: Grove Press.

Musick, D. (2001). *An introduction to the sociology of juvenile delinquency*. Albany, NY: State University of New York Press.

————. (1995). *An introduction to the sociology of juvenile delinquency*. Albany, NY: State University of New York Press.

Nathan, S. (2000). The prison industry goes global [Online]. Available: www.yesmagazine.org/issues/is-it-time-to-close-the-prisons/the-prison-industry-goes-global.

National Correctional Industries Association (2015). Prison Industry Enhancement Certification Program: Quarterly Report [Online]. Available: www.nationalcia.org/piecp-2/quarterly-statistical-reports.

————. (2002). PIE Certification program [Online]. Available: www.nationalcia.org/piecp-2.

————. (2001). Final report – training & technical assistance project: private sector prison industry enhancement program (PIECP) [Online]. Available: www.nationalcia.org.

National Council of Churches (2001). People fleeing persecution held in "worse than prison" conditions in U.S. [Online]. Available: www.ncccusa.org/news/01news38.html.

National Institute of Corrections (1998, September). Current issues in the operation of women's prisons. Longmont, CO: National Institute of Corrections.

National Institute of Justice (2016, June 16). The National Law Enforcement and Corrections Technology Center (NLECTC) system [Online]. Available: https://www.nij.gov/topics/technology/pages/assistance.aspx.

National Park Service (2001). Alcatraz Island U.S. Penitentiary [Online]. Available: https://www.nps.gov/alca/learn/historyculture/us-penitentiary-alcatraz.htm.

National PREA Resource Center (2013). Prison Rape Elimination Act [Online]. Available: https://www.prearesourcecenter.org/about/prison-rape-elimination-act-prea.

NBC News (2012, September 20). 13 inmates hurt, shots fired during 'New Folsom" prison riot [Online]. Available: http://usnews.nbcnews.com/_news/2012/09/20/13981953-13-inmates-hurt-shots-fired-during-new-folsom-prison-riot.

NDAA (2001, June/May). NDAA update [Online]. Available: www.ndaa.org.

Nelson, L. & Foster, B. (Eds.). (2001). *Death watch: a death penalty anthology*. Upper Saddle River, NJ: Prentice-Hall.

New York Times (2011, January 28). Lethal injection and the F.D.A. Available: www.nytimes.com/2011/01/28/opinion/28fri3.html.

————. (2009a, October 4). Botched executions. Available: www.nytimes.com/2009/10/03/opinion/03sat2.html.

————. (2009b, September 28). High cost of death row. Available: www.nytimes.com/2009/09/28/opinion/28mon3.html.

————. (2007, August 6). The executioner's hood. Available: www.nytimes.com/2007/08/06/opinion/06mon2.html.

————. (2006, July 24). A warning about AIDS in Prison [Online]. Available: www.nytimes.com/2006/07/24/opinion/24mon4.html.

————. (2004, April 19). Foreigners on death row. New York: New York Times. Available: www.nytimes.com.

Nolan, K. (2012, November 6). The prison system and its relation to communicable disease presence in the United States [Online]. Available: https://nyutorch.com/2012/11/06/the-prison-system-and-its-relation-to-communicable-disease-presence-in-the-united-states/.

Noonan, M., Rohloff, H. & Ginder, S. (2015, August4). Mortality in local jails and state prisons, 2000-2013 – statistical tables [Online]. Available: https://www.bjs.gov/index.cfm?ty=pbdetail&iid=5341#.

Novak, D. (1978). *The wheel of servitude: black forced labor after slavery*. Lexington, KY: University Press of Kentucky.

O'Connor, A. (2010, September 24) Woman, 41, is executed in Virginia [Online]. Available: www.nytimes.com/2010/09/24/us/24execute.html.

Office of the Inspector General, U.S. Department of Justice (2015, May). The impact of an aging inmate population on the Federal Bureau of Prisons [Online]. Available: https://oig.justice.gov/reports/2015/e1505.pdf.

Oklahoma Department of Corrections (2005). The 1973 OSP riot and fire [Online]. Available: https://www.ok.gov/doc/documents/DOC%20History.pdf.

Oldach, B. (2016, February 26). Four correctional officers injured in women's prison fight [Online]. Available: http://whotv.com/2016/02/26/four-correctional-officers-injured-in-womens-prison-fight/.

Oppel, R. (2011, May 18). Private prisons found to offer little in savings. [Online]. Available: www.nytimes.com/2011/05/19/us/19prisons.html.

Organized Crime About (2001). John Gotti reportedly near death [Online]. Available: www.organizedcrime.about.com.

Ovalle, D. (2014, September 28) Inmate death in private transport van in Miami-Dade raises questions [Online]. Available: www.miamiherald.com/news/state/florida/article2287990.html.

Paczensky, S. (2001). The wall of silence: prison rape and feminist politics. In Sabo, D., Kupers, T. & London, W. (Eds.). (2001). *Prison masculinities*. Philadelphia, PA: Temple University Press.

Palast, G. (1999). Wackenhut's free market in human misery [Online]. Available: www.corpwatch.org/article.php?id=868.

Pankratz, H. & Mitchell, K. (2005, January 9). Prison gang built network of violence and intimidation. *The Denver Post*.

Parenti, C. (1999). The prison industrial complex: crisis and control [Online]. Available: www.corpwatch.org/article.php?id=852.

Parker, C., Greene, J., Libal, B. & Mazon, A. (2014, October). For-profit family detention: meet the private prison corporations making millions by locking up refugee families [Online]. Available: http://grassrootsleadership.org/reports/profit-family-detention-meet-private-prison-corporations-making-millions-locking-refugee.

Paternoster, R. & Brame, R. (2003). *An empirical analysis of Maryland's death sentencing system with respect to the influence of race and legal jurisdiction*. Unpublished report.

Pavlo, W. (2012, February 14). Corrections Corp of America on buying spree – State prisons for sale? [Online]. Available: www.forbes.com/forbes/welcome/?toURL=www.forbes.com/sites/walterpavlo/2012/02/14/corrections-corp-of-america-on-buying-spree-state-prisons-for-sale/.

PBS (2005). The Rockefellers: Attica prison riot – September 9–13, 1971 [Online]. Available: www.pbs.org/wgbh/americanexperience/features/general-article/rockefellers-attica.

Pear, R. (2004, July 8). Many youths reported held awaiting mental help [Online]. Available: www.nytimes.com/2004/07/08/us/many-youths-reported-held-awaiting-mental-help.html?_r=0.

Pelaez, V. (2014, March 31). The prison industry in the United States: big business or a new form of slavery? [Online]. Available: www.globalresearch.ca/the-prison-industry-in-the-united-states-big-business-or-a-new-form-of-slavery/8289.

Pens, D. (1998a) Virginia prisons open for business [Online]. Available: www.corpwatch.org/article.php?id=860.

———. (1998b). Oregon's prison slaveocracy [Online]. Available: www.corpwatch.org/article.php?id=857.

———. (1996). Out-celling the competition [Online]. Available: www.corpwatch.org/article.php?id=864.

Pew Charitable Trusts (2015, January 22). Fact sheet: growth in federal prison system exceeds states' [online]. Available: www.pewtrusts.org/en/research-and-analysis/fact-sheets/2015/01/growth-in-federal-prison-system-exceeds-states.

Pew Research Center for the People and the Press (2012, January 6). Continued majority support for death penalty [Online]. Available: www.people-press.org/2012/01/06/continued-majority-support-for-death-penalty/.

Philliber, S. (1987). "Thy brother's keeper: a review of the literature on correctional officers." *Justice Quarterly*, 4 (1), 9–33.

Physicians for Human Rights (2004a). Juveniles in adult prisons [Online]. Available: www.phrusa.org.

———. (2004b). The juvenile death penalty [Online]. Available: www.phrusa.org.

Piecora, C. (2014, September 15). Female inmates and sexual assault [Online]. Available: www.jurist.org/dateline/2014/09/christina-piecora-female-inmates.php.

Pitsch, M. (2004, November 20). 23 face charges in riot at prison [Online]. Available: www.courier-journal.com.

Plasket, B. (2001, April 25). Prison guard pleads guilty to civil rights violations. *Longmont Times-Call*.

———. (2000, June 1). Guards accused of inmate-abuse ring. *Longmont Times-Call*.

Pojman, L.P. (2004). Why the death penalty is morally permissible. In H. A. Bedau & P. Cassell (Eds.). *Debating the death penalty: should America have capital punishment?*. New York: Oxford University Press.

Porter, P. (1998). The economics of capital punishment [Online]. Available: www.mindspring.com.

Prendergast, A. (1996, December 19). The circle game: a "prisoner of war" plays ball with the feds – and gets beaned [Online]. Available: www.westword.com.

Prisoners' Advocacy Network-Ohio (2001). PUC orders MCI to refund overcharges to prisoners [Online]. Available: www.pan-ohio.org.

Prison Industry Authority (2015). About CALPIA rehabilitating offenders through job training [Online]. Available: www.calpia.ca.gov/About_PIA/AboutPIA.aspx.

Prison Legal News (2013, August 15). Florida's prison bond scheme obscures real costs of expansion [Online]. Available: https://www.prisonlegalnews.org/news/2013/aug/15/floridas-prison-bond-scheme-obscures-real-costs-of-expansion/.

Prison Policy Initiative (2015). Section III: the prison economy [Online]. Available: https://www.prisonpolicy.org/prisonindex/prisonlabor.html.

Prison Talk (2002, February). Older inmates prove expensive to keep [Online]. Available: www.prisontalk.com/forums/archive/index.php/t-25896.html.

Private Corrections Working Group (2015) TransCor rap sheet [Online]. Available: www.privateci.org.

ProCon.org (2012, March). Death penalty [Online]. Available: www.deathpenalty.procon.org.

Prodeathpenalty.com (2004, March). More than 2/3 of Americans support capital punishment [Online]. Available: www.prodeathpenalty.com.

Purdy, M. (2002, May 8). It takes a tough law to hold her [Online]. Available: www.nytimes.com/2002/05/08/nyregion/our-towns-it-takes-a-tough-law-to-hold-her.html.

Quinn, A. (2014, July 27). In labor, in chains. *New York Times*.

Quirini, P. (2000). Seek change in cell use [Online]. Available: www.global2000.net.

Rafter, N.H. (1990). *Partial justice: women, prisons, and social control*. 2nd edition, New Brunswick, NJ: Transaction Publishers.

Rantala, R., Rexroat, J. & A. Beck (2014, January). *Survey of sexual violence in adult correctional facilities, 2009–11 – statistical tables*. Washington, DC: U.S. Department of Justice. (NCJ 244227).

Rasmussen, F. (2000, July 13). Harry J. Patton, 85, curator, puppeteer and photographer. *Baltimore Sun* [Online]. Available: http://articles.baltimoresun.com/2000-07-13/news/0007130037_1_patton-puppet-photographer.

Rasor, D. (2012, May 3). America's top prison corporation: a study in predatory capitalism and cronyism [Online]. Available: www.truth-out.org/news/item/8875-corrections-corporation-of-america-a-study-in-predatory-capitalism-and-cronyism.

Reese, F. (2012, December 17). Prison rape and the atrocity of the American penal system [Online]. Available: www.mintpressnews.com/prison-rape-and-the-atrocity-of-the-american-penal-system/43198/.

Reiman, J. (1990). *The rich get richer and the poor get prison*, 4th edition, Boston: Allyn & Bacon.

Reiterman, T. (2004, August 11). Scathing report on prison doctors: a panel of experts ordered by court to review state system calls physician quality 'seriously deficient' [Online]. Available: http://articles.latimes.com/2004/aug/11/local/me-prison11.

Rendon, J. (1998) Inside the new high-tech lock-downs [Online]. Available: www.salon.com/1998/08/30/feature947623935/.

Revolutionary Worker (1997, June). Sisters behind bars: inside the women's prisons of California [Online]. Available: www.rwor.org.

Richissin, T. (2002, February 5). Juvenile justice official resigns [Online]. Available: www.sunspot.net.

Riddle, A. (2001, July 28). Boy, 14, gets 28 years. *Rocky Mountain News.*

Rideau, W. & Wikberg, R. (Eds.). (1992). *Life sentences: rage and survival behind bars.* New York: Times Books.

Rieger, D. (2005). Methicillin-resistant Staphylococcus Aureus (MRSA) in correctional settings. Indianapolis, IN: Indiana Department of Corrections.

Rierden, A. (1997). *The farm: life inside a women's prison.* Amherst: University of Massachusetts Press.

Riveland, C. (1999, January). *Supermax prisons: overview and general considerations.* Washington, DC: National Institute of Corrections.

Robbins, I.P. (1994). The prisoners' mail box and the evolution of federal inmate rights. In Roberts, J. (Ed.), *Escaping prison myths* (pp. 111–157). Washington, DC: American University Press.

Robbins, T. (2015, September 27). Guarding the prison guards: New York State's troubled disciplinary system [Online]. Available: www.nytimes.com/2015/09/28/nyregion/guarding-the-prison-guards-new-york-states-troubled-disciplinary-system.html.

Roberts, J. (Ed.). (1994). *Escaping prison myths: selected topics in the history of federal corrections.* Washington, DC: The American University Press.

Rohde, D. (2001, August 21). A growth industry cools as New York prisons thin [Online]. Available: www.nytimes.com/2001/08/21/nyregion/a-growth-industry-cools-as-new-york-prisons-thin.html.

Romano, S. (1996). If the SHU fits: cruel and unusual punishment at California's Pelican Bay State Prison [Online]. Available: www.law.emory.edu.

Roose, K. & Harshaw, P. (2015, February 3). Inside the prison system's illicit digital world [Online]. Available: http://fusion.net/story/41931/inside-the-prison-systems-illicit-digital-world/.

Rothman, D. (1979). *Incarceration and its alternatives in 20th century America.* Washington, DC: U.S. Government Printing Office.

Rudolph, J. (2012). Elderly inmate population soared 1,300 percent since 1980s: report [Online]. Available: www.huffingtonpost.com/2012/06/13/elderly-inmate-population-soars_n_1594793.html.

Ryan, G. (2004). I must act. In H. A. Bedau & P. Cassell (Eds.). *Debating the death penalty: should America have capital punishment?* New York: Oxford University Press.

Ryckaert, V. (2003, October 15). Inmate files suit against ex-guards [Online]. Available: www.indystar.com.

Sabo, D., Kupers, T. & London, W. (Eds.). (2001). *Prison masculinities.* Philadelphia, PA: Temple University Press.

Salter, J. (2014, May 1). Oklahoma execution reopens debate on death penalty. *Denver Post.*

Sample, B. (2008, August 15). Violence on the rise in BOP facilities [Online]. Available: https://www.prisonlegalnews.org/news/2009/aug/15/violence-on-the-rise-in-bop-facilities/.

Sampson, R. & Laub, J. (1996, June). Socioeconomic achievement in the life course of disadvantaged men: military service as a turning point, circa 1940–65. *American Sociological Review, 61,* 347–367.

Sanchez, R. (2010, June 18). Ronnie Lee Gardner executed by firing squad in Utah. Available: http://abcnews.go.com/GMA/Broadcast/convicted-killer-ronnie-lee-gardner-executed-utah/story?id=10949786.

———. (2002, April 22). Spirit of hospice clashes with purpose of prisons. *Rocky Mountain News.*

Sanko, J. & Woullard, C. (2004, July 23). State may examine finances at prison. *Rocky Mountain News.*

Sapien, J. (2014, January 23). Guards may be responsible for half of prison sexual assaults [Online]. Available: https://www.propublica.org/article/guards-may-be-responsible-for-half-of-prison-sexual-assaults.

Sawyer, K. (2000). A message to all Bureau of Prisons employees regarding privatization [Online]. Available: www.bop.gov.

Scalia, J. (1996, August). *Noncitizens in the federal criminal justice system, 1984–94.* (NCJ-160934). Washington, DC: U.S. Department of Justice.

Schiraldi, V., Holman, B. & Beatty, P. (2000). Poor prescription: the costs of imprisoning drug offenders in the United States [Online]. Available: www.drugpolicy.org/docUploads/PoorPrescription.pdf.

Schiraldi, V & Zeidenberg, J. (1997). The risks juveniles face when they are incarcerated with adults [Online]. Available: www.cjcj.org/uploads/cjcj/documents/the_risks.pdf.

Schlosser, E. (1998, December). The prison-industrial complex [Online]. Available: www.theatlantic.com/magazine/archive/1998/12/the-prison-industrial-complex/304669/.

Schmalleger, F. (2004). *Criminal justice: a brief introduction,* 5th edition, Upper Saddle River, NJ: Pearson Prentice Hall.

Schneider, M. (2001, May 17). Prison guards plead not guilty to killing inmate [Online]. Available: www.angelfire.com.

Schorsch, A. (1979). *Images of childhood: an illustrated social history.* New York: Mayflower Books.

Schreiber, C. (1999, July 19). Behind bars: aging prison population challenges prison health systems [Online]. Available: www.nurseweek.com/features/99-7/prison.html.

Segag.org (2011). Neta information, [Online]. Available: www.segag.org/ganginfo/frneta.html.

Sellin, J.T. (1976). *Slavery and the penal system.* New York: Elsevier.

Sengupta, S. (2003, September 26). Facing death for adultery, Nigerian woman is acquitted [Online]. Available: www.nytimes.com/2003/09/26/world/facing-death-for-adultery-nigerian-woman-is-acquitted.html.

Shelden, R., (2001). *Controlling the dangerous classes: a critical introduction to the history of criminal justice.* Boston: Allyn and Bacon.

———. (1991). "A comparison of gang members and non-gang members in a prison setting." *The Prison Journal,* LXXI (2), 50–60.

Sherman, M. (2015, January 24) Court to review execution drug. *Denver Post.*

Shichor, D. (1995). *Punishment for profit: private prisons/public concerns.* Thousand Oaks, CA: Sage Publications.

Sickmund, M. (2002, December). *Juvenile residential facility census, 2000: selected findings.* Washington, DC: U.S. Department of Justice (NCJ-196595).

Siegal, N. (1998, September 1). Slaves to the system [Online]. Available: www.salon.com/1998/09/01/cov_01feature_4/.

Silberman, M. (1995). *A world of violence*. Belmont, CA: Wadsworth.

Silverman, I. & Vega, M. (1996). *Corrections: a comprehensive view*. St. Paul, MN: West Publishing Company.

Silverstein, K. (1997). America's private gulag [Online]. Available: www.corpwatch.org/article.php?id=867.

Simons, M. & Weiner, T. (2004, April 1). Court tells U. S. to review death sentences. *The New York Times*.

Smith, B.V. (2006). Rethinking prison sex: self-expression and safety. *Columbia Journal of Gender and Law*. 185, 1–41.

Smith, C., Bechtel, J., Patrick, A., Smith, R., & Wilson-Gentry, L. (2006, June). Correctional industries preparing inmates for re-entry: recidivism & post-release employment [Online]. Available: https://www.ncjrs.gov/pdffiles1/nij/grants/214608.pdf.

Sneed, W.C. (1860). *A report on the history and mode of management of the Kentucky Penitentiary*. Frankfort, KY: J.B. Major.

Solotaroff, I., (2001). *The last face you'll ever see: the private life of the American death penalty*. New York: HarperCollins.

Sowers, C. (2002, February 11). Study: Arizona among 10 worst states for errors in death penalty cases [Online]. Available: www.arizonarepublic.com.

Sparrow, J. (2009). *Killing: misadventures in violence*. Melbourne, Australia: Melbourne University Publishing.

Speer, L (1997). *Portals to hell: military prisons of the civil war*. Mechanicsburg, PA: Stackpole Books.

St John, P. (2015, December 16). State investigators cite culture of abuse, racism by High Desert State Prison guards [Online]. Available: www.latimes.com/local/politics/la-pol-abuse-california-prison-20151216-story.html.

Stamoulis, A. (2001, August 28). Prison policy in a media-driven America. *LiP Magazine*: 1–3.

Staples, B. (2004, September 7). Fighting the AIDS epidemic by issuing condoms in the prisons [Online]. Available: www.nytimes.com/2004/09/07/opinion/fighting-the-aids-epidemic-by-issuing-condoms-in-the-prisons.html.

Starchild, A. (2001). AIDS testing problems in federal prisons [Online]. Available: http:///www.io.com.

Sterngold, J. (2002, February 16). Head of camp in Arizona is arrested in boy's death [Online]. Available: www.nytimes.com/2002/02/16/us/head-of-camp-in-arizona-is-arrested-in-boy-s-death.html.

Stevens, J. (2010, December 23) On the death sentence [Online]. Available: www.nybooks.com/articles/2010/12/23/death-sentence/.

Stewart, R. (2002). Death row prisoners with hepatitis C tortured by the California Department of Corrections (CDC) [Online]. Available: www.prisons.org.

Stillman, S. (2014, June 23). Get out of jail, inc: does the alternatives-to-incarceration industry profit from injustice? [Online]. Available: www.newyorker.com/magazine/2014/06/23/get-out-of-jail-inc.

Stohr, M., Lovrich, N., Menke, B., & Zupan, L. (1994, September). Staff management in correctional institutions: comparing Dilulio's 'control model' and 'employee investment model' outcomes in five jails. *Justice Quarterly*, 11 (3), 93–95.

Stop Prisoner Rape (2004a). The basics on rape behind bars [Online]. Available: www.spr.org.

————. (2004b). Prisoner rape spreads disease – inside and outside of prison [Online]. Available: www.spr.org.

Streib, V. (2004). The juvenile death penalty today: death sentences and executions for juvenile crimes, January 1, 1973–April 30, 2004. [Online]. Available: www.deathpenaltyinfo.org/documents/JuvDeathApril2004.pdf.

Struckman-Johnson, C. & Struckman-Johnson, D. (2000, December). Sexual coercion rates in seven Midwestern prison facilities for men. *The Prison Journal*, 80 (4), 379–390.

Stryker, J. (2001, March 26). Improving prison health care [Online]. Available: www.chcf.org.

Sullivan, J. (2003, April 21). Claims of beatings persist in a 1997 prison episode [Online]. Available: www.nytimes.com/2003/04/21/nyregion/claims-of-wide-spread-beatings-persist-in-a-1997-prison-episode.html.

Summers, C. (2001, August 10). America's most dangerous prisoner? [Online]. Available: http://news.bbc.co.uk/2/hi/americas/1393970.stm.

Sundaram, V. (2009, February 9). Why are we keeping old ladies locked up in prison? [Online]. Available: www.alternet.org/story/126041/why_are_we_keep-ing_old_ladies_locked_up_in_prison.

Sword, W. (1992). *Embrace an angry wind: the confederacy's last hurrah.* New York: Harper Collins.

Sykes, G. (1958/1966). *The society of captives.* Princeton, NJ: Princeton University Press.

Sykes G. & Messinger, S. (1960). Inmate social system. In Cloward, R., Cressey, D., Grosser, G., McCleery, R., Ohlin, L., Sykes, G. & Messinger, S. (Eds.). *Theoretical studies in social organization of the prison.* New York: Social Science Research Council.

Szalavitz, M. (2001, September 4). Coerced treatment: too many steps in the right direction [Online]. Available: www.alternet.org/story/11425/coerced_treatment%3A_too_many_steps_in_the_right_direction.

Takei, C. (2014a, September 29). The Wal-Mart model: not just for retail. Now, it's for private prisons, too! [Online]. Available: https://www.aclu.org/blog/wal-mart-model-not-just-retail-now-its-private-prisons-too.

————. (2014b, May 20). Karma: private prison company throws shade and fails, badly [Online]. Available: https://www.aclu.org/blog/karma-private-prison-company-throws-shade-and-fails-badly.

Tankersley, J. (2005, June 20). Prison firm made political donations. *Rocky Mountain News*, 5A.

Tardy, D. (2003, September 26). Two women file suit against the Dept. of Corrections for sexual harassment [Online]. Available: www.firstcoastnews.com.

Taylor, T. (2000). Camp Douglas: 'Eighty acres of hell' in a confederate prison camp [Online]. Available: www.prairieghosts.com.

Taylor, W. (1993). *Brokered justice: race, politics, and the Mississippi prisons, 1798–1992.* Columbus, OH: Ohio State University Press.

Tennessee Department of Correction (2002, December). Older inmates under TDOC supervision [Online]. Available: www.state.tn.us/correction/planning.

Tesfaye, S. (2015, July 2). New report lays bare the horrific reality of youths detained in adult prisons [Online]. Available: www.salon.com/2015/07/02/new_report_lays_bare_the_horrific_reality_of_youths_detained_in_adult_prisons/.

Texas Department of Criminal Justice. (2013, February). *Texas Department of Criminal Justice correctional capacity & population, fiscal year 2012*. Austin, TX: Texas Department of Criminal Justice.

———. (2001a). Frequently asked questions [Online]. Available: www.tdcj.state.tx.us/faq/index.html.

———. (2001b). Contract facility operations: management of institutional division private prisons [Online]. Available: www.tdcj.state.tx.us.

———. (2000). Closing a millennium – reviewing the past decade [Online]. Available: www.tdcj.state.tx.us.

Texas Lawyers in Support of a Moratorium (2002). Support the ABA moratorium resolution in Texas [Online]. Available: www.moratorium.info.

Tharp, P. (2001). Prison cos. get hot [Online]. Available: http://nypost.com/2001/10/04/prison-cos-get-hot-terror-threat-fueling-firms-stocks/.

The Clark County Prosecuting Attorney (2002). The death penalty: methods of execution [Online]. Available: www.clarkprosecutor.org/html/death/methods.htm.

The Discovery Channel (2001). *On the inside: maximum security prisons*. (Cassette Recording). New York: The Discovery Channel.

The Economist (2010, August 24). The perverse incentives of private prisons [Online]. Available: www.economist.com/blogs/democracyinamerica/2010/08/private_prisons.

The Geo Group, Inc. (2015). Welcome to the Geo Group, Inc. [Online]. Available: www.geogroup.com.

The Greeley Tribune (2014, April 30). Inmate dies after botched execution. *The Greeley (Colorado) Tribune*.

The History Channel (1998a). *The big house: Sing-Sing*. (Cassette Recording). New York: The History Channel.

———. (1998b). *The big house: San Quentin*. (Cassette Recording). New York: The History Channel.

———. (1998c). *The big house: Leavenworth*. (Cassette Recording). New York: The History Channel.

———. (1998d). *The big house: Alcatraz*. (Cassette Recording). New York: The History Channel.

The Learning Channel (1999). *Supermax prisons*. (Cassette Recording). New York: The Learning Channel.

The Marshals Monitor (2000). Marshals museum shares agency's vast legacy [Online]. Available: www.usdoj.gov/marshals/monitor.

The November Coalition (2001). The gulaging of America!: federal prison population report [Online]. Available: www.november.org.

———. (1999, September/October). New federal prisons: recently completed or under construction [Online]. Available: www.november.org.

The Sentencing Project (2012a). Fact sheet: trends in U.S. corrections [Online]. Available: www.sentencingproject.org.

———. (2012b). Incarcerated Women [Online]. Available: www.sentencingproject.org.

———. (2003). Factsheet: women in prison. Washington, DC: The Sentencing Project.

Thomas, C. (2001). Private adult correctional facility census [Online]. Available: http://web.crimufl.edu/pcp/census/2001.

———. (2000). Correctional privatization in the United States: an examination of its modern history and future potential [Online]. Available: http://web.crim.ufl.edu/pcp/research/Kansas.

Thomas, D., Blatt, D., Levi, R.S., Lai, S., Mariner, J. & Ralph, R.E. (1996). All too familiar: sexual abuse of women in U.S. state prisons [Online]. Available: https://www.hrw.org/reports/1996/Us1.htm.

Thompson, D. (2004a, February 14). Schwarzenegger struggling with prison crisis in California [Online]. Available: www.detnews.com.

———. (2004b, January 26). Guards at prison formed own gang, report concludes [Online]. Available: www.dailyreviewonline.com.

Thompson, G. (2004, September 26). Shuttling between nations, Latino gangs confound the law [Online]. Available: www.nytimes.com/2004/09/26/world/americas/shuttling-between-nations-latino-gangs-confound-the-law.html.

Thrasher, F. (1927). *The gang*. Chicago: University of Chicago press.

Tiffin, S. (1982). *In whose best interest? Child welfare reform in the progressive era.* Westport, CT: Greenwood Press.

Timberg, C. (2001, July 31). Documents show use of force at Va. Prison. *Washington Post.*

TransCor America, LLC (2015) TransCor America – respect, trust, loyalty, integrity [Online]. Available: www.transcor.com.

Trombley, S. (1992). *The execution protocol: inside America's capital punishment industry.* New York: Crown Publishers.

Trombley, S. & Wood, M. (1992). *The execution protocol.* (Cassette Recording). New York: First Run/Icarus Films.

Townes, C. (2015a, January 13). Florida inmate killed 36 hours after being placed with notoriously violent cellmate [Online]. Available: https://thinkprogress.org/florida-inmate-killed-36-hours-after-being-placed-with-notoriously-violent-cellmate-c86dc90ea371?gi=a7bdb748f3.

———. (2015b, July 6) Days of rioting showcase Arizona's private prison failures [Online]. Available: https://thinkprogress.org/days-of-rioting-showcase-arizonas-private-prison-failures-a3fc7bdf5668.

Turner, J., Singleton, Jr., R. & Musick, D. (1984). *Oppression: a socio-history of black-white relations in America.* Chicago: Nelson-Hall Publishers.

United Nations Commission on Human Rights (1999). Reports on the abuse of women in U.S. Prisons [Online]. Available: www.cfdp.ca/boje.htm.

Urban/Rural Coalition Against Prisons (2001). Farms not jails [Online]. Available: www.farmsnotjails.com.

Urbina, I. (2014, May 24). Using jailed migrants as a pool of cheap labor [Online]. Available: https://www.nytimes.com/2014/05/25/us/using-jailed-migrants-as-a-pool-of-cheap-labor.html.

U.S. Bureau of Prisons (2004). Executions of federal prisoners since 1927 [Online]. Available: www.bop.gov.

———. (2001). Executions of federal prisoners since 1927 [Online]. Available: www. bop.gov.

———. (1999). Special Confinement opens at USP Terre Haute [Online]. Available: www.bop.gov.

U.S. Department of Justice (2016, January 13). Two U.S. Bureau of Prisons corrections officers plead guilty to assaulting a prison inmate and falsifying reports [Online]. Available: https://www.justice.gov/opa/pr/two-us-bureau-prisons-corrections-officers-plead-guilty-assaulting-prison-inmate-and.

———. (2015). *Justice Expenditure and Employment Abstracts 2012* (NCJ 248628). Washington, DC: U.S. Department of Justice.

———. (2014a, September, Revised September 30, 2014). *Prisoners in 2013*. Washington, DC: U.S. Department of Justice.

———. (2014b, September). *Prisoners in 2013*. Washington, DC: U.S. Department of Justice (NCJ-247282).

———. (2012, December, Revised April 30, 2014). *State Corrections Expenditures, FY 1982–2010*. Washington, DC: U.S. Department of Justice.

———. (2011a, December). *Capital Punishment, 2010 – Statistical Tables*. Washington, DC: U.S. Department of Justice.

———. (2011b, February 3). National Standards to prevent, detect and respond to prison rape. *Federal Register* 76 (23), 6248–6302.

———. (2004a, June). *Data collections for the Prison Rape Elimination Act of 2003*. Washington, DC: U.S. Department of Justice.

———. (2004b, February 6). *United States Attorney issues statement responding to governor Schwarzenegger's request concerning 2002 Folsom state Prison riots*. Sacramento, CA: U.S. Department of Justice.

———. (2002). *Sourcebook of criminal justice statistics – 2001*. Washington, DC: U.S. Department of Justice (NCJ-1964380.

———. (2000a). *Sourcebook of criminal justice statistics – 1999*. Washington, DC: U.S. Department of Justice (NCJ-1837).

———. (2000b, August). *Prisoners in 1999*. Washington, DC: U.S. Department of Justice (NCJ-183476).

———. (2000c, December). *Capital punishment 1999*. Washington, DC: U.S. Department of Justice (NCJ-184795).

———. (1998, February 26). Eight officers indicted for civil rights violations at Corcoran State Prison in California [Online]. Available: www.usdoj.gov.

———. (1997). *Capital punishment 1996*. Washington, DC: U.S. Department of Justice (NCJ-167031).

———. (1996). *Sourcebook of criminal justice statistics – 1995*. Washington, DC: U.S. Department of Justice (NCJ-158900).

———. (1995). *Sourcebook of criminal justice statistics –1994*. Washington, DC: U.S. Department of Justice (NCJ-154591.

———. (1993a). *Correctional populations in the United States, 1991*. Washington, DC: U.S. Department of Justice.

————. (1993b). *Sourcebook of criminal justice statistics – 1992*. Washington, DC: U.S. Department of Justice.

————. (1990). *Sourcebook of criminal justice statistics – 1989*. Washington, DC: U.S. Department of Justice.

————. (1987). *Sourcebook of criminal justice statistics – 1986*. Washington, DC: U.S. Department of Justice.

————. (1977). *Sourcebook of criminal justice statistics – 1976*. Washington, DC: U.S. Department of Justice.

U.S. Department of Justice, Bureau of Justice Statistics (2010, August). *Sexual Victimization in Prisons and Jails Reported by Inmates, 2008–09*. Washington, DC: Bureau of Justice Statistics.

————. (2010, June). *PREA Data Collection Activities, 2010*. Washington, DC: Bureau of Justice Statistics.

————. (2006, July). *Sexual Victimization in State and federal Prisons Reported by Inmates, 2007*. Washington, DC: Bureau of Justice Statistics.

————. (2006) *Sexual Violence Reported by Correctional Authorities, 2005*. Washington, DC: Bureau of Justice Statistics.

Useem, B., Camp, C., Camp, G. & Dugan, R. (1995, October). *Resolution of prison riots*. Washington, DC: National Institute of Justice.

U.S. General Accounting Office (1997). Death penalty sentencing: research indicates pattern of racial disparities. In H.A. Bedau (Ed.). *The death penalty in America: current controversies*. New York: Oxford University Press.

Utah Highway Patrol (2005). Prison riots [Online]. Available: www.highwaypatrol.utah.gov.

Van Den Haag, E. (1997). The death penalty once more. In H.A. Bedau (Ed.). *The death penalty in America: current controversies*. New York: Oxford University Press.

Walker, D. (1988). *Penology for profit: a history of the Texas prison system 1867–1912*. College Station, TX: Texas A&M University Press.

Walker, R. (2005). Prison gangs [Online]. Available: www.gangsorus.com.

Walker, S. (1980). *Popular justice: a history of American criminal justice*. New York: Oxford University Press.

Walsh, D. (2002, December 30). The prison is locked down after inmates attacked the guards [Online]. Available: www.sacbee.com.

WAPT News (2012, May 21), Corrections officer killed, 19 injured in prison riot [Online]. Available: www.wapt.com/article/corrections-officer-killed-19-injured-in-prison-riot/2078958.

Ward, D. (1994). Alcatraz and Marion: confinement in super maximum custody. In Roberts, J. (Ed.). *Escaping prison myths: selected topics in the history of federal corrections* (pp. 81–93). Washington, DC: The American University Press.

Washington State Institute for Public Policy (2005, January). Correctional industries programs for adult offenders in prison: Estimates of benefits and costs [Online]. Available: www.wsipp.wa.gov/ReportFile/894/Wsipp_Correctional-Industries-Programs-for-Adult-Offenders-in-Prison-Estimates-of-Benefits-and-Costs_Full-Report.pdf.

Waters, R. (2004, March/April). Adult time for adult crime: have we lost faith in rehabilitating juvenile offenders? *Psychotherapy Networker*, 19–20.

Watterson, K. (1996). *Women in prison: inside the concrete womb.* Revised Ed., Boston: Northeastern University Press.

Weber, M. (1998, March/April). "Probing look at 'capital punishment industry' affirms expertise of Auschwitz investigator [Fred A.] Leuchter." *The Journal for Historical Review* [Online]. Available: www.ihr.com.

Weed, W. (2001, July 10). Incubating disease: prisons are rife with infectious illnesses – and threaten to spread them to the public [Online]. Available: www.motherjones.com.

Welsh-Huggins, A. & J. Salter (2014, April 6). In most states, secrecy shrouds death penalty. *Denver Post.*

Wessler, S. (2015, June 23). The true story of a Texas prison riot [Online]. Available: https://www.thenation.com/article/the-true-story-of-a-texas-prison-riot/.

White, J. (2004, March 21). Sniper trial took toll on attorneys. *Washington Post.* Available: www.washingtonpost.com/wp-dyn/articles/A11426-2004Mar20_2.html.

Wicker, T. (1975). *A time to die.* New York: Quadrangle/New York Times Book Company.

Wikberg, R. (1992). The Farrar legacy. In W. Rideau and R. Wikberg (Eds.), *Life sentences: Rage and survival behind bars* (pp. 9–22). New York: Times Books.

Wilgoren, J. (2003, January 12). Governor assails system's errors as he empties Illinois death row [Online]. Available: www.nytimes.com/2003/01/12/us/citing-issue-of-fairness-governor-clears-out-death-row-in-illinois.html.

Wilkinson, T. (2000, March/April). Shocking discipline [Online]. Available: www.motherjones.com.

Williams, T. (2015) The high cost of calling the imprisoned [Online]. Available: www.nytimes.com/2015/03/31/us/steep-costs-of-inmate-phone-calls-are-under-scrutiny.html.

Williams-Harold, B. (1998). Facts and figures: A costly matter of life or death. *Black Enterprise,* 26–27.

Wilson, B. (1927). Folsom Prison riot, 1927 [Online]. Available: www.militarymuseum.org/FolsomPrisonRiot1927.html.

Wilson, J. (1975). *Thinking about crime.* New York: Basic Books.

Winter, C. (2008, July 21). What do prisoners make for Victoria's Secret? [Online]. Available: www.motherjones.com/politics/2008/07/what-do-prisoners-make-victorias-secret.

Wisely, W. (1998). The bottom line: California's Prison Industry Authority. In Burton-Rose, D., Pens, D. & Wright, P. (Eds.). *The celling of America: an inside look at the U.S. prison industry* (pp. 140–144). Monroe, ME: Common Courage Press.

WIVB TV4 (2004, July 30). Three officers hospitalized after attack [Online]. Available: www.wivb.com.

Wolff, N., Shi, J. & Siegel, J. (2009). Patterns of victimization among male and female inmates: evidence of an enduring legacy [Online]. Available: https://www.ncbi.nlm.nih.gov/pmc/articles/PMC3793850/pdf/nihms168246.pdf.

Wood, G. (2014, October). How gangs took over prisons. [Online]. Available: https://www.theatlantic.com/magazine/archive/2014/10/how-gangs-took-over-prisons/379330/.

World Health Organization (2007). Preventing suicide in jails and prisons [Online]. Available: http://www.who.int/mental_health/prevention/suicide/resource_jails_prisons.pdf.

Wright, P. (1997). (1998). Dying for attention: the atrocity of prison health care. In Burton-Rose, D., Pens, D. & Wright, P. (Eds.). *The celling of America: an inside look at the U.S. prison industry* (pp. 78–87). Monroe, ME: Common Courage Press.

———. (1997, March 1) Profiting from punishment [Online]. Available: www.corp-watch.org/article.php?id=854.

Yardley, J. (2001, September 2). Oklahoma retraces big step in capital case [Online]. Available: www.nytimes.com/2001/09/02/us/oklahoma-retraces-big-step-in-capital-case.html.

Yee, D. (2003, October 17). Inmate skin infections becoming a concern [Online]. Available: www.prisontalk.com/forums/showthread.php?t=29515.

Zack, B. (2004, May 6). From our communities to our jails/prisons and back: sex, drugs, and infectious diseases [Online]. Available: www.centerforce.org.

Ziedenberg, J., & Schiraldi, V. (2000). The punishing decade: prison and jail estimates at the millennium [Online]. Available: www.cjcj.org/uploads/cjcj/documents/punishing.pdf.

Zoukis, C. (2013, June 15) TransCor may face punitive damages for prisoner's death. *Prison Legal News.* 24 (6), 34.

Zoukis, C. (2014, August). The dirt wars: An intimate look at convict culture in American prisons [Online]. Available: http://www.huffingtonpost.com/christopher-zoukis/the-dirt-wars-an-intimate_1_b_5672848.html.

Zvekic, U. (1994). *Alternatives to imprisonment in comparative perspective*, Chicago: Nelson-Hall.

Index

Page numbers in bold refer to tables.

William C. Holman Correctional
Facility 183
Williams, Stanley "Tookie" 161
Wilson, Woodrow 50, 54
Wisconsin 3
Wobblies 50
women inmates *see* female inmates
Wood, Joseph Randall 107
Wyoming 3

Wyoming Territorial Prison
18–19

Young, C. C. 176
Yousef, Ramzi 62
Youth Services International 133